AYA
Life's Garden Manual
As You Are

Jamie Sloan

Glue Pot Press
New Orleans, Louisiana

Copyright © 2025 Jamie Sloan All Rights Reserved

No part of this publication may be reproduced, distributed, or transmitted in any form or by any means, including photocopying, recording, or other electronic or mechanical methods, without the prior written permission of the author, except in the case of brief quotations embodied in critical reviews and certain other noncommercial uses permitted by copyright law.

ISBN: 978-1-7379423-9-9

AYAGardenbooks@gmail.com

Acknowledgments

This book has been shaped by garden gurus, teachers, mentors, and a wealth of experiences. At its core, it is a culmination of knowledge and wisdom passed down through time and toil. A few years ago, I realized that compiling much of humanity's repurposed, recycled, and reused teachings into a manual of sorts may benefit future generations.

As an active horticulturist and retired professional gardener, many of my greatest teachers were my esteemed clients. They generously shared their knowledge, vision, and hope for a more beautiful world, and I was honored to serve as an instrument in bringing those visions to life within their landscapes.

May this book find its way into the hands of those who embrace its message: to create a better world by becoming better humans. May it inspire a shift in the trajectory of injustices inflicted upon the planet, sparking a revolution that reshapes our future for the better. We can build a new world founded on principles and virtues that reconnect society with its shared humanity.

Special thanks to my editor, Michele VanPelt. While I may never fully harness the power of writing in an active voice, the humbling experience of correcting countless errors has been invaluable. The remaining presence of any mistakes brings a smile to my face—a reminder that perfection was never the goal. What matters is the creation of something that will continue to take root and grow in the landscape of life, for myself and for others who may find meaning in it. For that, I am deeply grateful.

Jamie S. Sloan

Jamie Sloan

The nature of this flower is to bloom.

~Alice Walker

AYA Preface

The AYA Garden Manual blends philosophy with practical insights, offering a holistic approach to gardening, personal development, and self-discovery—As You Are. Much like life, gardening is an ongoing journey with unpredictable outcomes, creating a unique space for growth. Wherever you find yourself, this manual meets you there, allowing you to honor your current self while recognizing your potential for transformation. Similar to a garden, life's meaning is found in its being. Your life's garden aims to connect with the emergence of your natural, sovereign, authentic self, a journey of growth and transformation within your reach.

This manual serves as a valuable resource to help shape our inner and outer reality. It also serves as a reminder that the ongoing journey of growth and self-discovery can enrich our lives and positively impact global consciousness and the health of the planet. Once we recognize that nature is a diverse source of healing, we can draw on this knowledge to nurture life within and around us. Embracing what nature provides allows for a deeper connection to our true selves, leading to more fulfilling life experiences. Being present while creating reality will enable us to notice and appreciate the gifts offered each day in our life's garden.

The universe embodies the garden of life, where every creation reflects the essence of existence. Each element contributes to the garden's abundance, reminding us that all forms of life are interconnected. Just as a gardener nurtures each plant according to its unique needs, we can intentionally cultivate all areas of our lives. In this space, we are not mere observers; we are the gardeners, actively tending to our inner and outer landscapes, part of a larger, interconnected whole. We are all born as gardeners, given a life in which to grow.

Gardening is a mindset—one that cultivates patience, nurturance, growth, resilience, adaptability, presence, balance, experimentation, harmony, and abundance. When you plant a garden with an abundant mindset, you align with nature's innate tendency to thrive. Just as it is a flower's nature to bloom, a garden will produce and flourish, though it may sometimes require care and support. A garden simply exists, yet it grows because that is its essence and its nature. This mirrors the mindset of the gardener: "I can grow, and I will, because growth is my essence and my nature."

As gardeners, we tend to more than plants—we shape our thoughts, emotions, and spiritual experiences like a fertile patch of earth. We nurture our passions by planting seeds of intention while carefully weeding out the negativity that stifles growth. Seeds of inspiration surround us, brimming with potential to blossom into dreams that expand our horizons. Some may fall on barren ground, be consumed by scavengers, or be carried away by the wind. Yet others will find fertile soil, sprouting into vibrant, viable ideas that grow and bear fruit.

Life is a garden of dreams where aspirations and goals are the seeds, and nurturing them brings fulfillment. By aligning seeds of intention, awareness, and purposeful action with the rich soil of our experiences, we nurture natural growth in our garden of life. When we envision our lives as a fertile landscape, we transform ideas into a burgeoning garden of joy and abundance. Using the tools of our awareness and innate abilities, we step into our life's garden, plant seeds of creativity, and master the art of living.

At its core, gardening is about nurturing life within ourselves and the world around us. Consider the impact of tending to a flower-filled edible garden. If a significant portion of people grew even a small part of their own food, it would greatly contribute to a healthier and more sustainable planet. Whether through self-sufficiency practices like gardening, permaculture, biodynamic farming, agronomy, or food forest ecosystems, any method that promotes harmony with nature benefits the earth and its diverse communities. By coexisting with nature, creating habitats, supporting ecosystems, enriching soil, and building resilient spaces, we establish environments where humans and nature can grow together in balance.

Actively and attentively engaging with the land transforms our lives across multiple magnitudes—environmental, personal, social, conscious, physical, and emotional. This echoes the timeless wisdom of Indigenous peoples: when we care for the land, the land cares for us in return. The soil serves as our shared connection, providing the foundation for life. Healthy soil nourishes not only our bodies but also our spirits and communities. True growth isn't about producing as much as possible but cultivating what is sustainable, meaningful, and achievable.

Every effort to connect with the land brings value, but meaningful endeavors often come with challenges. Creation demands work, time, perseverance, and patience before the results fully emerge. Yet, as we find fulfillment in these efforts, we gain the opportunity to share the fruits of our labor with others. Through this sharing, the community prospers as a connected whole—rooted in reciprocity, gratitude, and appreciation.

Embracing food autonomy empowers us to tackle the ongoing threats of environmental and economic instability. Diverse challenges drive us to adopt self-sufficiency practices, including seed saving, propagation, farming, food preparation, storage, canning, preserving, and cultivating herbs and medicinal plants. These actions help us prioritize our health and develop the skills to heal. By nurturing the land and waterways, we actively heal ourselves, strengthen our communities, and restore balance to nature.

In the face of modern challenges, learning self-sufficiency has become a necessity rather than just an option. Our reliance on commercialized industrial food is increasingly uncertain due to ongoing threats like chemical contamination, genetic modification, artificial ingredients, preservatives, dyes, nutrient deficiencies, and pesticides. These issues contribute to the decline of our health, society, and the environment. In today's world, the responsibility for safeguarding our well-being falls entirely on us—no one else will come to our aid. Additionally, climate change presents significant challenges for food production.

The fundamental aspiration shared by all species in the natural world is growth in becoming and evolution. As gardeners, we embrace the idea that life is for living and commit to nurturing it. Food agriculture has always been a driving force in advancing human life on our planet. When we plant a garden, we weave together threads of life and create ecosystems. A garden becomes a unique gift, providing a tangible connection to our intrinsic desire for growth and transformation. It serves as a means for personal development in a natural and fulfilling way. A garden is a dynamic space filled with biodiversity, continuity, reciprocity, and interrelationship. It emphasizes the beauty of life's interconnectedness, teaching us about growth, balance, and our place within the natural world.

A single flower can grow well independently, but it draws nourishment from the soil, water, and sunlight. Similarly, trees gain strength from the wind. Each entity is connected to a network of interdependence that sustains its survival. A species draws even greater strength from its interactions with the beneficial elements of its environment. The entire ecology of a landscape emerges through the contributions of all its residents. Though a single bloom may appear solitary in the garden, it is intricately linked to the web of the ecosystem. Similarly, humanity relies on healthy natural environments, nourishment, and connection. Independence is possible, but true progress comes through connection and collaboration.

When we come together as a community, we can work towards creating a cleaner, healthier environment that benefits everyone. This collaboration is especially important in urban areas, where community gardens are vital. A garden is a small ecosystem; the more significant its diversity, the more life prospers. Biodiversity not only boosts the vitality of a garden but also supports a wide variety of species. In this way, gardening becomes a conscious act of conservation.

Gardening mirrors the daily flow of life. According to legend, life began in a garden, where sustenance and curiosity coexist. Each living thing grows, blooms, bears fruit, and eventually returns to the soil, contributing to the greater whole. Though flowers may belong to specific genera, each is unique, needing its own conditions to blossom. Not all seeds germinate, and not all reach their full potential. Yet, with understanding, effort, patience, and care, we can create an environment that nurtures and supports one another's growth, yielding abundant rewards.

This guide serves as a manual designed to enrich and enhance the beauty of our world, both within and around us. It explores various concepts through practical methods and allegory. The primary goal is to help you create a purposeful life that nourishes your soul and contributes to the well-being of our planet. It also offers insights on how to cultivate your ideal garden.

Regardless of age or experience, your garden is open for participation and appreciation. You can embark on this journey with no prior knowledge of horticulture. The garden of life will teach you, and you will learn through experimentation, trial, and error. Each page will meet you where you are, as you are, within life's garden.

If you seek tangible and profound fulfillment, open your mind to the limitless possibilities of cultivating a beautifully abundant life.

We begin with a simple question: 'What would you like to cultivate in your garden?'

Every act of creation is first an act of destruction.

~Pablo Picasso

Chaos Before Order

If cultivating a physical garden isn't feasible, tend to the gardening principles within. Each of us holds an internal garden that invites our wonder, where we can reap a bountiful harvest—one that's not only possible but inevitable. Neglecting the life allotment bestowed upon us at birth impacts the quality of life we create through experience. When we consistently cultivate meaningful intentions, we will eventually witness their blossoming. The garden within is our true home—a place of respite, always accessible. It's never too late to clear the weeds and sow seeds for future flowers. Remember, gardening often gets messy and chaotic before we establish order.

From a young age, we create and practice maintenance habits that naturally evolve—they must. Everything has a purpose, and each of us has the potential to fulfill it. Weeds, often disguised as thoughts or stories we tell ourselves, require uprooting and tossing. We must clear space for new growth and fresh ideas. Repeating the same thoughts in the same ways drains the fertile ground of creativity, leaving us stagnant. Just as the soil needs amendments and nutrients, we must nourish the soil of our body, mind, and spirit.

Scattering seeds of desire into our daily routines often leads to growth, provided the right conditions. We can effectively manifest ideas into reality. Transforming mindfulness and self-awareness into a routine becomes a powerful tool for sustaining continuous growth. Unveiling our true nature requires us to listen to our inner dialogue and observe our reactions to life—decoding whether we are the victor or the victim in our victory garden.

Reflect on how your thoughts shape your feelings; often, the decisions that lead to peace are the ones worth nurturing. Breathe deeply, relax, and awaken to your potential. While growth is inevitable, its expansion depends on your clarity. Grab your tools, free yourself, and embrace growth beyond your expectations and perceived limitations.

Nature does not hurry, yet everything is accomplished.

~Lao Tzu

Nature's Path

The natural world is an integral part of the human experience, a connection that has endured since the dawn of humankind. To ensure life thrives, we must maintain respect for it. Nature endures and creates chaos with powerful determination and grace, expressing universal conscious energy. What may seem lifeless to the human eye often teems with energy. Consider a fallen tree, classified as 'dead' once it topples. Yet, it continues to live in a different form, nourishing the soil, sustaining neighboring plant roots, and providing shelter for insects. This cycle, in turn, supports birds, fish, and other wildlife, weaving an intricate web of existence. In this profound interplay, the circle of life transcends death and stands as a vibrant testament to nature's resilience and interconnectedness.

A garden is a community of life that represents the energetic exchange between nature and our conscious selves. It offers a space to harmonize our mind, body, and spirit. The Earth provides healing, offering resources and wisdom that support the growth of all living beings. Engaging with this ancient knowledge helps us achieve balance and alignment.

As a sacred creation, nature regenerates, restores, grows, connects, and sustains. The profound connection between humanity and nature bridges our outer world to our inner beings and simultaneously opens our inner selves to realities beyond our limited perception.

Gardening, whether on a small or large scale, is more than just a hobby—it's a transformative journey that taps into our creativity. It has the propensity to become an expression of higher love and a collaborative creative endeavor with life itself. Through this process, we expand our perception and embrace new visions of what is possible.

Feeling good on a daily basis is an attainable goal. We can make this a reality by practicing mindfulness and incorporating physical activities.

When we consciously release worry, we restore faith. Change begins with trust, hope, and self-belief as we challenge outdated thoughts and perceptions. Our mindset can either manifest wonderful things or block them from happening.

Humans are born creators, and nature accepts us as we are. We are also inherently entrusted with the role of being Earth's caretakers, charged with the sacred task of ensuring the well-being and growth of both our inner selves and the world that surrounds us. This calling is not bound by dogma or religion but rather intricately linked to the enlightenment of human consciousness and the indomitable spirit of humanity. It's a responsibility that empowers us to positively impact our environment.

An expansive and boundless exchange of reciprocity unfolds between the gardener and the garden. Whether tending to a modest arrangement of succulents or nurturing a sprawling and diverse edible landscape, ecological systems naturally flourish and harmonize when the right conditions are established. Not only do beneficial insects, birds, and predators find sustenance, but the hidden microbiomes within the soil food web also pulse with vibrant life. The soil food web is the living system in the soil where a world of communal activity lives beyond the visible surface. Feeding the soil is a necessary, inherent aspect of gardening. Good soil begets a good foundation for life.

Gardening is a natural evolution, an intricate dance of stewardship where the gardener assumes the role of being a custodian of nature and, in turn, reap a bountiful harvest of rewards. These benefits offer expanded knowledge, nourishment, a pleasurable environment of beautiful aesthetics, radiant blooms, abundant crops, moments of respite and joy, a profound sense of fulfillment and satisfaction, ecological equilibrium, and a wellspring of wisdom—to name a few. The optimal time to build a garden is now, even if it means developing the idea into a plan. The best place to start is from the ground up.

Garden Alternatives

Every individual possesses unique strengths and gifts, and sharing these gifts is a meaningful way to contribute to life. While gardening may not be for everyone, numerous ways exist to positively impact and support environmental and land stewardship. Start by buying from local organic farmers and independent grocers. Joining a CSA (Community Supported Agriculture) network for produce, shopping at farmer's markets, or gathering fruits and berries from U-Pick farms keeps currency in local markets and out of the industrialized food market. Utilize compost bins, if available, to help build soil for sustainable food production.

Protecting wildlands by staying on designated trails is critical. Learn about other species and discover ways to help protect their habitats. Use organic methods to combat weeds and avoid harmful pesticides. Adopt roads and waterways and pick up litter when hiking or boating. Support beneficial insects and pollinators by leaving particular lawns and fields to grow without the intrusion of mowers or string trimmers. By taking these actions, you improve the environment's health and help create a sustainable future.

A tree that is unbending is easily broken.

~Tao Te Ching

Bring To Light

Let's confront some challenging truths. Adversity is not an enemy; instead, it is necessary. It serves as the wind that strengthens trees. As the saying goes, the most rigid trees may snap, but those that bend with the wind survive the storm. The winds of change don't have to render us barren, for we can always begin anew. Sometimes, the metaphorical gusts and gales that come our way help us grow stronger by sinking our roots deeper. Life is a series of lessons in resilience and adaptation. The sooner we accept what is, the quicker we can overcome our resistance and fear of what could be. Eventually, we realize peace can be found in acceptance, and progress can be achieved through adaptation.

The 3 A's—awareness, acceptance, and action—actively guide us in navigating challenges and moving forward. Widely explored in personal development and psychology, this framework highlights the importance of recognizing reality, embracing it, and taking purposeful steps forward. Like a spider rebuilding its web after damage, enduring adversity can lead to remarkable growth. The spider, unfazed by its circumstances, accepts reality and immediately transitions into action, tirelessly rebuilding.

The wisdom we gain from facing adversity becomes a source of strength we can draw upon during future challenges. Even if our inner selves are the only ones to recognize this growth, we shape a solid and resilient internal landscape as the foundation of our inner home. Adversity acts as a consequential amendment to the soil of our souls, promoting profound personal growth and transformation. It enriches our character and equips us to navigate life's difficulties with greater resilience and insight.

In our modern age, we must honor nature in all its forms. The Earth breathes and pulses with life, functioning as a self-sustaining organism beyond our comprehension and limits. Continuously regenerating and reconstructing, it births new species while others are extinguished, often due to adverse human actions and interference. Earth seeks balance, yet humanity incessantly challenges her, forcing her to compensate for our carelessness. The imbalances in nature always reflect imbalances in society. We live a co-creative existence.

A co-creative existence acknowledges the interdependent relationship between humans and nature, where both influence and shape each other. We are not passive recipients of the Earth's processes but active participants who impact the environment through our actions. At the same time, nature shapes our lives, providing resources and sustaining us.

In this relationship, we take responsibility for making choices that promote harmony rather than disruption. By working with nature—whether through sustainable practices, protecting biodiversity, or embracing eco-conscious innovation—we actively contribute to its regeneration. A co-creative existence calls us to live in partnership with the Earth, recognizing that our well-being intertwines with the planet's health. This collaboration shapes a more balanced, thriving future for all.

We have contemplated these truths since the dawn of the Industrial Age. The sustainability of a healthy life now teeters on environmental uncertainty. Healthy, well-tended soil sustains all life, while clean water, fresh air, and sunlight drive continuous growth. It is time for humanity to confront its fate and take responsibility for ignoring nature's warnings.

Help us to be ever faithful gardeners of the spirit, who know that without darkness nothing comes to birth, and without light nothing flowers.

~May Sarton

Leap Of Faith

Every gardener tends to develop a personal approach to planting. Some talk to their seedlings or add coffee grounds to roses. Others bury fish heads and banana peels under their tomatoes. Some even sing to their landscapes and find joy in companion planting. Gardening is more than a sensory experience; it's a conscious one. This manual also explores the invisible force of several virtues and essential elements worth reflecting on, considering, and embracing to make the journey more enjoyable and manageable.

The foremost virtue that every gardener must possess, regardless of experience, is faith. This statement isn't meant to challenge anyone's beliefs or be taken lightly; it pertains to an inner quality within us. Faith holds significant importance because gardening, like life, offers no guarantees. Obstacles are inevitable, and there's no assurance that seeds will sprout, roots will grow, or fruits will set. We recognize that we cannot control everything beyond our actions; external factors such as weather, critters, insects, and spores follow their agendas. Instead, we invest our faith in our ability to put forth our best effort.

When we collaborate with the ephemeral nature of creativity, we co-create. With the assistance of co-creative forces and external influences, gardeners can make steady progress while acknowledging and learning from their imperfections. This growth may not always be immediately apparent, but it undeniably occurs. This same faith can guide us through perseverance, becoming our guiding light and helping us navigate uncertainty in challenging times.

Opting to quit is always a choice and sometimes a necessity, but it is often the least favorable, especially in the garden. Knowing when to step back is not the same as giving up. Don't give up on your being; let go of what causes stress. When we quit, weed seeds spread, overshadowing potential growth and leading to disappointment.

Learning from our trials and errors is necessary to avoid repeating them. Every gardener encounters moments of devastation, but harboring resentment towards perceived outcomes proves unproductive.

Of course, trials and tribulations are challenging, but they provide the necessary fuel and grit for meaningful improvement. These difficulties offer a wealth of knowledge and wisdom, serving as silver linings during challenging times. Instead of viewing these moments as setbacks, we can take accountability and embrace our mistakes, allowing them to transform into opportunities for growth—much like compost enriches the soil for healthier development. Just as gardeners tend to their plants, we can cultivate our inner garden —our mind, body, and spirit—by nurturing the virtues of patience and trust, allowing it to blossom and grow.

In the garden, nature offers countless opportunities to learn from its rhythms and our essence. A seed buried in darkness must crack open to sprout, change, emerge, and reach toward the light. This seed becomes a plant that matures and blossoms. By accepting the pain and challenges of growth, we become more adept at navigating them in healthier ways—this, too, is a part of personal evolution.

It may seem unconventional, but the ability to think with our heart and feel with our mind holds the wisdom of the ancients—those who survived by understanding the natural world and aligning their actions with the lessons learned through observing nature and their acts of trial and error. We can move with greater freedom and grace when we consciously connect to our inner joy and integrate the mind with the heart. This is a form of faith in action, a source of inspiration and enlightenment.

Cultivating grace is an important virtue to practice daily; it allows us to accept losses more easily than contempt ever could. The essence of grace lies in compassion. When a plant fails to grow well, we don't blame it; instead, we examine its environment, consider what may have hindered its growth, and make necessary adjustments. Nature often presents challenges, yet it forgives our interference by persisting despite our actions. Similarly, we must learn to compassionately forgive our mistakes as part of our inner work toward success. Grace is a gift we give ourselves and others when life doesn't go as planned, empowering us to recover and continue our journey of growth and resilience.

The garden of your world has no limits except in your mind.

~Rumi

Life's Garden

Gardening transcends everyday pleasures, providing a profound sense of personal achievement and satisfaction throughout the growing season. Sitting amidst nature's bounty and savoring a meal straight from the vine offers a fulfillment that is hard to describe—it's the taste of success. Observing the first bud burst on a rose shrub evokes an inexplicable sense of peace and wonder, filling the heart with hope for even more joy. These are the moment-to-moment pleasures of being present in our co-creative environments.

Working with soil and nurturing a garden are among the most rewarding and laborious endeavors. A burgeoning garden teeming with bees, birds, butterflies, and countless other beneficial creatures lifts us from the doldrums and fills us with awe and gratitude. Our efforts help the local ecology and awaken sustenance for other beings, eliciting a profound sense of satisfaction and a deep connection to the world around us.

Gardening is an act of the heart that defies full explanation and must be lived to be truly understood. Words alone cannot capture its depth; only personal engagement can reveal its true power. Working with the land creates a connection with nature, sparking a deep, contagious desire to continue.

Similar to all living beings destined for their evolution of growth and personal discovery, we are born into the unknown and nurtured in the unyielding embrace of life's challenges. The full spectrum of what hinders or propels our growth remains mysterious until experience bestows its gifts of wisdom. Within these gifts lie deep stillness and self-awakening—a rebirth unto oneself, where conscious awareness emerges and begins to bloom. During these times, life is enriched in unseen ways and is usually only noticeable in hindsight.

We are born into a state of perfection, set against the backdrop of a complex and sometimes unforgiving world. Like seeds, each person possesses immense potential for growth and fulfillment; however, this potential remains dormant until we nurture it. By giving attention and care, we transform potential energy into active becoming—whether through the pursuit of knowledge, happiness, ingenuity, expressions of love, the building of wealth, or even inspiration. Clarity of perception through consciousness releases the ego and allows freedom to meet love. When guided by love and compassion, this newfound freedom becomes a powerful force for positive transformation within oneself and the world, bringing deep satisfaction and accomplishment. Just as plants flourish in sunlight, individuals prosper in the warmth of positive thoughts, attitudes, and actions.

We can't precisely measure how much effort is needed to be effective, as we can't guarantee that the seeds we plant will grow or be harvested. Yet, we move forward with faith that something positive will emerge and hope to enjoy the fruits of our labor eventually. Embracing life's virtues enriches our experiences more than trying to control outcomes. We relax and trust that our efforts contribute to a collaborative creation. We must step into our power, stay focused and present, and let creative inspiration guide us.

Each unique and sovereign flower in life's garden is a part of the whole, adding beauty and richness to the landscape. We must uncover and nurture our energy throughout our development to achieve and possibly surpass our potential. While our interactions and connections with others often influence our journey of self-discovery and personal growth, it isn't solely dependent on them. Nevertheless, collaboration and mutual support can help us navigate life's challenges and amplify our impact on the world. Everyone benefits when we help each other grow.

Goodness should become human nature because it is real in nature.

~Jean-Jacques Rousseau

Reap What We Sow

The energetic seeds we sow are what we will eventually reap. What we believe shapes what we create. Limiting beliefs will, indeed, limit our abundance. Tuning into our energy, especially during periods of change, is important for maintaining awareness and alignment within ourselves. Our emotions serve as signals that reflect our balance and overall state. When we engage in actions that resonate with our true selves, we gain clearer insights and can develop a deeper sense of internal peace. Achieving this peace through alignment is an ongoing internal practice that requires daily attention and adjustments. This focus is a fundamental aspect of our soul's journey, complementing our pursuit of creative expression. Energy is our most valuable resource, and nurturing a sense of peace is a form of personal wealth that holds priceless value. Peace is powerful.

Dedication and participation are the water to our bloom. Committing to ourselves can help us develop healthy routines that align with our intentions, balancing discipline with repeat practice. Consistency is a powerful force that connects us with our inner goodness, establishing a sense of contentment and acceptance of life without being easily swayed by challenges. By nurturing these routines, we enrich the soil of our soul and improve the health and vitality of our life's garden.

Staying in the present moment is not just a practice; it is a way of life. It heightens our awareness and control over our thoughts, while helping us connect more deeply with our hearts and emotions. When we lose focus on the present, we often become preoccupied with thoughts of the past or future, leading to uncertainty and distraction. As many authors have noted, walking the path of the heart is our most valuable journey. By staying present, we can experience our lives as they are, beyond what was or what might be.

Experiencing moments of feeling stuck can lead to creative solutions.

Nurturing peace and relaxation during these periods of stagnation can be quite beneficial. Time often serves as an excellent incubator for new ideas. Sometimes, clarity emerges from allowing yourself space to be as you are. It also provides time to prune outdated thoughts and beliefs—similar to how a plant needs pruning to grow more abundantly.

True confidence, free from ego, emerges when you are willing to know and love yourself fully, including the shadow aspects of your character. It takes courage and focus to challenge and change limiting beliefs, nurturing your spiritual awareness. You liberate yourself when you pursue actions without attachments to the outcomes. As a seed of source energy, authentic power grows from a strong foundation of acceptance, and this power cannot be taken from you. Each individual has a unique growth process; discovering what works for you is an integral part of your evolution.

Nothing changes unless we change, so we must shift our perception of reality to achieve different results. One practical approach is to direct our imagination toward how we want our situation to be. By focusing on the elements that bring us joy and make us feel good, we can harness that energy to transform our surroundings. As we become more aware of our mental, emotional, physical, and spiritual growth, a shift in perspective creates positive momentum, guiding us toward the purposeful life we desire. Our imagination draws in what we need to create the reality we want.

Appreciating everything, from minor details to the grandest aspects of our lives, can help us align with more positive feelings about our reality. Gratitude for our abilities and faculties is a good starting point when our perspective becomes distorted. Simply being alive and having another day in our life's garden is a powerful motivator to make space for new, inspired thoughts. We are responsible for what grows in our mental space, and if anything threatens or obstructs our growth, we can find ease by shifting our perception.

Regularly nurturing our inner landscape strengthens the foundation for building our character. Life presents numerous challenges that shape our successes by eliminating unstable support systems. Embracing these experiences allows us to grow stronger and more resilient, enabling us to navigate future obstacles with confidence and grace.

Focus on activities that bring joy and satisfaction. Engaging in physical movement can help alleviate mental stress that often feels repetitive. Aim to exercise daily to release stagnant energy and impurities—sweating through movement is an excellent daily practice. Work toward feeling better without placing conditions on your improvement.

Your experience of life originates from within. The source of your creativity, power, and strength is internal. It is important to recognize your sensitivity to the world around you. Engage with your passions without attachment to specific outcomes; instead, immerse yourself in the dynamics of the present moment. Embrace the flow of experiences as they arise, allowing yourself to feel and understand what is happening.

We possess the power to choose how we respond in each moment. Indecision and confusion can act like weeds, suffocating our ability to take action and leading us into a cycle of stagnation. Dr. Ellen Langer states, "Rather than waste your time being stressed over making the right decision, make the decision right. Randomly choose…there's no way of knowing if the choice would have been worse, better, or the same as the other; that's why regret is so mindless—because the choice you didn't take, you're presuming, would have been better." (Langer, Dr. Ellen. Interview with Rich Roll, YouTube, February 13, 2024).

Your Mind's Garden

Be mindful of your thoughts. Choose the ones you want to grow, and actively tend to the garden of your mind each day. Eliminate the weeds of worry and fill your mental space with positive, uplifting thoughts. Just as you decide what to cultivate in a garden, decide what to nurture in your mind. Take ownership of your thoughts. Delusional thinking disrupts your mental flow and leads to detours. Stay open to learning so you can experience an abundance of clarity.

You belong here, and universal energy responds to your beliefs. Choose your beliefs wisely, as they shape your reality. A belief is simply a thought you keep thinking is true. Believe in your abilities and become the person you aspire to be. Repeating negative, self-deprecating beliefs harms your well-being. Improve your thinking and treat yourself with kindness, even when it's hard to find kindness elsewhere. Conscious mindfulness nurtures the tiniest ideas to bloom. Sowing the seed of a good-feeling thought can transform your entire mental landscape.

By making conscious choices and prioritizing joyful activities and feelings, you can break free from negative cycles and create greater personal fulfillment. Ultimately, you are the sole caretaker of your mental garden, where thoughts can nurture blossoms of creativity or allow pessimistic weeds to take root. It is up to you to tend to this garden, cultivating positivity and self-worth while removing anything that hinders your potential. You live there, so why not make it a place where you feel good? Be joyful as you are.

> The love of gardening is a seed once sown that never dies.
>
> ~Gertrude Jekyll

Back To School

Life offers multiple avenues of free education, but the critical requirement is to show up and participate. Respecting nature is a course requirement, and restoring it without destroying it is the long-term goal. Before taking the spade to the soil, become familiar with desired plant selections, native species, seasonal changes, available growing space, soil fertility, water sources, and sunlight.

Harnessing and exercising the power of imagination is indispensable to nurturing creations. From this point forward, view yourself as a student in the Garden School of Life. The daily practicum involves experimentation. Your initial classroom is the land you envision, which you can continually improve and expand. This is where your journey begins. Life will provide the necessary teachers, tools, and resources. There will be challenging moments and times of despair, and you might even feel like giving up, but these experiences are also part of the journey in the garden of life.

There is no wrong way to proceed, as learning occurs through every experience. There are no wrong questions, and there usually are many acceptable answers. Everything is fluid and ever-changing. As you nurture your nature, your vision will naturally expand. Engaging with the land teaches you about yourself, revealing a connection that should be explored with respect. Every gardener has a unique approach to growth, and the garden serves as an ideal classroom. Cultivating life is entirely in your hands and your responsibility; it is your creation. Seeking and incorporating help when needed is part of the process—it broadens your perspective, tempers pride, and builds character.

Trial and error and observation are valuable tools for improving gardening practices over time. By identifying and reflecting on planting mistakes, gardeners can improve their techniques, increase crop yields, and support plant health. This ongoing process of experimentation and adjustment is key to becoming a skilled and knowledgeable gardener.

Gardening is a multifaceted practice that evolves rather than a final goal. The aim is to improve just a bit each day. The results are naturally continuous, as is evolution.

Nature is our greatest teacher, offering education that benefits humanity. We gain a deeper understanding of freedom through serving others and tending to a growing garden. Mutual reciprocity flows naturally through the services we provide and the harvests we receive. Abundance comes to us in many unexpected ways. Learning to give is as important as learning to receive; both shape the journey through life's garden.

Each day we commit to something beyond our own needs, we grow as Master Gardeners of Life and scholars of stewardship. We are here to plant our gardens. Every garden, no matter its size, holds immense significance, reflecting the value and interconnectedness of all life. Our existence is intricately linked with others, often in unseen ways. Not everything we plant will be reaped or enjoyed by us; some benefits are meant for others to discover. We must have faith in our existence without being attached to fulfilling a specific purpose. Inspiration is a magical, fluid energy that transforms ideas into creation and thoughts into action.

Even a simple container filled with greens or flowers can positively impact the local ecology in subtle and often unseen ways. The intention to grow contributes to the greater good, even if our awareness of its impact is limited. Through this process, we become stewards and teachers, whether we recognize it or not. The gifts of expanded awareness and applied knowledge enrich our growth journey, transforming our lives and potentially influencing the lives of others.

Living life is different from merely existing. While being alive requires only the essentials—oxygen, food, water, immunity, and warmth—truly living involves both circumstantial and intentional states of being. Creating a life worth living and truly feeling alive demands purposeful action. It begins with an idea, a vision, or a dream. Like a gardener who carefully plants seeds rather than scattering them aimlessly, deliberate effort is necessary to yield a bountiful harvest. Growth takes time, making patience an equally valuable virtue.

Like life, gardening involves risks. The next best step becomes more manageable once we accept that everything carries some risk. We must recognize that no amount of planning can shield us from natural or unforeseen forces. As life progresses, we realize much of it lies beyond our control. Therefore, we must keep moving forward, managing what we can while adapting to the unknown. This leads us to another valuable virtue—trust.

Faith and patience, like trust, play an important role. Negative thoughts, much like bindweed in the garden, choke potential. Trust requires fearless surrender and roots itself in the quiet stillness of the mind. Without it, we depend on blind faith, leading to uncertainty and misunderstanding. Doubts disrupt our intuition, creating anxiety and despair. However, when we release fear and cultivate trust, we realize there isn't a right or wrong way to proceed—only different paths to explore. Some journeys may involve frequent detours as we gain clarity about our true intentions. Meditation becomes valuable here; over time, it clears away the weeds of unwanted and confusing thoughts, allowing for greater focus and understanding.

Trusting ourselves involves building confidence and embracing the unknown with each breath. We nurture our gardens and live on faith in life's timely provisions. We can endure, overcome, and survive the harshest storms like a garden. Time is a series of moments, each marked by temporary circumstances. A flower's bloom may be fleeting, but it is significant. Similarly, setbacks can be profound yet are also temporary. Strategizing and rebuilding are integral aspects of life, even if it means transplanting and establishing roots elsewhere. Nothing remains static, and a garden vividly reflects this truth every day.

Gardening doesn't follow strict rules but relies on practical methods and procedures. A seed will germinate under the right conditions, whether planted intentionally or randomly. Gardening, much like life, is mainly about experimentation. Different approaches produce different results; the key is discovering what works best to achieve the desired outcome. Each season builds upon fundamental knowledge, increasing experience and leading to wisdom through practice. Experimentation opens up possibilities, introduces variety, and brings unexpected joy, but it may also lead to occasional setbacks.

Perseverance is another valued virtue in life's garden, empowering individuals to confront challenges with courage and determination. It embodies resilience in the face of adversity. In gardening, failures can take many forms, including lost crops, pest infestations, disease outbreaks, climate challenges, poor planting choices, and neglect. To "fail forward" means to persist, recognizing that setbacks are temporary pauses in the journey. Perseverance encourages a mindset that views failures as learning opportunities, understanding that errors are minor detours rather than obstacles. This approach cultivates adaptability and innovation in problem-solving. Practicing perseverance builds discipline, grit, and inner strength, shaping a well-rounded character and enhancing self-worth.

Sometimes, in our journey, we feel the urge to "fix" something or intervene because we are dissatisfied with what is unfolding. Although intervention may sometimes be necessary, it is encouraged to thoughtfully consider actions in advance. This principle also applies to the mental fears that disrupt our progress. When we let chaotic thoughts or justifications for our fears hold us back, we stagnate and stray off course, leading to a detour. However, this detour can ultimately guide us back once we have learned the lessons intended for our journey.

In this dynamic process, it becomes evident that making adjustments is an important part of the journey. Attuning our approach is a flexible strategy that adapts to the garden's ever-changing landscape. With a resilient mindset, gardeners persevere, viewing each challenge as an opportunity to refine their skills and deepen their understanding of the intricate patterns in the garden and life.

Most of us don't begin life with a clear sense of purpose or singular passions, although those who discover their interests early on are fortunate. Life often feels like a game of odds, with each of us holding the energetic dice. Many navigate their paths by scattering seeds of intention, hoping something will take root and grow. Favorable conditions sometimes lead to unexpected, positive outcomes, showing that exploration and openness bring surprising rewards. Embracing this uncertainty creates opportunities for growth and discovery.

However, an experienced gardener understands that a garden is constantly evolving and can be unpredictable from season to season and year to year. Beginning with intention is necessary; however, remaining flexible and open to change as growth unfolds is beneficial. Gardening is a lifelong journey, so relax, enjoy the process, and stay receptive to the opportunities that arise along this co-creative adventure—embracing the journey with curiosity and adaptability.

Life begins the day you start a garden.

~Chinese Proverb

The Power Of Choice

Life is a garden of choices, where each decision is a seed planted, and its outcome shapes the landscape of our journey. The power of choice deeply connects gardening and life. Choosing to cultivate a garden is an enriching decision that brings countless benefits. Each seed and plant we nurture mirrors the many choices we make in life. These choices shape our journey, as well-tended plants create a vibrant and fruitful garden. Decisions drive growth, bring fulfillment, and harvest meaningful rewards in life and gardening.

A bountiful harvest may be the ultimate goal, yet the journey holds far more than simply producing a fruitful crop. Through trial and error, we gain understanding and knowledge, which can evolve into wisdom if we learn from our experiences. This process mirrors life, where we uncover our true desires by letting go of what no longer resonates. In our gardens, we decide what to nurture and what to remove, allowing the desired plants to grow by clearing away the unwanted. Similarly, making choices often requires letting go of old habits, relationships, or beliefs that no longer support our growth. It's about weeding our inner landscape to create space for personal development and happiness.

By making intentional choices, we can create meaningful change, overcome challenges, and align our actions with our true desires. Even when we feel we've made poor decisions, those choices often teach valuable lessons. Shifting our perspective allows us to see the gifts in our initial choices and uncover the insights they offer. Adversity typically brings important lessons that prepare us for what we genuinely desire.

Perception is often seen as a choice because it reflects how we interpret our experiences through our senses and thoughts. We choose how to view situations, and two people can experience the same event but perceive it differently based on their beliefs, past experiences, and mindsets.

Our mindset plays a significant role in shaping our perception. A growth mindset encourages us to view challenges as opportunities for learning, while a fixed mindset can lead us to see them as insurmountable obstacles. Growth becomes evident when we choose to respond rationally to our perceptions. Instead of reacting with frustration or fear, we can take a moment to reflect and opt for a more constructive response. While emotions serve a purpose, they can also be misleading.

Reframing our thoughts involves consciously shifting how we view a situation to change its emotional impact. These moments encourage us to explore what our fears can teach us. By recognizing that our choices shape our perception, we can become more intentional in interpreting and responding to the world around us.

The Soil Of Soul

You might be wondering how all this connects to gardening. Similar to how a gardener cares for plants, we can care for our souls, nurturing inner well-being and spiritual growth. When envisioning your ideal garden, it's often shaped by your desires, past experiences, and preconceived ideas. Likewise, when designing the garden of your life, it's important to leave space for the unknown to unfold. In simple terms, stay open to the possibility that life may exceed your expectations. Just as a garden can grow beyond your initial vision, your life can expand when you welcome new possibilities, remain flexible, and make intentional choices.

When planning your garden, consider cultivating what nourishes your soul and body. Explore new sources of joy and fulfillment, discovering beauty and sustenance in diverse options. Just as a balanced diet supports physical health, your choices shape the richness of your life. Adversity feels less overwhelming when your personal power is deeply rooted—this power, your inner strength, is the foundation for growth. Surrendering it weakens your potential, while embracing it strengthens your resilience. The quality of your life depends on the strength of your inner power and your decisions, which is why self-awareness is so transformative.

Making choices is often one of the most challenging aspects of beginning any endeavor. Yet, hesitance can quickly extinguish the flames of possibility. Resisting change tends to create struggle and pain, whereas making a decision ignites change, bringing clarity, progress, and, ultimately, freedom. Making a decision encourages the flow of movement.

The gardener's soul is deeply connected to the garden. Your choices, creativity, and actions breathe life into it, reflecting and enriching your personal journey. The care and effort you invest in your garden often mirror how you care for yourself. Self-care involves recognizing and meeting your needs, such as staying active, eating nourishing foods, getting enough rest, practicing mindfulness, and engaging in hobbies. It also means setting healthy boundaries, seeking support, and making time for relaxation and self-reflection. By nurturing yourself, you cultivate balance, resilience, and the strength to overcome challenges—both in your garden and in life.

Take a moment to examine your inner garden. What have you been nurturing within yourself? Reflect on the beliefs, thoughts, and emotions you've been cultivating. Are there areas in your inner garden that need more care and attention? What has been neglected? Have weeds of negativity, doubt, or complacency stifled growth? Just as you thoughtfully design and tend to your outer garden, you can shape and cultivate your inner landscape. Enrich the soil of your soul with positive thoughts, intentional words, and mindful actions, creating a space where growth and fulfillment can actualize.

Nature's Way

One of the most enchanting aspects of gardening is the sense of abundance it offers. A well-tended edible landscape often yields more than enough to share, nourishing ourselves and the local ecosystem. Life reflects this pattern: acts of service grounded in care, love, generosity, and compassion create an abundant life meant to be shared. When we give from a mindset of abundance, expecting nothing in return, sustenance flows freely. This generosity sustains the cycle of prosperity, nurturing growth and fulfillment.

Before sowing the first seed, recognize that nature will always claim its share. Accepting that around 20% of the yield will return to nature helps maintain balance and respectful reciprocity. All life is connected to the soil and thrives on its productivity. Before taking drastic measures to prohibit or destroy natural beings that consume co-created provisions, remember that nature's survival depends on its ability to continue living. Nature provides, and it is equally necessary to provide for nature. Many animal habitats have been destroyed, displaced, and severely impacted, disrupting ecological balance. Make peace when natural forces take the occasional fruit or vegetable; this is part of nature's way of surviving against incredible odds.

A challenging but inherent lesson we can observe in nature is the concept of sacrifice. Sacrificing part of our harvest is a virtuous act of charity that benefits other beings in the garden, contributing to their well-being without significantly impacting our yield. Sacrifice is an idea that includes various insights, but it is ultimately up to each person to acknowledge and embrace these experiences as meaningful. For example, when we plant more crops than we need, we give back to the earth and support the ecosystem.

Sacrificial crops for nature refer to plants explicitly grown to support ecological balance and biodiversity. These crops may be used in practices such as permaculture or agroecology to enrich soil health, attract beneficial insects, or restore habitats. By planting these crops, farmers and gardeners can contribute to the ecosystem's resilience, helping to maintain or improve natural processes. This approach emphasizes giving back to the earth, recognizing that sustainable practices benefit nature and agricultural productivity.

In essence, sacrifice is a pathway to deeper understanding, empathy, and connection with ourselves and the world. It encourages us to look beyond our immediate desires and consider the broader impact of our actions. Recognizing what we give up makes us appreciate what we have even more deeply. Sacrificing for a cause or a greater good can lead to significant social and environmental change. This way, sacrifice can strengthen our connection to nature and build community. By sharing what we have, we nurture the environment and cultivate empathy and appreciation within ourselves. Cultivating empathy is like planting seeds of understanding and compassion, growing a garden of interconnected and harmonious relationships. The cycle of giving enriches the ecosystem and deepens our understanding of interdependence in the natural world.

Sometimes, letting go of certain relationships may be necessary to gain a clearer sense of self. Although we all have flaws, prioritizing personal well-being over these connections requires careful reflection on values. Knowing your worth means recognizing and valuing your abilities, qualities, and contributions. It involves understanding your intrinsic value, independent of external validation or comparisons with others.

Earth stewards learn and teach the importance of respecting and protecting ourselves, each other, and the natural world. Since experience often teaches more than manuals, we navigate challenges as they arise. When difficulties emerge in nature or life, asking, "What can I learn from this?" can uncover valuable insights. Embracing quiet stillness, especially in nature, brings clarity and perspective. This practice of self-care and reflection helps us heal and cope with disappointments, nurturing the soil of our soul as nature intended.

Interconnectedness

Modern societies have shifted their focus from the natural world to increasingly artificial environments. Technology has turned life into a continuous experiment, raising a pressing question: how far can humanity deviate from the natural order before the scales of balance tip?

Humanity is interconnected in many ways: environmentally, economically, culturally, historically, spiritually, and socially. Changes in the environment, whether beneficial or harmful, impact everyone. For instance, climate change alters weather patterns, agriculture, and health on a global scale, demonstrating our shared environmental ties. Local actions can also have wide-ranging effects. Pollution in one area can affect air quality worldwide, and conservation efforts in one region can benefit biodiversity globally.

The Earth is a rich source of creation, and tapping into its energetic flow begins with recognizing our interconnectedness. By embracing a spirit of abundance in daily life, you can share your knowledge, time, or resources with others in a balanced and supportive way. Cultivate gratitude by acknowledging the abundance already around you—scatter seeds of gratitude throughout your day. Keeping a daily gratitude list, even reflecting on it verbally, can deepen this practice. These habits lay a strong foundation for growth and personal development, nurturing yourself and those around you.

Our individuation complements our sense of communal connection. By connecting internally, we can attune to our thoughts, emotions, values, and intuition. This inner alignment guides us to make honest choices and navigate life's challenges with clarity. When we join forces with others who maintain a balanced internal connection, we drive meaningful global change.

The soil is a beautiful example of interconnectedness. Beneath the surface, extensive networks of mycorrhizal fungi form symbiotic relationships with plant roots. These fungi are significant in both plant and soil health. They facilitate nutrient uptake, particularly for nutrients like phosphorus that are otherwise hard for plant roots to access. This partnership allows for efficient nutrient exchange between fungi and plants. Additionally, mycorrhizal fungi improve soil structure, increase aeration, and reduce erosion, which is a pivotal reason behind the benefits of no-till gardening. Tilling disrupts the mycorrhizal network and the natural processes that contribute to soil health. Minimizing soil disturbance helps maintain soil health, and adding soil amendments is vital for soil enrichment.

Sometimes, we encounter a plot of land with nutrient-deficient, compacted soil. In these cases, we must intervene to rebuild the soil. Tilling helps break the compaction, allowing us to introduce soil builders like compost, organic matter, earthworms, and mulch. After aerating the soil and adding amendments, further tilling is usually unnecessary. Instead, using seasonal cover crops, practicing crop rotation, and occasionally using a garden fork or aerator will continue to improve the soil's nutrient profile and structure. Building soil takes time, but consistently adding organic materials increases gradual growth.

Understanding our role in this interconnected universe helps reduce our potential for harm. Knowledge becomes powerful when applied effectively. Embracing our interconnectedness can lead to greater empathy, cooperation, and a sense of shared responsibility, encouraging actions that benefit not only individuals or nations but all of humanity. Your vision for your garden reflects your power to shape life through imagination, choice, and action. As you journey through the Garden School of Life, remember that you hold the seeds of possibility. Choose carefully where to plant them, nurture them thoughtfully, and watch them blossom into a life rich with beauty, purpose, and prosperity.

One of the worst mistakes you can make as a gardener is to think you're in charge.

~Janet Gillespie

Rooted in Balance

Before we dig into the fertile soil of life and gardening, it's necessary to understand a few foundational principles. Life force is a potent and wondrous energy, with nature playing a central role in orchestration. As soil and soul gardeners, we aim to harness this vitality and offer our support when needed. We are called to take action but not to engage in excessive toil. The basics for growth are simple: soil, sun, water, warmth, and immunity. However, sowing virtues of life can elevate growth to a dynamic and expansive level.

The best things in life grow organically. Similarly, it is important to understand that love cannot be forced or demanded. Trying to compel affection for something that doesn't resonate with you is often unproductive. Instead, focusing on appreciating and learning from its presence is far more beneficial. Embracing resistance can help prevent wasted efforts and foster a more developed sense of self-worth and personal integrity. Resistance acts as a signal, indicating that there may be an unknown factor requiring further exploration or a different approach. By acknowledging this resistance, you open yourself to new insights and possibilities, ultimately cultivating a more sincere connection with yourself and the world around you.

Just like in gardening, excessive force is not the solution. When a tool encounters an obstruction in the soil, it signals the need to pause and reassess. Overexertion can fatigue us and risk damaging tools or hidden utilities beneath the surface. Similarly, nature does not yield to coercion. While the effects may not be immediately visible, Newton's Third Law of Motion reminds us that every action has an equal and opposite reaction. Using our mental or physical energy constructively helps maintain balance and prevents the strain of forcing our will.

In nature, life proliferates through a delicate web of symbiotic relationships that maintain ecological balance. A forest exemplifies this intricate network. When logging occurs, it disrupts the entire ecosystem, altering the web of life irreparably. Though young saplings may be planted later, the original symbiotic harmony is irreversibly disrupted. The consequences are widespread, affecting everything from the microbial life in the soil to bird migration patterns and the survival of native wildlife. Erosion caused by topsoil removal and land degradation leads to loss of soil fertility, reduced agricultural productivity, and ecosystem damage. This disruption is a harsh and often concealed reality that the logging and timber industry tends to downplay. Similarly, the relentless extraction of fossil fuels exposes significant ecological imbalances and damage.

In gardening and daily life, humility and an awareness of our place within the natural world are necessary means for connecting with the land. We can only be accountable for our own choices. By choosing to benefit life, we become stewards and collaborators with the natural world. The garden of life blossoms when we embrace this partnership, co-creating with our environment, treading lightly on the earth, and nurturing the soil beneath our feet and the essence of our being.

The Language Of Nature

Nature speaks through mathematical expressions, embodying mathematical principles in structure and behavior. Plant growth, for instance, follows logarithmic spirals, with parts often aligning to the golden ratio to optimize growth. The Fibonacci sequence appears in the arrangement of leaves, seeds, and petals, while symmetry is evident in animals, flowers, crystals, and snowflakes. Fractals, or self-repeating patterns, manifest in tree branches, cloud formations, and coastlines, showing how smaller patterns resemble the whole. The laws of physics, such as gravity and thermodynamics, follow mathematical equations governing everything from planetary orbits to light bending. The constant Pi (π) governs the geometry of circles, as seen in planets and flower petals. Waves, from oceans to light, follow predictable mathematical patterns. Mathematics provides a universal language to understand nature's intricate, often hidden, patterns, offering insight into its complexity and beauty.

The mathematical patterns in nature also reflect our potential for balance and growth. Just as nature follows laws that create harmony, we can align with these principles to find balance in our lives. Understanding these patterns helps guide our personal growth and decision-making, encouraging a harmonious relationship with the natural world. Recognizing these connections allows us to live more consciously and cultivate balance in our inner and outer worlds.

In seeing ourselves as part of this vast, intelligent design, we begin to understand that we are not separate from nature but expressions of it. The same patterns that govern galaxies and guide the unfolding of a fern also shape the rhythms of our breath, relationships, and growth. When we align with these natural principles—seeking balance, embracing cycles, and honoring complexity—we return to a more grounded, meaningful way of living. In this alignment lies personal transformation and the potential for collective healing and a more harmonious existence with the world around us.

> **Half the interest of a garden is the constant exercise of the imagination.**
>
> **~Mrs. C.W. Earle**

Open Your Mind

Now, let's take a significant step toward creating your masterpiece—your ultimate garden. Picture your plot of land, where you can design and cultivate a garden filled with your chosen selections, varieties, and designs. Set aside any concerns about money, feasibility, or limitations for this exercise. Embrace the limitless nature of what's possible.

With an open mindset to limitless possibilities, begin using your imagination to envision the future of your garden plot. Start by projecting concepts from your mind and gradually shape your grandest ideas. Use this space to jot down your initial thoughts on what you'd love to enjoy in your garden. Once you have a clear sense of your vision, move on to the next page.

Gardens are a form of autobiography.
~Sydney Eddison

Here is a quiz. You are ready.

1. Where is your garden plot located?
2. How big is your garden plot? Is it a patio, backyard, acreage, or hectares?
3. Is it flat, or does it have elevation changes?
4. Does it have square dimensions, or are there curvatures in the design?
5. What is growing in your plot? Are there flowers, edible varieties, specimens, trees, and vines?
6. Have you chosen a specific color palette for your garden? How do these colors make you feel?
7. Do you want to surround yourself with specific scents or fragrances?
8. Are there pathways, sitting areas, hammocks, or swings?
9. Does it consist entirely of vegetation, or are there hardscapes?
10. Are there any art installations or trellises, treehouses, or other structures?
11. Are there any cultural or historical inspirations for your garden design?
12. How do you envision your garden changing with the seasons?
13. Does it have a bird bath, water feature, or pond?
14. Are there fences or gates, and if so, what materials are they made of?

15. Will there be any animals or livestock in an area of your garden?

16. Is your garden designed to be formal, natural, or a combination?

17. Have you considered the overall atmosphere or mood you want your garden to evoke?

18. What outdoor activities or gatherings do you envision in your garden?

19. How does your garden reflect your personality, values, and priorities in life?

20. Are there a variety of gardens within your landscape: kitchen garden, Zen garden, rose garden, herb garden, secret garden, etc.?

No single sort of garden suits everyone. Shut your eyes and dream of the garden you'd most love, then open your eyes and start planting. Loved gardens flourish; boring ones are hard work.

~Jackie French

Reflecting On The Quiz

Now, let's pause for reflection. Did many of the questions align with your initial brainstorming vision? Were there ideas that went beyond the scope of the questions? Did this exercise ever feel overwhelming, or did you experience a sense of excitement about the possibilities?

This quiz is a multifaceted exercise designed to expand and harness one of your greatest gifts—imagination. Its purpose is to encourage you to contemplate options that may not have previously crossed your mind. Remember, this quiz is a tool to assess your ability to explore your unlimited potential, not as a means for self-judgment or criticism. Such attributes can be counterproductive, stifling the growth of your creative process.

Self-judgment often traps us in a deceptive loop, causing us to perpetuate distrust by deceiving ourselves. Imagination offers a powerful way to break free from this cycle, opening doors to greater possibilities and opportunities. While our goal isn't merely to fall in love with potential, we are here to engage in thoughts that uplift and expand us, helping us to embrace and love our reality.

Every intentional step helps us move away from stagnant energy and brings us closer to clarity. This clarity enables us to make thoughtful decisions and act on them effectively. In contrast, self-judgment and criticism cloud our clarity. Keep in mind that our imagination is the key to exceeding our potential. We will now use deliberate thought and intention to cultivate a metaphorical or literal garden where you can grow well beyond your imagination.

People sometimes fail to live because they are always planning to live.

~Alan Watts

Get Off The Ground

The gardening journey begins with careful planning long before the spade touches the earth. However, there comes a time when action must take precedence. Excessive planning can lead to overwhelming thoughts, and before panic sets in, it's helpful to ask, "Where and how do I begin?" The answer is refreshingly simple: start precisely where you are, just as you are. You set your journey in motion by making a conscious decision and taking the next step forward. As in life, your garden will evolve, and so will you throughout the process.

Just as we learn to take baby steps before making long strides, starting with an approach that emphasizes ease is important. The point is to start small and gradually expand. Begin by assessing the site where you plan to grow. Success begins with choosing the right environment. A location with clean water, good airflow, and plenty of sunlight holds the same importance as quality soil. Consider what you want to cultivate and what your environment can realistically support. By observing your surroundings before planting, you can refine your choices.

For example, if the soil is heavy with clay and challenging to work with, starting with a raised bed or a few potted plants might be a practical solution. Some plants do well with minimal care, while others challenge even experienced gardeners. To connect with the local ecology, it is imperative to research native species that are suited to the environment. By embracing nature's wisdom and focusing on regional native plants for your landscaping, the garden will benefit from their natural resilience, lower maintenance needs, and more significant support for local wildlife.

To grow a garden successfully, assess your environment. Identify your space—an outdoor plot, an indoor area, pots on a patio, or a community garden. Begin your gardening journey with your existing resources and build from there. For example, if you only have a balcony or a sunlit window, use it as your starting point. While indoor gardening can be challenging without a dedicated greenhouse, experimenting with hydroponics, terrariums, growing leafy greens, or placing select plants near a sunny window can still produce satisfying results. Determine what works best for the available space and needs.

We will focus on outdoor gardening, but you can apply the same principles to any growing space, whether indoors or outdoors. These core themes—transforming life into a productive and abundant source of joy—remain relevant in every gardening context.

Scratching The Surface

Another practical approach to understanding garden space is to conduct a soil test to measure nutrient density. To grow nutrient-dense food, build nutrient-dense soil. To get a soil test, collect a soil sample from the garden. Use a clean garden trowel to take samples from several different spots in the garden, ideally from the top 6 to 8 inches of soil. Combine these samples in a clean bucket to create a representative composite sample. Remove debris, such as roots or stones, and allow the soil to dry completely before placing it in a soil testing bag or container.

Next, find a local extension service, agricultural laboratory, or garden center that offers soil testing services. Some institutions provide mail-in kits that include instructions for sending a sample. Follow their guidelines carefully to ensure accurate results. The lab will analyze the sample for various factors, including nutrient levels, pH, and soil texture. You will receive a report detailing the soil's current condition and recommendations for amendments to improve soil fertility and health.

Amending the soil annually is a valuable practice for maintaining a healthy garden. To rejuvenate the soil's composition and structure, incorporate quality compost, aged manure, untreated grass clippings, and biodegradable mulch. These additions improve soil fertility, stimulate better plant growth, and help sustain the overall health of your garden.

Some plant species, including edibles and herbs such as garlic, chives, kale, and thyme, are well-suited to poor soil conditions. Additionally, plants like peas and beans can help improve soil quality by fixing nitrogen. Enriching it with organic matter like compost or aged manure can significantly enhance the soil profile when working with nutrient-poor soil. This adds essential nutrients and builds soil texture. Mulching further supports soil health by conserving moisture and gradually improving soil quality.

Understanding soil pH is critical to selecting the proper plant amendments. For instance, lavender grows best in alkaline soil, whereas blueberries and tomatoes thrive in slightly acidic conditions. Each soil type supports different plants, so knowing your soil's characteristics helps you grow your plants more effectively. Local Master Gardener programs and soil conservationists can assist in interpreting soil test results and identifying the necessary adjustments for optimal plant health.

Site planning helps minimize potential issues affecting your garden's success. Before you start planting, observe the sunlight patterns in your space. Pay attention to any shadows created by plants, trees, or structures, which can help ensure better growth later. Remember, gardening often involves learning from mistakes—what seems like an error at first may prove beneficial in the long run. A little preparation before you begin can lead to more successful results.

It becomes clear that there is always more to learn and more to do. The best approach is to tackle one task at a time, starting with what you have and what you already know or want to learn. Assistance is readily available from numerous sources, including local Master Gardener extension services, the Internet, libraries, and community groups.

Gardening is the work of a lifetime: you never finish.

~Oscar De La Renta

Keep It Simple

This manual emphasizes creating a functional and enjoyable living garden within one's space, internally and externally. Learning the art of living, being self-sufficient, and growing your own food are rewarding energy investments. Gardening is a continual, seasonal journey, constantly evolving and full of surprises. Take it one step at a time, and as you progress, you may notice the remarkable similarities between your daily life and your experiences in the garden.

For now, start with simplicity. Determine the type of experience you want from your garden. Are you looking to harvest fresh produce or prefer a serene space filled with vibrant colors and delightful fragrances? Perhaps you want a blend of both and more. The good news is that you can achieve all these, though not all at once. With time and dedication, you can surpass your expectations. Everything begins with the soil, where the magic of growth truly starts. Soil is the great alchemist, turning death and waste into life energy.

Start small and build from there. Try to begin with a pot of edible greens or grow edible flowers like nasturtiums or pansies. It's important to understand specific needs for optimal growth. Just as in life, the environment portends struggle or success. As mentioned, factors such as soil, light, water, and climate are primary considerations. Perfect conditions may be ideal, but they're not always attainable. Gardeners often improvise and adapt, making the most of what's available.

The size of your growing area influences your gardening options, but simplicity is key. Progress often comes naturally when you keep things straightforward. Inspiration can arise from unexpected sources, and the ability to improvise is a valuable skill in gardening. You'll be amazed at how resourceful you can be with just the basics. Additionally, there are many ways to optimize your space. Techniques like trellising, vertical gardening, layering, and succession planting can all help to increase growth and yield.

Understanding the nuanced and specific needs of plants helps determine their placement. For example, lettuce and parsley require partial shade to avoid wilting or bolting. **Partial shade** refers to areas that receive 3 to 6 hours of sunlight but are shaded for much of the day, often by structures or trees. Plants that thrive in partial shade are more sensitive to prolonged exposure to intense, direct sunlight. It can also refer to areas that receive indirect or filtered light throughout the day. Cool-season crops like greens do well in partial shade, so planting them under taller plants can boost their production.

Plants like kale, arugula, and Swiss chard perform well in partial sun, with some shade. **Partial sun** requirements apply to plants that can tolerate locations receiving 3 and 6 hours of direct sunlight daily. Many such plants benefit from morning or late afternoon sun, which is less intense than midday light. The difference between partial sun and partial shade is sunlight intensity and duration. Understanding the requirements of the plants you want to grow will significantly improve spatial efficiency and boost overall productivity.

One Day, It Will Happen

Remaining open to possibilities helps transform potential into reality over time. Working within our abilities helps us recognize our strengths. Showing gratitude for the opportunity to grow aligns us with the energy needed to progress. This gratitude extends into the garden, creating a reciprocal relationship where we give to the earth, and the earth gives back to us. By nurturing this cycle, we become powerful co-creators. Remember, asking for help when needed is a sign of strength, not weakness. One day, we may become the support someone else needs. Stay persistent and open-minded with your vision; you'll witness your garden's potential unfold.

In the garden, our senses are invigorated, enriching our development. The scent of the earth strengthens our connection to it, and the more we engage with our gardens, the deeper our connection to our own lives grows. Watching a butterfly land on a flower and sip nectar can inspire us to attract more of these delicate creatures. By planting milkweed and food sources for specific species, especially vulnerable Monarchs, we help sustain their life cycles—a garden benefits not just ourselves but the broader ecosystem.

Active gardeners often find their ideas converging and evolving, creating specialized gardens dedicated to attracting beneficial insects like butterflies, bees, and hummingbirds. Adding a water feature or birdbath can further enrich your garden, providing essential resources that support a diverse range of wildlife and help them cope with rising temperatures.

In life, noticing what or who we attract helps us understand which qualities we are projecting that draw attention—whether they are positive traits or less favorable ones. Self-reflection becomes a valuable tool for identifying and removing unwanted elements, allowing us to focus on areas that elevate growth. It's important to remember that it's not only about what we attract but also about what we choose to engage with that ultimately shapes our outcomes and experiences.

Discernment is as important as having a good pair of hand pruners. It helps us remove what doesn't positively contribute to our environment. By understanding our options, we can make informed decisions while staying open to and imagining our desired experiences. Practical discernment can lead to more significant growth and expansion. As we shape our gardens, identifying and focusing on our priorities will eventually bring them to life. It begins with ideas, followed by actions that produce the desired results.

Focusing on food as a fundamental aspect of our gardens and dedicating space to grow what we wish to eat is a meaningful and necessary endeavor. Nurturing our body and soul through our gardens anticipates sweetness in the days ahead. Regularly tending to our desires helps us map steps toward our goals and ultimately enjoy the rewards. It's important to practice patience and allow time for progress without rushing for immediate results. Trust that progress is happening, even if it's not immediately visible. Not every crop will succeed, but no effort is wasted. Every action in the garden serves a purpose, even if it's simply a moment of fresh air.

A garden is not a place. It's a journey.

~Monty Don

A Fresh Start

Every outcome starts with a beginning. The path to deliberate growth begins with an honest evaluation of our current situation. Identifying our goals ignites the drive needed to move forward. Fear and overwhelm can paralyze us, suffocate our dreams, drain our energy, and halt our progress. Despite this, life continues to move forward with great force. Therefore, it's important to be kind to yourself and take small, manageable steps. Sometimes, staying still is the bravest choice until we're ready to move ahead.

Begin by identifying what you want to grow, then research viable options. Just as becoming a neurosurgeon requires knowledge and practical experience, understanding horticultural practices increases your chances of success. For example, blueberries need specific conditions—they won't thrive in desert soil. However, they can flourish in a well-managed greenhouse with the right soil and environment. Even deserts, though unique ecosystems, can be transformed into highly productive gardens. Understanding what's practical for each environment is key to successful cultivation.

Continuous learning facilitates growth and expansion. Creativity and adaptability are also inherent aspects of the growth process. Finding new solutions and adjusting to changing circumstances often form the foundation of progress. As we gain knowledge, we become more skilled at exploring new areas. Understanding which crops are best suited for each season is an integral part of this learning. Timing plays a critical role; planting too early or too late can lead to poor results due to weather conditions and frost. Seasonal frost and planting dates may shift as climate change continues to affect different regions.

Soil temperature plays a key role in plant growth and health. It influences seed germination, root development, disease resistance, growth rates, and how well plants emerge from the soil. Each plant species has specific temperature requirements, so knowing the optimal soil temperature for different crops is necessary for successful planting throughout the seasons. Seed packets often provide this information. By understanding these temperature needs, gardeners can ensure that seeds germinate efficiently, roots develop properly, and plants grow vigorously without being hindered by unsuitable conditions. This knowledge also helps prevent diseases that thrive in certain temperature ranges, supporting overall plant health and productivity.

Seasonal Crops

Cool-season crops should be planted first, thriving in the cooler temperatures of early spring or fall, while warm-season crops prefer the summer heat. Knowing the approximate frost dates for your region is necessary for determining the best times to plant each crop type. This information can save time and money and help avoid potential setbacks. Planting within the window defined by these dates ensures the best chance for successful growth.

Winter-hardy vegetables are great for gardeners who want to extend their growing season into the colder months. These hardy crops can tolerate heavy frost and often grow well in cooler temperatures. Kale is a prime example, known for its resilience to frost and cold weather. Other good choices include radish, onion, leeks, Brussels sprouts, broccoli, turnips, parsnips, rhubarb, fava beans, spinach, and garlic. Many of these vegetables can be directly seeded into the ground as soon as the soil is workable in early spring, late winter, or fall, depending on the climate.

In addition to winter-hardy vegetables, there are also semi-hardy cool-season crops that can tolerate light frost. These crops, which include carrots, beets, chard, peas, lettuce, endive, radicchio, cauliflower, and potatoes, are suited to cooler weather but are not as resilient to extreme cold as winter-hardy varieties. Plant these semi-hardy crops early in the spring to make the most of them. This allows them to grow and develop before the warmer summer temperatures arrive, which can benefit their overall health and yield. Early planting ensures these crops have ample time to mature in the cooler weather before facing summer heat.

Some cool-season crops can be planted during warmer months, but their growth and flavor often suffer, and they are more likely to bolt. Crops like lettuce, spinach, and cilantro are prone to bolting in the heat, especially if exposed to full sun. Bolting happens when these plants sense stress, such as high temperatures, and respond by quickly producing flowers and seeds. This process leads to bitter-tasting leaves and can reduce the overall yield.

Warm-season crops require higher temperatures to develop and produce a good harvest. These crops include tomatoes, peppers, eggplant, sweet potatoes, pumpkins, melons, squash, snap beans, cucumbers, and sweet corn, and they typically grow well in warmer weather conditions and longer daylight hours.

Planting warm-season crops at the right time in spring ensures they receive the warmth and sunlight needed for proper growth and maturation. Planting many of these crops after the last frost date in your region ensures that they won't be exposed to potentially damaging cold temperatures.

Understanding each crop's specific needs and preferences is pivotal for successful gardening. While it's tempting to plant a wide variety of vegetables throughout the year, it is important to consider the optimal growing conditions for each plant. This ensures that each crop has the best chance to grow well and produce a successful harvest.

Cucumbers highlight the importance of timing in planting and harvesting. Several factors can cause cucumbers to taste bitter, with one major culprit being cucurbitacins—compounds that contribute to bitterness, especially when plants are stressed. Irregular watering, extreme temperatures, or poor soil conditions can increase cucurbitacin levels, making cucumbers taste more bitter. Overripe cucumbers left on the vine are also more likely to develop a bitter flavor. Additionally, some cucumber varieties are naturally more prone to bitterness. Harvest cucumbers before they become too large or turn yellow to minimize this issue. Peeling cucumbers can also help, as the skin often holds the highest concentration of cucurbitacins. Consistent watering and avoiding stress are essential for keeping cucumbers flavorful. For the best results, plant cucumbers in late spring or early summer, after the last frost, and once the soil has warmed to at least 60°F (15°C). This timing ensures cucumbers grow well in their preferred warm temperatures, reducing the risk of bitterness.

There is no gardening without humility. Nature constantly sends even its oldest scholars to the bottom of the class for some egregious blunder.

~**Alfred Austin**

Down To Earth

Knowledge and growth are closely connected. Knowing everything from the start is impossible, but as we gain experience and interact with others, our understanding deepens, and our skills improve. Learning from others in our local community or those familiar with our plant hardiness zone can provide valuable insights and practical tips, helping us save time and effort.

Intentionality is the cornerstone of success in gardening and life. When we approach our garden with purpose and commitment, we tackle challenges more effectively and strengthen our connection with the natural world. Thoughtful planning builds momentum that drives us towards our goals. Growing our own food goes beyond providing sustenance; it's a powerful act of self-sufficiency and a way to honor and respect the Earth's abundance.

Harvesting the fruits of our labor with gratitude is a genuinely transformative and humbling experience. It reminds us of the natural cycles of abundance and scarcity, deepening our appreciation for life's resilience and beauty. Just as the growth rings of a tree reflect years of plenty and hardship, our experiences shape us, contributing to our growth and resilience. The passage of time leaves its marks, shaping our character and building wisdom.

The more we interact with the land, the more we uncover the universal truths it reveals. One such truth is that renewal frequently follows significant disruption and upheaval periods. Just as a garden may go through messy phases and seasonal changes before reaching its full potential, life also gets messy at times, and part of the process involves cleaning up and navigating through these challenges.

Nature's capacity to regenerate life is a powerful expression of consciousness. However, human actions often disrupt this delicate ecological balance. Practices such as mono-cropping, building river dams, clear-cutting forests, and mining disturb the natural equilibrium. The essence of life and nature depends on freedom and diversity, yet human activity often restricts this wildness through imposed boundaries of ownership. This paradox is evident in our frustration with wildlife, which is merely acting on its instincts and behaviors.

Human activities disrupt natural habitats, yet we can cultivate pockets of wildness in our gardens. These spaces nurture diverse ecosystems, support vibrant life, and create safe havens for nature to flourish. Even with careful planning, unforeseen events can upend our efforts and reshape our future endeavors. Promptly shifting and adapting saves time and prevents prolonged stagnation.

Nature's resilience and persistence often surpass human understanding, demonstrating a remarkable determination to live. The sun rises daily in life's garden, and the wind blows, perpetuating the endless cycle of life and death. This ongoing process of renewal and regeneration defines the essence of existence, infusing it with purpose. Nature embodies the spirit of life, maintaining harmony among all species. By collaborating with nature—planting seeds and nurturing growth—we sustain life and deepen our connection with the natural world.

Humility is a powerful virtue we experience often but rarely fully understand. When we approach life humbly, we are better equipped to learn from our mistakes rather than fixating on our losses. Letting go of the need to be right or to prove ourselves can help reduce stress and create a more relaxed mindset. Humility creates openness and compassion, nurturing relationships and community by encouraging others to recognize their strengths and contributions. This supportive atmosphere builds trust and connection, empowering individuals to succeed together.

Humble leaders tend to be more effective. They prioritize their team's needs, listen actively, and inspire trust and respect. By practicing humility, we shift our focus away from comparison and competition. Additionally, humility nurtures authenticity by allowing individuals to be true to themselves, leading to more genuine interactions and a stronger sense of identity.

Where there is love, there is life.

~Mahatma Gandhi

Labor Of Love

By now, you may have noticed that tending to your garden is a meaningful way to connect with the natural world and the life around you. This connection becomes more evident with consistent practice. As you continue, you begin to understand your role in the broader context of life. This deeper insight often ignites a profound curiosity and sense of discovery, leading to the most significant virtue of all—love. There is immense satisfaction in connecting with the wholeness and unity of love, which is the quintessence of life.

We begin life as beings of love, but society obscures our true essence over time. Only after straying far from our natural selves do we begin the journey back to love, rediscovering who we truly are.

To embody love is humanity's greatest gift to the world. This invisible force guides us in nurturing life's garden and cultivating a more harmonious existence. Love defines who we are and who we can choose to become again.

By approaching life with intention and curiosity, season after season, we facilitate healing and reveal interconnected realms that extend beyond our immediate awareness. The Earth, our home, lives in our hearts, where the beauty of the unexpected constantly unfolds, reflecting nature's essence. We discover unexpected friendships and hidden potential in places once thought barren. Love deeply connects to healing, as support and connections often arise unexpectedly to aid our growth. Life surprises us by aligning in ways that create opportunities for personal development. By staying flexible and open to new experiences, people, and ideas, we uncover possibilities that resistance might otherwise block.

Love and fear cannot coexist because their energetic frequencies are inherently incompatible. While love possesses the power to transform fear, they cannot exist together simultaneously. Fear, the absence of love, can overshadow and hinder love's growth. However, we create space for love to expand by choosing to nurture a different perspective and raise our energetic frequency. In this way, our thoughts are like seeds and our actions determine whether they will grow. Kind and loving thoughts, especially about ourselves, nourish the garden of our lives. Our life's garden is a labor of love, and when we align with nature's flow, we act with faith that transcends uncertainty.

Mindfully sowing our seeds helps us appreciate the growth process, especially when it comes to the subconscious mind. Repeating positive affirmations and mantras effectively programs the subconscious, much like an organic weed barrier. These uplifting statements fill the space that anxious or misleading fears might occupy. By cultivating a positive subconscious, we make it easier to enter a creative flow, nurturing love in life's garden.

Cultivating our inner garden with love as its foundation paves the way for growth, abundance, and fulfillment. Love inspires positive intentions and guides us to make choices that align with our highest good and the well-being of others. Just as a gardener carefully selects and nurtures seeds, we can choose our thoughts and actions, planting seeds of love and compassion that yield abundant blessings. Our choices shape who we become, and consistently embracing the higher energies of love creates fertile ground for growth and manifestation. This mindset attracts positivity, harmony, and abundance into our lives.

Self-discipline is a powerful expression of self-love at a high vibrational frequency. It serves as the mortar for every brick we lay on the pathway toward becoming our best selves, helping us to prioritize long-term benefits over short-term pleasures. Like the body needs exercise for optimal performance, mental well-being also requires attention, and meditation is vital for aligning the mind, body, and spirit. Over time, meditation improves clarity, enabling us to make wise choices and thoughtful decisions. While 'sleeping on it' allows for a reflective pause, meditating before making significant decisions helps us align more deeply and energetically with our choices.

Meditation is dwelling in presence so fully that we begin to experience the being within our becoming. Here, in the quiet between thoughts, the illusion of separation between what is and what is unfolding dissolves. In this still awareness, being is not fixed, nor is becoming merely a future state— they are intertwined aspects of consciousness revealed in real time. Through meditation, we come to know ourselves not as static entities, but as living processes: aware, evolving, and whole.

Seeds Of Love

Establishing a disciplined daily meditation practice is like watering a garden regularly; it strengthens the foundation of manifestation. The key to manifesting lies in intention, which drives our will and shapes our desires. Just as a gardener visualizes what to grow, we also focus on our goals and the fruits they will bear. Begin bringing goals to life, understanding that growth takes time. Believe in the possibility of success, for it is nature's gift.

When you ground yourself in a loving internal space and clearly understand what you want, you align with life's natural flow and the co-creation process. This alignment leads to manifestations, even if the results aren't immediately visible. Trust the process, stay present, and avoid becoming overly attached to specific outcomes. Just as overwatering can damage a garden by hindering root development and wasting energy, excessive attachment to results can disrupt the manifestation process and undermine your efforts. If some ideas fail to take root, remember that new seeds of thought are always ready to be planted.

Tend To Your Garden

We cultivate a relationship rooted in love as we learn, grow, and connect with the land. By recognizing our role as protectors and caretakers, the land responds by offering us support in return. Over time, we understand how the land sustains us and how our connection deepens based on our consistent and respectful approach. Nature, our constant companion, offers everything we need for our well-being. However, our relationship with nature requires care and balance, as it involves growth and challenges, with significant consequences if we fail to manage it responsibly.

All relationships require some form of reciprocity to blossom, including our connection to the land. If we take resources from it, we must also give something back. The land offers countless benefits, yet humanity has often taken them for granted, leading to environmental harm. Our waterways are filled with chemicals and waste, forests are cleared for development, mountains are decimated, and the situation grows more dire. Society unconsciously allows corporations to extract nature's resources, offering little in return—sometimes leaving behind monuments like Mount Rushmore or overplanted tree farms. However, by actively creating garden spaces, we nurture and strengthen our relationship with the land, helping to restore balance and deepen our connection to nature.

Much like love, a garden reflects our intentions, will, and care. Its energy grows and expands, often in subtle ways. Life can grow in the shadows, as some plants do well in indirect light. However, direct exposure to sunlight energizes plants and initiates the process of photosynthesis. Sunlight, a fundamental element of most ecosystems, provides the energy necessary for all living organisms. In this sense, the sun symbolizes nature's love.

Love operates as an emotion and a guiding force, deepening our understanding of ourselves and the world around us. One of the greatest gifts we can offer the world is healing our relationship with ourselves, for when we nurture self-love, we radiate positive energy that touches others. Nature, pulsating with life and wisdom, inspires us to explore the many dimensions of love. It constantly offers us inspiration and knowledge, urging us to reflect, learn, and grow. By immersing ourselves in nature's rhythms, we tap into its transformative power, allowing love to shape our journey.

Gardeners eagerly anticipate the unexpected in their gardens, recognizing that the ever-changing nature of a garden ensures nothing remains the same. Nature adapts, giving everything time to live, grow, and die. Similarly, love evolves, adjusting to shifting circumstances and needs. Even subtle changes contribute to a continuous flow from soil to sky. This flexibility reflects an intelligent response to life's complexities, allowing nature and love to grow and transform.

Nothing reveals the power of love more than its absence. When humanity unites in love, we become a formidable force capable of addressing injustices, cleaning shorelines, rebuilding habitats, and revitalizing neglected areas. This unity can transform lives across the global community. Unconditional love for life creates space for freedom, and every heart beats stronger with the strength that freedom provides and the love it imbues.

You can sow seeds of love with your first thoughts each day. As you awaken, take a moment to smile and fill your mind with gentle, loving thoughts. Express gratitude for the opportunity to experience another day of life's unknown. Speak words of affirmation and engage in actions that build a loving momentum. Meditating in the morning is an effective way to start—whether through walking meditation as a pleasant ritual or sitting in the garden to listen and observe. Breathe deeply, stay present in each moment, and give yourself the gift of loving yourself exactly as you are.

These practices cultivate a positive internal tone, guiding you through challenges that arise. Life becomes a journey of course corrections, where you let go of negative thoughts. Allow worries about yesterday and tomorrow to drift away like leaves carried by the wind. Stay grounded and embody love. Positive thoughts nourish your soul, invigorate your mind, and enrich your life. Regardless of how the world responds, continue to share your love through acts of kindness. Expect nothing in return but trust that you are cultivating love in a world that desperately needs it. Love is the water that nourishes blooms in an arid desert. As it has been sung, plant your love and let it grow.

The seed has all its potential within – the gardener helps unlock it.

~Sue Stuart-Smith

True Nature

Becoming conscious and aware of ourselves and the world around us helps us align with our desires, dreams, and, ultimately, our purpose—goals that often elude us throughout our lives. The garden teaches us to live more fully each day and to tend to our spiritual landscape. Gaining clarity, re-centering, reflecting, and finding peace amidst the world's noise and chaos requires personal space. Conscious awareness of our feelings acts as an internal compass guiding us toward our true North—our true nature, the constant point of authenticity.

When we tune into the feelings of our mind, body, and spirit, we become conscious of them. How we feel reflects the energy we create and embody. The better we feel, the more aligned we are. Though many paths lead to our goals, each person follows a unique journey, becoming a distinct expression of self. We are like flowers in life's garden, each with our own purpose. Awareness of personal growth helps us align with our true potential.

Navigating the garden of life becomes more fulfilling when we embrace certain principles that elevate our experiences and support our growth. Just as a thriving garden relies on consistent care, diversity, proper nutrition, sunlight, and water, our lives can blossom when cultivated with mindfulness. Like petals unfolding in their own time, self-discovery and original expression gradually reveal the true essence of who we are.

Life provides us with tools to navigate uncertainties and discover our individual paths. Our bodies offer valuable insights, guiding us as we learn to recognize signs of needs, imbalances, and changes over time. These cues become an integral part of how we understand ourselves and our journey. Our relationship with our bodies profoundly shapes our overall life experience. The integration of mind, body, and spirit forms the foundation of our existence, with each aspect requiring equal attention, awareness, care, and respect. When we stay attentive, we begin to recognize life's tools, which often appear unexpectedly yet always arrive when we need them most. By tuning in to the signals of our bodies, minds, and spirits, we can better align ourselves with the flow of life and embrace the lessons it brings.

Conversely, imbalances manifest in various ways when we feel disconnected internally. Physically, we may become clumsy or accident-prone—bumping into things, tripping, or dropping items. Mentally and emotionally, we might feel scattered, unfocused, or overwhelmed. Spiritually, we may experience a sense of being lost, empty, unappreciative, or bored. Avoiding self-reflection or introspection keeps unresolved issues at bay, fueling internal conflict and turmoil. By staying aware of these signs, we can address imbalances before they grow, allowing us to regain harmony within ourselves.

This disconnection can make it difficult to make decisions, manage stress, or find fulfillment in our daily lives. Recognizing these signs is important because it prompts us to pause and reflect on their underlying causes—whether external stressors, internal conflicts, or neglect of our self-care and introspection needs. By acknowledging these signals, we can take proactive steps to restore balance and reconnect with our true selves.

Sanctuary

Natural beauty arrests us because it hints at the realm of the sacred; seek it and let it split you open. Gardening is an act of beautification, creating spaces that are visually appealing and nourishing to the soul. Similarly, self-care involves nurturing an inner sense of beauty that emerges naturally through self-acceptance.

A genuine smile reveals internal radiance. Cultivating acts of self-care into our daily routines removes what is tired and spent and prepares space for rejuvenation and renewal. In this way, we consistently nurture an inner sanctuary.

Re-establishing internal connection involves practices such as mindfulness, self-reflection, meditation, gratitude, and engaging in activities that bring us joy and fulfillment. These approaches help us reconnect with our inner selves, clarify our values and goals, and cultivate a more profound sense of purpose and resilience. Without honest self-reflection, we risk perpetuating patterns of self-sabotage. Understanding why we repeat these behaviors often requires deep introspection, which includes evaluating our choices, identifying when these patterns began, and examining their development and purpose to determine if they serve us.

Sometimes, clearing the way for new growth requires addressing old, fear-based behaviors at their root. Without doing so, these patterns may persist like tenacious Yucca plants despite our efforts to eliminate them. We often need to dig deep to overcome limiting beliefs and establish new foundations based on truth. When old foundations crumble, we can rebuild on more solid ground.

Across many cultures, integrating a more holistic approach to self-awareness and life improvement is accessible through simple, mindful practices. However, the journey towards further development begins with an honest and reflective account of self-awareness. Ultimately, nurturing and strengthening our internal connection allows us to navigate life's challenges with greater authenticity, clarity, and resilience, cultivating our personal development and well-being in profound ways.

Observe And Notice

Nature is a beautiful place to practice silent observation and witness life's mysteries. We can learn much from nature and its cyclical flow revealed through the changing seasons and life cycles. Gardening imparts many lessons, with timing being a significant one. It is both an active and a passive pursuit. There are moments when we need to be fully engaged in the process, but there are also important times to step back, observe, and enjoy what unfolds. Balancing these two approaches enriches our gardening experience and deepens our connection to the natural world.

For a gardener, observation is a critical tool. Paying close attention to the surroundings helps maintain a healthy environment. While observation may seem like another task, it becomes invaluable for understanding and responding to needs over time. When you notice something unusual, resist the urge to fix it immediately. Instead, take the time to observe, make notes, and continue gardening. Often, what appears to be a problem signifies a deeper issue. Keep a list of items that need attention. This approach helps maintain stability and manage challenges before they become overwhelming.

Understanding cause and effect requires a broad perspective rather than a reactive one. Use foresight to avoid creating additional problems if something needs attention or repair. Consider whether changing one element will positively affect another or lead to other unwanted issues. Weigh options carefully and proceed without expecting to achieve perfection.

Observation practice can take many forms and doesn't adhere to any particular rules. It's your space; you get out of it the effort you put into it, which can vary daily from sitting quietly with a beverage and attentively surveying your surroundings to strolling around and absorbing your space. These simple yet practical approaches to connecting with your gardens enable you to notice transformations or degradations in your environment, placing you in a powerful position to make informed decisions.

Over time, you'll become more skilled at spotting different aspects of garden life. Regular observation helps you understand plant health, growth patterns, soil conditions, light and shadow effects, pest activity, weed growth, watering needs, drainage, microclimates, companion planting effects, crop yields, and wildlife activity. Pay attention to these details and appreciate the unique aspects of your garden.

Focusing on observation shifts your perceptions and may spark new questions. Let your thoughts flow naturally, and pay attention to what stands out. Are there unwelcome visitors disturbing the peace? Are there new signs of growth or blooming? Are shadows obstructing areas that need more light? These are some things to watch for when evaluating the garden's health. Observing closely helps you better understand your environment and your role in maintaining it.

In essence, assessing our internal garden through self-reflection is a form of self-care that helps us build greater awareness, clarity, intention, resilience, and well-being. It also supports emotional regulation by encouraging us to explore and understand our emotions. This practice enables us to manage stress better, improve self-control, and develop healthier relationships with ourselves and others. By regularly dedicating time to introspection, journaling, or other mindful activities, we empower ourselves to navigate life's challenges gracefully and purposefully.

Assess

To cultivate your garden successfully, start by assessing the current situation with a clear understanding of what is real. In your growing space, as in life, this assessment is critical. Examine the essential elements of the environment: Do you have adequate sunlight, water, fertile soil, suitable plant selections, and enough space? These elements are usually non-negotiable. If any are missing, you will need to make adjustments.

Consider alternatives like community gardens or greenhouses, which might provide the right conditions. Assessment acts as a guide, helping you make informed decisions and refine your goals. Regularly reviewing your progress can also serve as a strong motivator.

There's no intrinsic growth without self-reflection. Regular self-reflection is like tending to the garden of our minds—it helps weed out negative thoughts and emotions while nurturing positivity and growth. You can better manage your responses and maintain balance by assessing your energy and emotional state, especially during challenging times. Striving for homeostasis and neutrality provides a deep sense of equilibrium, allowing you to observe situations clearly and respond thoughtfully rather than impulsively. Ultimately, we learn and practice healing the relationship with self.

It's important to recognize that what you allow often becomes what you accept. Honest self-reflection and emotional assessment provide clarity, motivating you to make meaningful changes. This daily practice is a valuable form of self-care. As mentioned earlier, your well-being reflects your choices and the power to make better ones is always within your reach. Stay mindful of what you are willing to choose and accept, for each decision shapes your journey.

Attune

Engaging in direct physical contact with the Earth, such as walking barefoot on soil, grass, or sand, can quickly realign and attune your energy. The primary scientific theory behind grounding is that direct contact with the Earth allows for the transfer of electrons from the Earth's surface into the body. The Earth carries a negative electric charge, and its electrons act as antioxidants. They neutralize free radicals—unstable molecules that cause oxidative stress and damage cells. Studies, such as those published in *The Journal of Inflammation Research* (Oschman, Chevalier, Brown—Volume 8, 2015), show that grounding helps reduce oxidative stress and inflammation. Spending time barefoot outdoors boosts energy levels and vitality, while grounding relieves pain and discomfort. Additionally, grounding practices regulate cortisol levels, improving hormonal balance.

Similarly, working with bare hands in the soil has been found to heal both body and mind. Some studies suggest that this connection with the Earth might boost immune function, reducing the risk of illness and supporting overall health. Research indicates that these practices provide a range of health benefits. For instance, connecting with the Earth can help reduce stress by promoting relaxation and a sense of calmness.

Moreover, grounding has been linked to improved sleep quality and duration, leading to more restful and rejuvenating sleep. Science shows that simple physical contact with the Earth can significantly benefit our well-being, supporting physical, mental, and emotional health.

For older adults, gardening, in particular, can also benefit cognitive health. Research published in *The Journal of Gerontology: Medical* Sciences (July 2024) found that gardening was associated with better cognitive functioning and a lower risk of cognitive decline in elderly individuals. Engaging in gardening has been linked to improved mental health outcomes. A study in *The Journal of Environmental Horticulture* (January 27, 2023, Volume 33, Issue 2) reported that gardening activities can reduce symptoms of depression and anxiety among older adults, offering a sense of accomplishment and reducing stress.

Attune to nature, the environment, and personal vision to harness foresight and guide actions with clarity and purpose. By practicing attuning through mindfulness and self-awareness, you can align your goals and actions with your inner truth, saving time and resources while surpassing expectations. Through this attunement, you can identify weaknesses and stressors, enabling you to address them proactively and quickly. Ultimately, attunement empowers you to navigate life's challenges with simplicity and effectiveness.

As we engage deeply in gardening tasks, we often become absorbed, momentarily forgetting about the broader world and its issues. Immersing ourselves in gardening serves as a form of meditation, sharpening our awareness of what is happening and what is not.

Meditation is an effective method for connecting with stillness and silence, where all potential resides. In this quiet state, the mental noise fades, allowing us to align our thoughts, emotions, and actions. This alignment sets in motion a process that moves us toward achieving our goals, dreams, and sense of purpose. Just as everything begins from nothingness, we bring our ideas to life through our unique talents and abilities, helping them grow and develop.

Align

Inner alignment harmonizes your thoughts, beliefs, values, and emotions—these roots eventually reveal the blossoms of wholeness. It signifies unity within, leading to a deep sense of well-being and balance. Like attunement, meditation sharpens your ability to align holistically with your innate self in mind, body, and spirit. Intentional alignment is the alchemy that transforms energy by cultivating awareness of yourself in each moment.

By quieting the mind through meditation, you open a portal to your heart—a connection point to your spirit. This process embodies liberation and love, forming the stability necessary for heightened success. When aligned with all aspects of your being, you can accept yourself as you are with greater awarencss. Alignment begets harmony, and aligning with the facts liberates your mind from the clutter of worry, allowing you to see things more clearly and envision what they could become. It acts as the bridge between reality and possibility—where true magic happens!

Aligning your thoughts, goals, and objectives sharpens your sense of purpose and makes your approach more effective. This increased focus develops your decision-making skills and helps minimize conflicts, whether they occur within yourself or with others. When working with others, clear alignment improves communication and boosts overall efficiency. As a result, you experience greater morale and a sense of daily achievement, contributing to a deeper understanding of satisfaction and personal well-being.

In the context of gardening, alignment not only prepares the gardener for optimal production but also ensures sustainable growth over time. Alignment is not an end goal but rather a form of daily maintenance involving constant adjustments inherent in gardening. Aligning with the needs for maximum growth and developing an approach to fulfilling those needs allows you to focus, perhaps going further by creating a plan of action. This plan ensures you synchronize all components to achieve the desired outcomes and focus only on one task. Doing so reduces the propensity for overwhelm. Life in the garden is ongoing and ever-evolving, so there's no need to rush. You do the best you can with the time you are given.

Once you experience the transformational impact of alignment through the gathered knowledge of awareness, you will see it as a powerful tool for further development. It becomes another pillar in your foundation, creating a stable environment for maximum yields. It is paramount to understand how to utilize your tools effectively and when to apply them. Daily maintenance is, at first, a practice until it becomes a routine.

Ascend

Expanding and ascending from the unknown into the awareness of the known within is like a flower simply being in its existence. Its nature is to bloom fully, ascending past the darkness of being a seed. Giving yourself to the earth by gardening is a profound healing act that connects the individual's soul with the spirit of nature. This connection improves your relationship with yourself and positively impacts your interactions with life. Your intuition and awareness grow as you observe life within and beyond the garden. Stress and worries diminish, giving way to a profound sense of unity and interconnectedness with all living beings and the universe. This sense of oneness cultivates deep peace, love, and compassion for all life forms.

Life cycles towards the blossoming of your ascension. Every generation expresses survival traits and adaptations. The more you lighten your being from the weight of survival, the more life transforms. The collective inner being reflects the external reality. When you radiate in high vibration, you bring light into your world. Collective light is a radical movement. You are an energy-light being; part of your purpose is to re-member your wholeness within the light and to ascend in frequency and energetic vibration. We are Hue-man resonating frequencies of light and all of the colors of the rainbow.

Observing progress is akin to witnessing personal growth unfold, like watching a flower bloom over time. Your actions drive movement and change, reflecting your advancement ascending toward your goals and the evolution of your being. Keeping a clear and balanced perspective throughout this transformative journey is necessary, as the ego can often interrupt the natural flow of development. Compassion for self and others is an inherent aspect of your becoming whole.

Remember, though there are outcomes, the process is continuous, so moving with steady intention is wise. Much like life, gardening is a perpetual journey without a final destination. Instead, it is a spiraling, cyclical fulfillment of numerous accomplishments and milestones. As gardeners, we patiently and gradually pursue incremental results. This ongoing process evolves into a spiritual adaptation, a harmonious interaction with nature, where we learn and grow alongside the plants we nurture.

Life undoubtedly presents challenges, but as you expand your consciousness and ascend in your growth, you can experience ecstatic joy amid the struggles. Simple pleasures, such as the first ripe tomato or the blooming of a flower, offer a satisfaction that no substance can match. This sense of fulfillment comes from nurturing your garden, facing trials, and savoring the sweet reward of success. Such experiences elevate your growth and satisfaction, opening you to deeper fulfillment.

As you ascend through life's joys and challenges, remain engaged and inspired, allowing yourself to yearn for more. Life's gardens are a continuous work in progress. Although there is no end, embracing steady progress with awareness and accepting yourself as you are nurtures continuous dynamic growth. Detours will arise, each serving a purpose and offering opportunities for development and future insights. As you continue learning and growing, it becomes evident that it is part of your soul's journey to ascend to the next level of your becoming. Creating enjoyment along the way accelerates your development. This is your responsibility to yourself.

Meditation is a way for nourishing and blossoming the divinity within you.

~Amit Ray

Co-creation Through Meditation

Meditation is an act of radical surrender—of the mind (I Am), body (I Am Here), and spirit (I Am Within). It creates space to experience the unity of co-creation with a life force—an energy sparked by inspiration, curiosity about what could be, and a deep appreciation for what is. Letting go of the need to control outcomes and allowing life to meet us along the way enables us to develop beyond what we had initially believed. Often, when we step back from control and worry about how things might be or ought to be, we find that life brings us more than we could have imagined. Attuning to our part in the oneness of life creates space for trust, acceptance, and receptivity.

Meditation practice serves as a daily reminder of the joy within. Everything you seek resides inside you, but you must slow down and be mindful of where you direct your energy. Carry the power of awareness, allowance, and acceptance that you've developed through meditation into every aspect of your life. Even in brief moments of stillness, you'll gradually experience greater internal pleasantness. Recognize that this inner sanctuary within your life's garden is always accessible, offering peace and effortless joy. Regularly assess your mood and disposition, attune to your inner state, align with your peace, and ascend beyond preconceived notions or illusions. Meditation is a precious gift that nurtures internal growth and self-awareness, embodying love, care, and connection while guiding your path to conscious evolution.

There are many forms of meditation, and finding the one that resonates with you can simplify building a consistent practice. Committing to daily meditation is a powerful way to cultivate harmony by aligning your mind, body, and spirit. Starting with 15-30 minutes daily can lay a strong foundation for your meditation journey. Consistency is critical, as regular practice deepens your connection with yourself and enhances the benefits of meditation. As you become more attuned to the present moment and develop mindfulness, meditation may become a cherished and integral part of your daily routine, enriching your life in countless ways. It is ideal to incorporate meditative practices in your garden space.

Naturally, some days are rife with busyness and distraction. Being mindful of your energy will prompt you to ground and calm yourself. If life interrupts your meditation practice, a quick check-in can help you regain balance. An easy remedy involves taking at least three deep breaths through your nose. Close your eyes, internally look up at the center of your forehead, and silently say, "I am within." Repeat this practice as often as needed. This mini-meditation helps you reconnect wholly with your mind, body, and spirit.

Approach your meditation practice with an open mind and heart, allowing whatever arises to flow naturally. Release judgment of your thoughts, knowing they do not define you. Let your breath flow freely, recognizing that you are not your mind—you are the observer. You exist beyond thought and form, simply witnessing your field of energy and awareness.

Trust in the process and recognize that each moment of meditation brings you closer to your true essence and inner wisdom. Some believe your spirit resides in your body, while others suggest that your body resides in your spirit. In either case, the chakras within the energetic body actively transmit the frequencies of supreme consciousness, forming a spiritual energy system available to everyone as free energy. Unconditional love represents the highest energy frequency and resides at the core of your being, simply as you are.

AYA Roots And Shoots Meditation

A simple yet transformative daily meditation practice involves sitting comfortably with an extended spine. Visualize a beam of light extending from your root chakra (Muladhara) into the earth's core, up through the shoot of the crown chakra (Sahasrara) towards the sun. If needed, support your back to ensure your head can move freely. Gently engage your sacral chakra (Svadhisthana) while lifting your solar plexus (Manipura) and heart (Anahata) chakras. Make a conscious decision to relax your body: face, jaw, lips, throat chakra (Vishuddha), tongue, and eyelids. Keep your chin pulled in and level, roll your shoulders back, and position your arms relaxed and open.

Release thoughts and judgments, allowing yourself to be as you are. Breathe deeply through your nose, letting thoughts and emotions come and go without attachment. When distractions arise, gently bring your focus back to your steady breath—your breath is your anchor. Maintain a sense of observation, and if needed, focus on a consistent source of white noise, like a fan or hum. Acknowledge external sounds and thoughts without attaching a response to them.

With your eyes closed, direct your inner vision to the space behind the center of your forehead, where the pineal gland is located (Ajna chakra), and silently say, "I am within." If distractions arise, again, observe them without attachment, return to your breath, and continue to affirm, "I am within" quietly. Encourage an inner smile, adding more freedom to your practice. With each breath, inhale serenity and exhale tension. See yourself as the energetic conduit between the heavens and Earth, deepening your connection with all that is with every breath.

Inner smile, inner vision, inner voice: "I am within." Let this affirmation resonate deeply as you embrace your internal wholeness and acceptance, just as you are.

Garden Reciprocity Meditation

For this meditation practice, you can sit comfortably but, ideally, stand barefoot in your garden. Plant your feet into the soil to connect with the earth. As you stand in physical alignment, building your foundation from your feet upwards, face the sun and breathe deeply. You can place your hands in a prayer position at your heart or let them rest and relax gently at your sides. With soft, open eyes, take a moment to express gratitude for your life and the offerings you've helped nurture. Allow the garden to witness you as you witness it. Smile. Give appreciation and receive appreciation in return. Express gratitude to the land for providing you with a place to grow. This is a timeless practice: be at peace in the garden for as long as you desire.

Heart Over Head Meditation

Another effective meditation practice involves placing the forehead, where the pineal gland (Ajna chakra or third eye) is, directly on the Earth. For best results, choose natural ground over concrete. Kneel and bow forward, bringing the heart over the head, and rest the forehead gently on the ground. Use a blanket if needed. This position aligns the heart above the head, creating a grounding connection. Let the Earth support the weight of your head as you inhale through your nose, connecting with its energy. Allow the Earth to absorb any arising emotions—tears, sounds, or feelings. Surrender your thoughts and control, letting go as you exhale through your mouth. Sit up and repeat the breathing, bowing, and releasing process when needed. If you wish, add healing mantras to deepen the experience.

If kneeling is uncomfortable, lay flat or sit with the root chakra (Muladhara chakra) connected to the earth. Aim for at least twenty minutes for your meditation practices, though it may take time to build up to this duration.

To augment this practice, hum to generate more energy. Higher-pitched humming, similar to a bee, tends to be more effective. Humming is a simple yet powerful practice that supports mental clarity, emotional balance, and spiritual growth. Many spiritual and healing traditions incorporate it to promote well-being and deepen your conscious connection to the universe.

High-pitched humming stimulates the vagus nerve, promoting calmness and relaxation. It also stimulates the release of serotonin and dopamine, which can elevate mood and elevate feelings of happiness. This practice sharpens concentration and focus, helping center the mind and deepen awareness. You can hum anytime and anywhere you feel safe and undisturbed—whether driving, cooking, or bathing.

Heartbeat Meditation

This practice can be done in your garden or in a bath. Lay flat on the earth or in the water and listen for your heartbeat. Begin by taking deep breaths and focusing on the sound of your heartbeat. Breathe steadily in and out through your nose. Place your hand over your heart to connect with the rhythm. You might also visualize your heartbeat pulsing like a star in the night sky. If your mind wanders, gently bring your focus back to your breath and the rhythm of your heart. Rest deeply, staying connected to both your heart and breath. You can practice this for any length of time—of course, the longer, the better.

When you're ready, release your focus, slowly open your eyes, and bring your awareness back to your surroundings. Take a moment to notice how you feel.

Meditation In Movement

Grounding and meditation practices don't have to be stationary; incorporating body movement offers many benefits. Moving the body helps reduce feelings of detachment and dissociation, allowing you to focus on physical sensations that anchor you in the present moment. Gentle movements deepen your connection to your breath and body, boosting self-awareness and supporting trauma healing.

Meditation in movement can take many forms, such as gardening, walking, yoga, dancing, mindful movement, Qigong, and Tai Chi. Some practices involve specific fluid movements, while others feature unchoreographed, free-flowing movements like ecstatic dance, pulsating rhythms, or somatic shaking. These activities help release stagnant energy and tension. Engaging in body movement can also facilitate the expression of suppressed emotions. Additionally, movement reduces stress and improves mood by releasing endorphins.

Freedom of movement can be practiced individually or in a group setting. The goal is to move energy through your body, alleviating feelings of being stuck and helping you harmonize and realign your mind, body, and spirit.

Inner Medicine

Daily meditation cultivates a deep sense of gratitude and appreciation for life, much like enriching the soil of your inner foundation. This gratitude, developed through mindfulness and meditation, is a therapeutic tool that rejuvenates your spirit, creating a veritable seed bank of ideas, dreams, and aspirations. Meditation practices are a commitment to your ultimate well-being. Each session acts as a form of medicine, nurturing growth and laying a solid foundation for your journey. Just as healthy soil supports strong roots, consistent meditation nurtures a clear path toward self-actualization, allowing full potential to unfold with each choice.

It is beneficial to use meditation practices whenever you feel compelled, even briefly, regardless of the duration. Remember, whether you're facing a stressful situation or experiencing joy, take a moment to close your eyes, breathe deeply, and direct your inner vision to the area between and behind your eyebrows. Mentally affirm, "I am within."

This act will help ground you, reconnect you to the present, and offer a meaningful form of self-care, requiring only your internal focus to engage with the external world.

As caretakers of our inner landscape, we can cultivate internal harmony and resilience through intentional meditation and mindfulness. This approach provides greater clarity for assessment, attunement, alignment, and ascension towards dynamic growth. By nurturing ourselves daily, we access a profound wellspring of inner strength and integrity that surpasses external pressures. Embracing our circumstances with empowerment allows us to rise above them, emerge stronger, and recognize that adversity can catalyze growth and resilience.

Embracing our whole selves enables us to find joy and fulfillment from within, regardless of the challenges or obstacles we face. Cultivating this inner contentment helps us stay calm and centered amidst life's inevitable storms, strengthening our resolve. With a solid foundation of inner peace, we gain the clarity and focus needed to navigate changing circumstances with grace and resilience. Instead of being swayed by external forces, we approach challenges with groundedness and perspective, confident in our ability to weather any storm or gather the courage to seek help when needed.

Sometimes, a simple shift in perspective is all it takes to move through feelings of stuckness. Rigid thinking can limit our growth potential, but by considering different viewpoints, we open space for healing and recovery. Exploring various perspectives helps us find relief and navigate obstacles with greater ease, creating a sense of freedom and progress.

Such inner work serves as medicine for our spirit. Through these practices, we approach life with open hearts and minds, understanding that every experience—whether joyful or challenging—nurtures the growth and evolution of our souls. By tending to the needs of our mind, body, and spirit, we ground ourselves and reconnect with our true nature, blossoming as a beautiful flower in life's garden.

Nature is the source of all true knowledge.

~Leonardo da Vinci

The Healing Power Of Nature

The garden is a living library, offering endless inspiration and a powerful way to connect with nature. It provides valuable knowledge gained through hands-on experience and thoughtful exploration. Forging a connection with nature is a direct pathway to profound self-awareness, and this bond serves as a solid foundation for personal growth, transformation, and expansion.

While society effortlessly connects to the internet, tapping into a vast global web of information, engaging with nature provides answers to questions and fills voids we may not even recognize. Immersing ourselves in the natural world reveals our inherent connection to its cycles, marking the genesis of true understanding. Over time, we begin to see ourselves as seeds of source energy planted within the garden of life.

Nature holds incredible healing potential and valuable medicinal resources. Integrating nature into our daily lives can significantly improve our well-being. It helps reduce stress, supports emotional recovery, boosts mindfulness, and strengthens physical health. Spending time in natural settings builds our cardiovascular and respiratory systems and encourages creativity, focus, and mental clarity. Additionally, working with soil can improve the immune system's ability to distinguish between harmful pathogens and harmless substances, which may lower the risk of allergies and autoimmune diseases and reduce stress-related inflammation.

The ability to grow our medicines poses a significant challenge to large pharmaceutical companies, leading them to control this knowledge and keep people dependent on their medical systems. This control represents a considerable injustice of our time. However, finding a balance between these extremes is possible, and it is up to individuals to choose what works best for them. Certainly, pharmaceuticals have their place, but overreach into personal health decisions has diminished many people's autonomy and independence. Experiencing the benefits of nature's remedies often makes reliance on artificial treatments less appealing. While some medications are necessary for health, the aim should be to establish habits and environments that minimize the need for drug dependence.

Nature offers extensive advantages, but maintaining a connection to the natural world can be challenging in a world full of distractions. This disconnection can lead to separation from ourselves and others, resulting in fractured communities and increased feelings of isolation. It is important to approach these distractions mindfully. Losing touch with nature means losing touch with our true selves, as we are intrinsically linked to the elements. We face a choice: to live in harmony and embrace our inherent power or to neglect this connection and accelerate our decline. Recognizing and appreciating the elements within us can be profoundly beneficial to accepting our interconnectedness with the land.

Cultures, religions, and belief systems offer diverse narratives about the origins of life. Yet, tracing our existence to the five classical elements grounds us in a shared truth. We come from the Earth—born of it and destined to return. Like the changing seasons, the life cycle unites all living beings. Whether bee, ant, fish, elephant, or human, we are all woven into this grand, interconnected cycle. The phrase "ashes to ashes, dust to dust" beautifully captures the eternal flow of life that transcends individual species.

The five classic elements—Earth, Water, Fire, Air, and Ether—sustain life by fulfilling our most basic needs, which should be freely accessible to all. These elements support and unite all living beings, forming the foundation of existence. Despite the claims of capitalism and colonization, no one can rightfully own, buy, or sell the classic elements. Life persists within the embrace of these timeless forces.

Classic Elemental Descriptions:

EARTH

Earth embodies nurturing, grounding, fertility, resilience, manifestation, stability, and solidity. Symbolically, it reflects aspects like our physical bodies, growth, the root chakra, death, rebirth, and the material aspects of life. The Earth is a teacher whose substrate is the foundation for all development. Soil acts as the Earth's natural skin, representing the essence and support of life. It provides nourishment and shelter; life depends on the soil's productive health.

Earth is a feminine element. Caring for the land with wisdom nurtures nature and safeguards our existence. Naturally, as we tend to the Earth, it reciprocates by meeting our needs. Innately connected to the Earth, it is our home, the foundational support upon which existence stands. Earth lives in our hearts and grounds our energy. Born of the Earth, we shall return to its embrace. We are the Earth, and Earth is life.

WATER

The qualities of water encompass fluidity, adaptability, renewal, purification, hydration, interconnectedness, the sacral chakra, and emotion. It symbolizes the flow of life, transportation, intuition, cleansing, and healing. Water serves as a teacher, embodying the essence of life as we know it. Its versatility is evident in its existence in various forms: liquid, solid, and gas. Cells, the basic units of life, are predominantly composed of water molecules, constituting approximately 75% of the human body. As a fundamental element for all living organisms, water is pivotal to biological processes, promoting the health of ecosystems and ensuring survival.

Water is a feminine element that moves energy. Human tears, primarily composed of water, flush the body of stress hormones and toxins. Crying actively soothes and cleanses the mind, body, and spirit. It improves mood and restores emotional balance from grief, stress, fear, or joy. Tears process strong emotions by releasing energies that need transformation, supporting emotional well-being, clearing debris, and lubricating the eyes. Sweat and urine, also primarily composed of water, help eliminate waste and regulate biochemical processes. Water cleanses, and cleanliness prevents disease.

Reflecting upon the element of water encourages us to move with the currents of our lives, accept what is, and go with the flow. As humans, we have the innate ability to adapt and change. When life signals a time for a shift, we can move toward the least resistance and continue our journey with the ease of fluidity. Water is the essence of life, a reminder that we are water, and water is life.

FIRE

The qualities of fire originate from its celestial source—the sun. These attributes encompass energy, passion, illumination, transformation, transmutation, regeneration, heat, the solar plexus, and digestion. The sun fills us with energy. Fire is a profound teacher, symbolizing both creation and destruction, often linked to purification and the spark of existence. It represents courage, inspiration, and spiritual enlightenment, playing a fundamental role in the forces of nature.

Fire is a masculine element. The sun, a primary source of life and existence, enables plants to photosynthesize and create the energy needed to grow. It influences countless natural processes, including electricity generation through solar power. Fire is metaphorically tied to our digestive system, gut, and passions. Some of the most passionate and determined individuals live with a "fire in their belly." Living beings are comprised of electrical charge, heat, and fire. Fire is life.

AIR

Air is a powerful symbol of connection and vitality, influencing our physical, mental, and spiritual states. It embodies qualities such as thought, communication, movement, freedom, and sound transmission. Air teaches us the essence of breath, respiration, transpiration, and the energy of the heart chakra while also connecting closely to intellect and mental clarity.

As the breath of life, air represents the intangible, dynamic aspects of existence. Air, as the element of mind and mental processes, reflects the boundless freedom of thought, the flow of ideas, and the exchange of energy in our interactions. Wind, a manifestation of air, symbolizes change, freedom, and movement in action, clearing stagnant energy and ushering in new possibilities.

Air is a masculine element, symbolizing action, clarity, and vitality. How we breathe is just as critical as the air quality we inhale. Practicing proper breathing techniques expands oxygen intake, expels stale air from the lungs, and supports the body's natural functions. These techniques help regulate the heart rate, lower stress hormones, and reduce blood pressure, promoting balance and calm. Fresh air invigorates the body, strengthens the immune system, improves circulation, and boosts overall well-being.

As we breathe in oxygen, a byproduct of photosynthesis from plants and algae, we fuel our bodies with the vital energy needed for life. In return, we exhale carbon dioxide, which plants absorb as they continue their photosynthetic process, producing oxygen again. This reciprocating cycle of give and take sustains the balance of life on our planet, illustrating the interconnectedness of all living beings and the importance of preserving our natural environment.

The breath is a profound expression of our essence, serving as a channel for our innermost thoughts, feelings, and intentions to manifest into the external world through speech, song, and sound. As air passes through our vocal cords and is shaped by our mouth, it creates the vibrations that form sound and language. This enables us to communicate, connect, and express ourselves. In this manner, our breath is a powerful means of sharing our unique essence and influencing our reality through the spoken word.

The rhythm of our breath influences the authenticity of our speech, allowing our words to resonate with sincerity and grace. When we communicate from a place of alignment, we express our genuine selves with a voice of truth. If we stray from this path, we can realign by recognizing and addressing our missteps. Using our voice to acknowledge and correct these errors strengthens our commitment to honesty and restores our grace. In this way, our words reflect our inner harmony, guiding us through life with clarity and compassion.

Like the wind, we are deeply connected to the air we breathe. This air sustains life in countless ways, from enabling respiration to regulating climate and facilitating energy transfer. Clean air is fundamental to our health and important for the well-being of ecosystems worldwide. By recognizing our shared bond with the air, we gain a deeper appreciation for its vital role in supporting all life on Earth. As stewards of our environment, we must protect and preserve the purity of the air for all living beings, both now and for future generations. Air is life.

ETHER

Ether, the fifth element, embodies profound qualities that transcend the physical realm. It represents intuition, consciousness, connection, and the spiritual essence of existence. Ether is considered neutral because it embodies the space or medium that connects all things. Often associated with the throat chakra and cosmic consciousness,

Ether is a teacher, guiding us to explore reality's unseen and infinite aspects. Unlike the tangible forms of the other classical elements, Ether symbolizes the intangible and formless aspects of existence, containing the raw materials for life itself. Ether connects us to the cosmos, carrying fundamental elements for life and reflecting the eternal, infinite nature of existence.

Understanding the elemental nature of life brings about a profound sense of respect and connection with all living beings. When we recognize that we are manifestations of the elements in human form, we tap into our inner wisdom and approach life with a renewed sense of empowerment. This empowerment helps us form meaningful connections and positively impact the world. Aligning our actions with our true nature makes it easier to overcome challenges.

When we align with our inner essence, we see purpose and value in every living being, moving beyond ego-driven projections and societal constructs. From this vantage point, we recognize that all beings are fundamentally equal, linked by the elemental fabric of existence. This awareness nurtures a profound sense of universal harmony, where everything is interdependent and deeply connected to the entire web of life.

It is the generous giving of ourselves that produces the generous harvest.

~Orison Marden

Growth And Virtue

A gardener's adage describes the process of a perennial garden actualizing by awakening and becoming unto itself: first, it sleeps, then it creeps until, finally, it leaps. This adage explains the first year of a young, tender garden or plant in its early stage of development. In the second year, roots begin to spread deeper and wider. By the third year, the garden or plant has matured enough to set fruit and display its full beauty.

Similarly, in the initial stage of our self-realization journey, we focus inward on our roots and contemplate what and how we want to develop. Understanding the 'why' behind our desire to establish will drive our roots deeper, assisting in anchoring into our newly realized foundation. It is unlikely that there will be many blooms of desires during this realization phase.

The second stage is when it creeps. This marks the awakening phase, where we intentionally occupy the necessary space to branch out. While our full potential may not be recognizable, we will begin to observe the emergence of new growth. Simultaneously, the roots of our knowledge and understanding will become stronger, more resilient, and grow deeper while our foundation continues to facilitate expansion. As we start noticing beneficial changes, we become more engaged in personal development and growth.

The third stage is when it leaps! This marks the moment when our root system is so well-established that our outward being is fully blooming. It is the culmination of our efforts reaching their full potential, propelling us towards self-actualization, and our intentions become clear. This entire process requires the virtues that the garden teaches: patience, faith, hope, trust, gratitude, kindness, courage, wisdom, integrity, diligence, grace, humility, generosity, and love.

This process may take a lifetime or remain unrealized, depending on our choices and our commitment to diligent exploration for growth and transformation. Few choose to live a moral and ethical life grounded in discipline and inclusion, but those who do experience rewards far beyond the ordinary. They find fulfillment in their journey, as their actions ripple out to inspire others and create a legacy of integrity, purpose, and lasting impact.

The secret to internal freedom lies in the practice of virtuousness. Aligning our actions with moral principles reduces guilt and inner conflict, creating peace and harmony. Virtue drives personal growth, strengthens communities, and creates a more meaningful existence. A life rooted in virtue builds a solid, unwavering foundation. Living without malice unlocks the door to internal peace, builds trust and compassion in relationships, and nurtures harmony. Virtue creates enduring value.

The foundation of ethics is rooted in moral behavior and decision-making. Integrity is choosing to do the right thing as the first option, rather than the last resort. Nature offers valuable lessons on virtuous living. The cycles of growth, decay, and renewal in nature emphasize the importance of change and transformation, reflecting the virtue of hope and the potential for new beginnings. Solid character development takes courage to start and fortitude to persevere. Practicing temperance brings balance and harmony to everyday life. Using discernment and reason encourages discipline by promoting prudence. Justice reflects fairness—what we give is what we receive.

One poor decision may steer us off course, but it doesn't eliminate our potential to become our best selves. Each person's journey is distinct, and life continues to evolve, often exceeding our expectations. Limiting beliefs may linger in our minds, but they are rarely accurate. We can confront the doubts—both ours and others'—because change is inevitable. Embracing the possibility of overcoming our mistakes fuels the energy that turns dreams into reality. Everything unfolds in its own time. As author and basketball coach Jerry Dunn states, it's not about limiting challenges but challenging limits.

Living a virtuous life doesn't involve being superior to others or striving for sainthood; it means fully embracing the human experience with all its complexities and imperfections. To live virtuously is to acknowledge our flaws and still strive to act with kindness, integrity, and responsibility. Life excels in the light and doesn't need to hide in the shadows. Through virtues, we cultivate benevolence in every moment—offering compassion, understanding, and support to others, regardless of their situation. Nature teaches us these lessons daily, showing us how to grow, adapt, and contribute to the well-being of the world around us. By embracing virtue, we align with life's natural rhythms, promoting harmony and growth in ourselves and our communities.

> As we look deeply within, we understand our perfect balance.
> There is no fear of the cycle of birth, life, and death. For when
> you stand in the present moment, you are timeless.
>
> ~Rodney Yee

The Gift Of Presence

Gardening is a sensory experience best approached as an experiment rather than a chore. Through our senses, we engage with the results of our daily efforts. Everything takes time, so by focusing on the present moment, we sharpen our awareness. We savor the feeling of air filling our lungs, the taste of vine-ripened berries, the scent of blooming earth, the sounds of nature at work, and the sight of slow, steady progress. These experiences bring moments of joy and a deep love for nurturing life. The enjoyment we gain from gardening rewards us in ways beyond measure. There's magic in the mundane. Adopting this mindset in life could transform our experience of it.

Idealism can be frustrating, particularly when life feels burdensome. Yet, this frustration often signals a misalignment with our true creative purpose. It's disheartening that the affliction of capitalism ensnares humanity; the necessity of paying for the fundamental right to live places an overwhelming burden on society. While some are fortunate to work in fields encouraging creativity and abundance, many struggle to survive daily.

Regardless of our circumstances, we can always take steps from where we are as we are. These actions inspire us to greet each new day with a sense of promise, reminding us that even in the face of challenges, there is always the potential for change, growth, and renewal. Maintaining a positive outlook requires more strength and courage than adopting a pessimistic one. The contrasting aspects of life guide us to reconsider and adjust the choices we repeatedly make, especially when they test our spirit.

Nurturing our internal garden begins with understanding our daily purpose. We must establish processes that support and fuel our growth. When distractions arise, we develop and strengthen our focus. We sharpen this focus by practicing mindful awareness and embracing personal accountability.

Cultivating a garden that enriches our mind, body, and spirit provides a wealth of abundance and elevates our experiences. This journey reflects the benefits of personal growth. Participate in activities that boost creativity and skills through hands-on practices like a trade or interpersonal skills such as active listening. The ability to see the human beyond their words sharpens understanding and becomes a powerful tool for communication. There is profound humility in genuinely listening to others and nature. An effective listener creates space for compassion, allowing people to feel acknowledged and affirming our shared humanity.

Understanding is an important part of effective communication. When comprehension is missing, connections can be a struggle. Being fully present and asking questions helps us grasp different perspectives and reasoning, making conversations flow more smoothly and encouraging further inquiries. It's important to recognize that we may not always reach agreement or complete understanding, but the strength of effective communication lies in the feeling of being heard.

When developing deeper interpersonal connections, people can only engage with us at the level they understand themselves. Many overlook their shadow side and fail to recognize the inner work required to address unresolved trauma. This lack of self-reflection and unawareness of the energy brought into interactions can create different communication dynamics. A person's ability to meet another with understanding, openness, or compassion is limited by their inner work, often resulting in superficial or surface-level communication. To find peace, avoid taking the actions or words of others personally. Accept them as they are, understanding that they may not yet be able to meet others where they are. We can extend the same perspective to others, just as we don't take it personally when a flower doesn't bloom.

Understanding yourself creates a pathway to a more meaningful and purposeful life, allowing you to live wholeheartedly and express who you truly are without fear of judgment. Self-awareness and the exploration of healing enable you to recognize the co-creative relationship between yourself and nature, enriching your experiences in life's garden. You can turn ordinary moments into extraordinary ones by practicing and refining your interpersonal skills.

Adaptability is another critical skill that bodes well in the garden. Nature is highly adaptable, birthing entirely new species in response to changing environments. Being open and capable of changing perspectives, approaches, and behaviors strengthens resilience and relationships with ourselves and others. Since life relies on a web of connections, adaptable individuals tend to communicate and collaborate more effectively, leading to stronger relationships with others.

Discipline is another valuable asset in our personal development toolkit and arguably the most challenging to master. It involves sacrificing temporary pleasures to work toward long-term goals, requiring a resolute mindset to follow through on our intentions. Although we may occasionally fall short, progress is inevitable as long as we maintain our integrity. Consistent commitment accelerates our progress, helping us avoid wasted efforts. Just as it's unrealistic to expect a full garden overnight, the same applies to achieving most of our goals. Discipline is a journey that supports all aspects of our inner being, guiding us toward success.

> We may think we are nurturing our garden, but of course, our garden is nurturing us.
>
> ~Jenny Uglow

Presence Is Power

When we savor our presence in the garden and move with intention, we find ourselves where neither the past nor the future can find us. Performing chores with mindful awareness is a form of meditation in motion, aiding in quieting the mind. In this state, we will discover the doorway to accessing the inner well of wisdom. Undoubtedly, there will be potentially stressful and disappointing moments, but how we address those situations transforms an amateur gardener into a master gardener.

Investing in a garden is closely linked to investing in ourselves. Gardening provides therapeutic benefits, supporting mental and emotional well-being through a connection with nature, physical activity, mindfulness, and a sense of achievement. The rewards significantly improve our mental, physical, and spiritual health. However, it's good to recognize that gardening demands attention, maintenance, and care, much like our personal spiritual landscape.

Daily maintenance in the garden brings rewards in the form of improvement and increased appreciation. Staying engaged requires commitment, with the effort needed to maintain balance depending on the garden's size. An established, productive garden typically demands less effort than the first three years of a new one. A few days of preparation, hard work, and weeding each season can keep it manageable. Once the initial groundwork is complete, the garden can excel with minimal intervention. Additionally, walking through the garden daily helps monitor its health and address potential issues early. Pulling visible weeds during these walks makes upkeep simple and ensures the garden remains beautiful and balanced.

Setting ourselves up for success increases the enjoyment of gardening. This can be accomplished through preventative measures such as mulching to suppress weeds, installing a reliable watering system, engaging in annual fall composting and soil amendment for optimal fertility, ensuring proper spacing and plant placement, using plant support structures, and practicing companion and succession planting. These effective strategies can lead to abundant yields and the occasional bonus of bumper crops. This is always a rewarding experience!

Conversely, if we consistently struggle, it may indicate an unstable environment that needs attention. Investigating and observing closely is important, especially if the main issue isn't immediately clear. The situation may become more apparent over time, particularly after trying a remedy. Seeking outside help could also be beneficial. Allowing the problem to continue without intervention can lead to future challenges.

Another significant and worthwhile advantage of cultivating a successful and productive garden is the joy derived from it. Some of the most delightful experiences can be found in moments of respite. Knowing when to retreat, recoup, and recharge cultivates wisdom and strengthens our capacity for rejuvenation. Similar to specific trees and plants settling into dormancy during the winter months, we, too, must take the time to slow down, gather our thoughts, and strengthen for rejuvenation. As the seasons change, we become aware of our role in the cyclical nature of life.

Life unfolds in seasons, mirroring the changing landscapes of a garden. Each season brings its own beauty, challenges, and opportunities. Just as gardens experience seasons, so do humans. We have times for planning and planting, nurturing and pruning, growth and abundance, healing and harvest. We will face periods of dormancy, isolation, and challenges along our journey. Each season is needed for growth and development. Resisting any of these stages can delay progress, but embracing the changing seasons allows our natural cycles of growth to continue.

How much seasonal gardening you engage in depends on your goals and environment. A lighthearted way to view the seasonal cycle:

Winter: Becoming Rested and Ready

Spring: Becoming Determined and Dirty

Summer: Becoming Hopeful and Happy

Autumn: Becoming Fulfilled and Fortified

> Look deep into nature, and then you will understand everything better.
>
> ~Albert Einstein

Tread Lightly

A significant portion of the population becomes increasingly detached from the natural world. The rapid expansion of cities, suburban sprawl, and the pervasive influence of technology have drawn many away from their innate circadian cycles and severed their connection with nature. This detachment extends to a point where some take the Earth and its resources for granted, while others display outright apathy toward the environment. This mindset is not limited to individuals but is also evident in the actions of corporations and governments. Regrettably, many have suppressed the profound indigenous philosophy that acknowledges the interconnectedness of everything. However, the indigenous peoples have increasingly made their voices heard about many environmental issues.

Some might argue that Earth is merely a rock covered with water and various life forms—a view that has some validity. However, the many awe-inspiring human experiences in nature suggest that life cannot be fully reduced to only tangible existence. Instead, it seems more plausible to consider life as an extrasensory experience with an underlying goal of developing earth consciousness.

Many native traditions worldwide convey a shared lesson about maintaining a balanced connection with nature. These cultural teachings show that our ancestors gained survival skills by closely observing the natural world and its creatures. Unfortunately, we rarely follow these ancient practices today, leading to the significant disconnection many people feel with nature, one another, and themselves.

Nature emerges as our primal and grandest teacher, offering us a pivotal choice: to collaborate and assist the natural world or recklessly control and dismantle it. Indigenous history vividly illustrates our true nature of living in harmony with the Earth, a stark contrast to viewing it merely as a commodified marketplace for harvesting natural resources. To expect our current challenges to resolve themselves without consequences is to embrace willful ignorance.

The Earth houses everything we need to prosper. This is an astonishing fact that is no coincidence. Interconnectedness and symbiotic relationships exist between humans and the natural world. While it's true that the Earth can flourish without human interference, now that we are here, we've become much more aware of and created systems and structures that host symbiotic relationships. A garden illustrates the grand picture of symbiosis between plants and those that rely on them. Pollinators need plants, and plants need pollinators. Their mutual dependence ensures their thriving through their active roles in each other's existence.

Humans often attach to ideas, beliefs, people, things, routines, and habits—inherent aspects of our nature. However, relying too heavily on these attachments can gradually diminish our confidence and undermine our independence and self-reliance. Linking self-worth to mental attachments undermines our true value. Our real worth lies in our character, wisdom, and how we treat other living beings.

Embracing impermanence helps us appreciate our experiences and let them go when their time is up. This awareness allows us to value the simplicity of each moment more intensely. Accepting the impermanence of all things is an act of kindness and self-awareness.

A garden exemplifies impermanence daily. Early spring flowers, for example, often have a brief blooming period, but this does not lessen their beauty or significance. Although we might wish that beauty could last longer, or even forever, this is neither realistic nor ideal. True beauty lies in the entire life process of all living things; otherwise, it remains fleeting and somewhat superficial. Beauty is inherently transient and subjective. And yet, it is precisely this impermanence that gives beauty its poignancy. What passes reminds us to pay attention. The brevity of a blossom teaches presence, gratitude, and reverence. To witness life in motion—never static, always becoming—is to be invited into deeper intimacy with existence itself. In this way, impermanence is not a loss, but a gift: the very condition that makes everything meaningful.

> The soil is the great connector of our lives, the source and the destination of all.
>
> ~Wendell Berry

Soil Food Web

The soil food web is a complex network of organisms that functions through a series of interactions. Each organism has a role in breaking down organic matter, cycling nutrients, and maintaining soil structure and health. It encompasses a range of organisms, from microorganisms to larger soil animals, all interconnected through their relationships with plants and each other. This network supports plant growth, strengthens soil structure, and contributes to ecosystem sustainability.

In the grand scheme of life, the Earth's soil is a foundational element that connects existence from its origin to its end. This vital layer, composed of minerals, organic matter, and microorganisms, creates an environment where plants grow and survive. Life's balance is disrupted without this rich soil, affecting everything from microorganisms to large trees.

Soil is the source of life and is pivotal in supporting biodiversity. Although methods like hydroponics, terrariums, and epiphytes have their place, soil remains the fundamental element that connects the entire web of life. The complex composition of soil substrate and its vast capabilities are beyond complete comprehension. What happens beneath the surface is a veritable universe that sustains life as we know it.

Termed as a "living network," the soil food web is an intricate system. It consists of a complex and interconnected community of organisms within the soil ecosystem. This community encompasses diverse life forms, including bacteria, fungi, nematodes, algae, insects, worms, and numerous other organisms that interact. These organisms fulfill vital functions in nutrient cycling, organic matter decomposition, and soil fertility preservation.

The exchange and connection among these elements contribute to establishing a dynamic and well-balanced ecosystem. As land stewards, we are responsible for restoring and improving the land with vegetation and fertile soil. The more we nourish the land with organic materials, the more we enrich the web of life beneath the surface. Recognizing the soil as a "sacred connector" emphasizes the reverence and care it deserves in our efforts to sustain life and biodiversity on our planet.

Soul Of Creation

Everything begins with the soil, so we must understand the soil profile we cultivate to recognize our garden's potential. Soil is the soul of creation; gardeners manage, amend, and enrich it with nutrients to sustain life's growth. Maintaining a healthy soil profile is a key gardening duty. Not all soil is created equal. Each region boasts its unique blend of nutrients and structural composition.

Unfortunately, industrialization and monocropping have significantly depleted vital nutrients in the soil across many regions. Extensive extraction and mining of Earth's substrates have left once-lush regions barren and lifeless. Additionally, the heavy use of chemicals in industrial processes has rendered vast expanses of land infertile—a bleak testimony to the consequences of such actions. Healthy soil is alive, breathing, and teeming with microbial activity.

Aerobic soils have sufficient oxygen for plant roots and soil microorganisms, while anaerobic soils have low oxygen levels or lack oxygen entirely. In many cases, anaerobic soils emit a foul, rotten odor, quite different from the earthy aroma of healthy soils. Gardeners and farmers can recondition soil by using sustainable ecological amendment practices.

Similar to many living organisms, soil undergoes a dormancy period for regeneration. Crops and harvests strip the soil of vital nutrients and alter its profile. During these seasonally dormant periods, adopting a "less is more" approach becomes proactive in aiding soil regeneration. Minimal disturbance to the soil is an excellent strategy for allowing it to rebuild and rejuvenate. As a living component of our environment, soil requires the same essentials as other living beings: food, water, air, and protection. These elements must be available in proper proportions to maintain health and ensure viable production of future crops.

Working With Nature

Cover crops offer valuable benefits in protecting and revitalizing soils post-harvest. However, nature's inherent defense against soil erosion and degradation is found in the persistent proliferation of what we commonly label "weeds." Driven by a near-compulsive habit, humans often feel the need to pull, till, or spray these weeds. Ironically, this well-intentioned effort can work against the inherent intelligence of nature itself.

Allowing weeds to take root in areas devoid of cover crops can aid in drainage and rebuilding soil structure. Another effective method to manage weed thresholds, especially during winter dormancy, is applying a straw layer over exposed soil, which assists in weed suppression and erosion control. The finer the straw, the more conducive it is to breakdown in composition. Following the preferred no-dig gardening approach in spring, incorporate the straw as an amendment by applying a thick layer of mulch on top. Over time, the straw will naturally break down.

The ease of maneuvering straw allows for pulling it aside, adding mulch directly to the soil surface, and then reusing the straw as a top dressing—an effective and efficient way to protect and feed the soil continuously. While straw excels as a soil protector and benefits soil structure, it is less potent as a nutrient provider. Interestingly, the weeds mulched into the soil contribute to nourishment and structure. This approach is most effective before the weeds start to flower and go to seed.

Nature's ingenious design generously provides a natural mulch annually through the fall foliage drop from trees and shrubs. As leaves create a protective blanket, nature protects forest floors from exposure and erosion. Over time, this leaf litter breaks down, gradually contributing to topsoil formation, known as leaf mold.

Unlike traditional composting methods that combine green and brown materials, leaf mold is made exclusively from decomposed leaves. It differs from conventional compost because it lacks nitrogen-rich green components. Although leaf mold isn't as nutrient-dense as some composts, it does enrich the soil with organic matter, gradually improving its fertility. Initially, leaf mold works best as mulch but can be mixed with nutrient-rich compost to support further development.

Leaf litter provides a vital habitat for many creatures, offering food, shelter, and camouflage. Insects, spiders, amphibians, small mammals, and mollusks live and feed among the fallen leaves. Fungi and various microbes, including bacteria, inhabit the decaying leaves, breaking them down and recycling nutrients. This process supports other creatures in the ecosystem. Fall leaves create a microhabitat that sustains a wide range of life and strengthens local biodiversity.

When choosing mulch materials, avoid high-lignin leaves, as they decompose slowly and may hinder the nutrient cycle in the garden. High-lignin leaves to avoid in edible garden beds include oak, beech, birch, holly, sweet chestnut, and magnolia. Also, eucalyptus and black walnut leaves should be avoided due to their natural herbicide content, which can inhibit seed germination.

Promoting sustainable gardening practices involves advocating for the use of organic mulches. Recycling a blend of chemically untreated grass clippings, aged crop residues, straw, and garden trimmings is an excellent mulching strategy for incorporating into garden beds throughout the year, with a particular emphasis on winter. As these materials break down, they contribute to the formation of new layers of soil.

Mulch And Compost

Recognizing the applications and necessity of both mulch and compost is fundamental for cultivating healthy, high-yielding crops. While both are vital, they differ in their roles.

Mulch functions as a protective layer on the soil surface, providing advantages like moisture retention and weed suppression. Its breakdown, illustrated by straw, may or may not contribute nutrients to the soil. Introducing "living mulches" through cover crops is among the most effective methods for soil building. Cover crops like clover, buckwheat, cereal rye, and legumes protect the soil by preventing winter topsoil erosion.

Conversely, compost is a fully decomposed, nutrient-rich material intentionally integrated into the soil to increase fertility. It contributes significantly to the overall nutrient content. Garden compost blends decomposed plant-based kitchen scraps, eggshells, coffee grounds, yard waste, aged manure, potash, sawdust, seaweed, and more. Ideally applied in autumn, compost provides numerous benefits for soil preparation, regeneration, and plant health.

Applying compost in autumn strategically aligns with the natural decomposition processes, microbial activity, and nutrient availability. This timing creates an enriched and fertile soil environment, laying the foundation for healthy plant growth in the coming seasons. The nutrients, regenerated through microbial activity and decomposition over the winter months, become readily available in spring.

Incorporating a balance between green materials (rich in nitrogen) and brown materials (rich in carbon) is paramount for building nutrient-dense compost. Regularly turning a compost pile and managing moisture levels are key factors promoting decomposition and maintaining airflow. To ensure a healthy compost pile, avoid adding diseased plants, weed seeds, meat, dairy, or pet waste, as these can introduce pests, odors, or pathogens.

Soil necessitates time for regeneration, emphasizing the importance of minimizing disturbances. Preparing garden beds in autumn and allowing the soil to rejuvenate during late fall and winter yields benefits throughout the upcoming growing season. Some disruption may occur during planting and harvesting, but to preserve the integrity of the soil profile, it is best to adopt a no-till approach to gardening. Typically, adding amendments as top layers is adequate, eliminating the necessity to till in organic material. Building upon the soil proves more effective than extensively working in the substrate. No-till or no-dig gardening aligns with sustainable practices and helps create a more resilient and productive garden ecosystem.

Soul Food Web

From our first breath, we become intrinsically connected to the web of all life. We are allowed to shape our path and grow in various ways. Initially supported by the people around us, we develop like trees, with roots spreading out and branches reaching upward over time. Often, we move through life focused mainly on survival. During significant change, we experience shifts in perspective, leading to necessary internal growth. These moments cause us to reevaluate our place and adjust how we see ourselves. Nonetheless, there is always potential for further learning development and self-discovery.

By cultivating our inner garden with mindfulness, intention, and deliberate choices, we can infuse our lives with greater meaning and creative purpose. With added care and dedication, we create a ripple effect of positivity and transformation that reaches beyond ourselves, enriching the shared human experience and contributing to the collective soul food web of life. By actively reducing our suffering and nurturing our inner selves, we cultivate conditions for a more joyful and fulfilling life experience. We do not need a reason to feel happy because we are the source of our happiness.

Our well-being is shaped by various factors: the foods we eat, our nutritional habits, physical activity, exposure to toxins, environmental conditions, sleep quality, stress management, and relationships, including our bond with nature. Just as healthy plants need rich soil, we need a solid foundation in these areas to support our overall health. The beauty of tending to our inner garden lies in the gifts it bestows internally and externally.

Just as we assess plant health by examining the roots and soil, we must evaluate the core elements of our lives and take appropriate action. Quick fixes aren't enough; we must tackle the underlying issues. True well-being is attainable when we build a strong foundation and address the root causes of any imbalances. Focusing on these deeper aspects can restore our health and vitality, starting from the core.

Just as enriching the soil leads to a better harvest, nourishing our minds through activities that expand our knowledge, deepen our understanding, and strengthen our connections with others supports our personal growth. Engaging in these pursuits helps us develop and grow our potential. By embracing our role in the broader web of life, we allow ourselves to occupy the space needed to pursue our goals and experiences. Our presence in the world is valuable, even if we don't always see the outcomes we expect.

Life's Compost: Nurturing Growth

Turning challenges into compost for personal growth is like transforming difficulties into fertile ground for resilience and wisdom. Just as compost, made from decaying organic matter, enriches the soil and nurtures plant life, our challenges strengthen our character and resilience. Compost transforms waste into vital nutrients that sustain plant growth, much like our adversities transform into valuable lessons that nurture personal growth, resilience, and empathy, enriching our lives in meaningful ways.

In both cases, the process can be uncomfortable and demanding. Composting requires the breakdown of organic matter while enduring life's challenges tests our strength and patience. Yet, just as compost enriches and revitalizes the soil, our hardships can strengthen our character, deepen our compassion, and equip us to create positive change in the world. Much like compost nurtures life, our struggles can transform us into better individuals, empowering us to contribute meaningfully to society and improve life for ourselves and those around us.

The composition of Earth's soil reflects the variety of life experiences. It mainly consists of humus from decomposed plants and animals mixed with disintegrated rocks and minerals. Similarly, our life's mix of challenges, mistakes, and achievements mirrors the soil's richness. These varied experiences offer valuable lessons and opportunities for further improvement.

Cultivating a curious mind and a willingness to learn is akin to ensuring the soil is fertile for new ideas and personal development. Just as the Earth's soil provides the foundation for abundant growth, our openness to new experiences and continuous learning nurtures the soil of our minds, allowing us to blossom into our fullest potential.

Benefits Of Soil

Studies have found a significant number of benefits when working with soil. For example, gardening and farming have been shown to provide both physical and mental health advantages. Physically, interacting with soil and even the smell of soil exposes individuals to beneficial microorganisms like Mycobacterium vaccae, which can stimulate serotonin production and positively influence emotions. Additionally, contact with soil is associated with improved immune function and lower inflammation, thanks to exposure to various microbial communities.

Scientific evidence supports the notion that digging in the dirt and harvesting food are effective ways to improve mood and reduce stress, anxiety, and depression. This involvement with nature develops a deeper understanding and respect for natural cycles and the interconnectedness of living organisms, inspiring more sustainable practices and a commitment to caring for the environment.

We create a mutually beneficial relationship with the land by investing time, money, and effort into growing a garden or farm. Actively tending to the soil and plants improves the environment's health while allowing us to enjoy clean, nutritious food. Harvesting fresh produce fills us with joy and inspires us to continue the physical work needed to maintain and care for our space. Over time, this relationship deepens our connection to the land and brings a meaningful sense of purpose.

Gardening is more than a leisurely pastime; it supports overall health, psychological well-being, and longevity. Tasks such as digging, planting, weeding, and harvesting require a range of movements that contribute to complete physical fitness. Gardening involves a variety of motions, such as bending, lifting, reaching, and squatting, which helps to improve flexibility, strength, and endurance. These activities support better joint mobility and increase muscle strength, particularly in the core, arms, and legs. Regular gardening maintains and improves physical fitness levels, especially for older adults who may benefit from activities that encourage balance and coordination.

The physical exertion involved in gardening also supports cardiovascular health. Activities like raking, cultivating, and pushing a wheelbarrow can elevate heart rate and contribute to aerobic exercise, which benefits cardiovascular fitness and overall stamina. Additionally, spending time outdoors in natural sunlight while gardening provides an opportunity for vitamin D synthesis, supporting bone health and immune function. Sunlight exposure also regulates circadian rhythms, improving sleep patterns and promoting overall well-being. Gardening is a fulfilling way to stay active while enjoying the therapeutic benefits of connecting with nature.

Keep a diary, and someday, it'll keep you.

~ Mae West

From Seeding To Feeding

Journaling transforms ideas and dreams into reality while offering valuable self-care and healing benefits. Writing down your thoughts boosts brain function, sharpens focus, and reduces stress. It provides a mental, physical, and emotional workout, turning the process into a pleasurable form of creative expression, similar to the therapeutic experience of gardening. A journal becomes a keepsake, preserving memorable moments that time might otherwise erase. As you journal, you'll notice how quickly time passes as you explore the many topics blooming in the garden of your mind.

Garden journaling sharpens your gardening skills by keeping detailed records from seeding to harvest, food preparation, and preservation. This practice improves effectiveness and efficiency in future seasons. It also helps you anticipate and prevent pests, fungi, and diseases. Over time, you'll observe how the process comes full circle, from the initial plant seeding to the rewarding act of feeding yourself and others.

A strong start is important for any plant, and having thorough information can make the difference between a plentiful harvest and a poor one. The success of future crops often relies on the lessons learned from past experiences. Garden journals are a valuable tool for gardeners, offering insights into what worked and what didn't in previous seasons. This accumulated knowledge helps refine future efforts, leading to ongoing improvement and a better understanding of the cultivation process.

Reviewing past experiences and learning valuable lessons strengthens the foundation for future endeavors. This reflective approach creates continuous improvement, leading to better results over time. By understanding the details of your growing history, you can make informed decisions that boost efficiency and success in your gardening efforts. In short, learning from the past is a valuable asset for creating more effective and rewarding practices in the future.

Although maintaining a garden diary takes time and effort, its long-term benefits are substantial. By diligently recording and analyzing your gardening history, you build a proactive defense against potential setbacks. This approach protects your plants and serves as a wise personal investment, reducing waste and future costs. The time spent on meticulous record-keeping becomes a strategic measure, ensuring a more efficient, sustainable, and successful gardening experience.

Clearing A Path

Writing is a powerful tool for clearing and connecting our minds with our hearts, and journaling offers many benefits. Regular writing helps align thoughts and feelings, clear repetitive thoughts, and record experiences. It provides a safe space to express emotions, which can lower stress and anxiety. Organizing your thoughts improves mental clarity, making it easier to move forward with decisions. Reflecting on your experiences encourages self-awareness and lays the foundation for continuous self-improvement.

Writing is one of many ways to sharpen the mind. The conscious mind is a tool that needs to be honed to function effectively over time. Our consciousness shapes our perception of reality, and by cultivating a strong mind, we can intentionally create our lives. We can manifest our desired reality when we train our bodies to align by feeling what our minds aim to create. Writing plays an important role in this process.

While writing about our challenges and daily struggles might be tempting, it's often more rewarding to focus on and detail the positive aspects of our lives. Emphasizing the good things helps to attract more positivity. Conversely, concentrating on negative aspects can lead to a cycle of negativity, reinforcing those thoughts and experiences. This tendency to dwell on the negative is common, but focusing on the positive can help break that pattern.

Naturally, being able to purge stale feelings of dissatisfaction is a good release. However, the idea is simply acknowledging troubling thoughts while focusing on the positive aspects and your goals. Allocating a specific amount of time to address negative disturbances is an effective strategy for limiting self–indulgence in pity, fear, and worry while maintaining mental and emotional balance. This practice allows you to express concerns without letting them dominate your focus. The goal is to release and manage feelings without becoming fixated on the problems. Journaling, in particular, supports this process. Reviewing entries provides a powerful way to track personal growth over time.

Plant seeds of happiness, hope, success, and love; it will all come back to you in abundance. This is the law of nature.

~Steve Maraboli

Seeds Of Purpose

Every person is a unique creation with inherent meaning and purpose that contributes to the continuity of life. While this concept is simple, our growth process is complex and influenced by many external factors. Ideal conditions for realizing our full potential are rare, and each individual carries distinct genetic coding. We all possess a range of purposes, each contributing to the vast and diverse garden of life.

Living without awareness of our being can lead to mental anguish and internalized doubt. Most of humanity grapples with finding a place of peace and purpose in our ever-evolving and changing world. However, each day, we all contribute to shaping the world. Some individuals drive change and progress, acting as catalysts for transformation. Others fill roles as peacemakers and mediators, working to create harmony and balance within our communities. Many people live reactively without awareness of various aspects of their existence.

No matter where we are on this spectrum, each of us has the potential to make a positive impact and enrich the collective human experience. We can choose what we nurture in the garden of our own lives, though there will always be surprises and unexpected events. Trust the seeds of your unique potential and nurture them with care and intention. Through self-awareness, growth, and self-discovery, we can all find our place of peace and purpose within.

Just as each tree in a forest tells its story through its rings, each person's life is unique, and their purpose is part of their destiny. Tree rings reveal the factors that shaped a year's growth, and similarly, our narrative is influenced by various relationships and experiences. Some influences are obvious, while others are less clear. Despite distractions, how we nurture our development is ultimately a personal choice. We all have ideas and dreams, and it's up to us to bring them to fruition and offer them to the world. Support from others often helps us grow personally and shape our evolving purpose.

Every day, we either grow closer to our truth or drift further away from it. Each choice and action shapes our alignment with who we truly are. By embracing authenticity, we nurture the connection to our deepest self, allowing it to unfold and guide us. On the other hand, when we ignore our inner truth or conform to external expectations, we lose touch with that essence, creating a disconnect that dims our clarity and purpose. In the small, daily moments, we either honor or neglect the path to our true selves.

The season of failure is the best time for sowing the seeds of success.

~Paramahansa Yogananda

Sowing Seed Needs

The required basics for sowing seeds indoors or outdoors:

<u>Viable Seeds</u>: Healthy seeds capable of germinating.

<u>Soil or Growing Medium</u>: A nutrient-rich medium that supports germination and root development.

<u>Light</u>: Some seeds require light to germinate, while others need darkness; check specific seed requirements.

<u>Water</u>: Seeds need consistent moisture to germinate, but avoid waterlogging.

<u>Oxygen</u>: Seeds need air for respiration during germination.

<u>Heat or Temperature</u>: The right temperature is critical for germination; different seeds have different temperature needs.

<u>Containers</u>: Suitable containers that provide drainage and space for seedling growth.

These factors are interconnected and primary for ensuring seeds germinate and grow into healthy plants.

Seeds Of Success

Indoor sowing and plant propagation are excellent methods for gaining a head start on future harvests. However, direct outdoor sowing is equally valuable for succession planting, a gardening technique designed to ensure a continuous harvest by planting new crops at intervals. This method involves sowing or transplanting seedlings in stages, allowing for a steady produce supply. For example, you might plant a new batch of lettuce every few weeks to keep a fresh supply coming. It also includes rotating crops and growing different types in the same area at various times to maximize soil nutrients and reduce the risk of pests and diseases. Additionally, using varieties with varying maturation times can extend the harvest period.

Overall, succession planting helps gardeners achieve multiple harvests from the same space, minimize gaps between harvests, and make the most of the growing season. It extends the harvest period while contributing to healthier soil. Remember, the Earth thrives on growth; so when in doubt, sow some seeds!

Succession planting relies on careful timing and crop rotation. Effective succession planting requires planning to ensure new crops are sown immediately after harvesting previous ones, fully utilizing the growing season. Factors like plant growth rates, local climate, and soil health also impact the success of this technique. However, with ongoing climate changes, much of the advice in traditional garden guides may no longer be reliable. Gardeners must remain attentive to their regional climate and adjust planting strategies accordingly.

Keeping a dedicated garden planner or journal is a valuable tool for tracking and managing ongoing cultivation methods and weather changes. It allows gardeners to record planting dates, climate temperatures, germination periods, and harvest schedules, helping to ensure that each planting stage is well-coordinated and efficient. Over time, the journal becomes an important reference for the success of future crops. Additionally, using information from seed packets can aid in planning. By incorporating these details, gardeners can better anticipate harvests, reduce guesswork, and create a more organized, successful gardening experience, improving their ability to excel at succession planting.

Considerations And Cautions

Indoor sowing requires careful attention to prevent pests and diseases. Early detection and intervention can prevent minor problems from becoming more significant issues. Damping-off, a fungal condition inhibiting seedling growth, often results from poor air circulation and excessive moisture. To avoid this, aim to create an environment that is not conducive to pathogens. Problems can quickly arise from overwatering, inadequate drainage, and insufficient airflow. Using a low-speed fan to increase air circulation around the soil can help prevent conditions that lead to fungal infections and root rot.

Some gardeners may apply cinnamon powder around the base of seedlings due to its antifungal properties. Adding sphagnum moss to the seedbed and lightly pressing it down for good seed contact and a thin layer of chicken grit can improve germination. Regularly monitoring seed pots to ensure the proper moisture levels, temperature, and germination progress is also good practice.

Germination is more reliable in a controlled environment. Many seed varieties, especially warm-season crops like tomatoes, peppers, and melons, need heat to germinate. A heating mat designed for placing under plants for indoor sowing can help with this process. Alternatively, a space heater that keeps soil temperatures between 65 and 75 degrees can also support germination with appropriate precautions. It's important to regularly check the conditions when using heat sources, as they can reduce soil moisture. Monitoring helps prevent seed pots from drying out and maintains the best conditions for germination.

Watering from below is the ideal method for seed germination and seedling development. Place seed containers in a shallow tray of clean water to rehydrate them. This allows the growing medium to absorb moisture from the bottom, minimizing disturbance to the seeds. When the seed pots start to dry out, water from below by letting them sit in the water for 15–30 minutes before removing them. Taking the pots out after this period is important to prevent issues like the premature death of delicate seedlings. A light spray from a water bottle can help if the soil's surface becomes too dry.

Stratification And Scarification

Some native and wildflower seeds need to break dormancy to germinate successfully. The protective coatings on these seeds can make germination difficult, requiring particular techniques, especially in controlled environments. Natural processes like stratification and scarification help these seeds overcome their barriers and enhance their chances of survival. These methods are evolutionary adaptations that ensure seeds grow and the species survives.

Stratification is a method used to break seed dormancy by exposing seeds to cold, warm, or moist conditions. These conditions naturally occur for native plants and wildflowers, where cold and wet winter weather helps break down the seed coating. This process prepares the seeds to germinate when spring arrives, and conditions are more favorable. Home gardeners can mimic this process by leaving pots outdoors in the winter or placing them in a refrigerator if the soil is moist and covered with plastic. Alternatively, seeds can be wrapped in a damp paper towel, put in a plastic bag, and stored in the refrigerator for 30 to 90 days. After this period, the seeds can be planted in the garden soil in the spring.

Scarification is a process that involves breaking the harsh seed coat through physical, mechanical, or chemical methods to allow water to penetrate and trigger germination. Historically, indigenous land stewards used techniques such as intentionally burning fields and forest brush for various land management purposes. These practices helped with wildfire prevention and scarified seeds and acted as part of integrated pest management (IPM) by killing fungi and bacteria and disrupting pest breeding cycles. Today, many wildfires result from inadequate land management. For instance, clearcut tree farms pose a higher risk of wildfires due to reduced vegetative diversity. Older forests, which could withstand and benefit from occasional fires, are now rare.

Wildfires assist with thermal scarification by using heat and smoke to create conditions that help seeds germinate. Certain seeds benefit from a combination of both stratification and scarification. To mimic these natural processes, gardeners and commercial growers use different methods to break the seed coatings of various plants, promoting better growth and successful germination.

Not all seeds require scarification, and using improper methods can damage them. Most vegetable seeds do not need scarification or stratification to germinate but must be healthy and viable. Seed packets and plant guides typically provide this information. Gardeners can determine whether seeds need stratification or scarification by researching the specific requirements of each plant species. Refer to gardening books or reputable online resources for detailed seed treatments.

Breaking Through

People go through processes similar to stratification and scarification to bring their ideas to life. Intense moments or pressure often trigger bursts of creativity and exploration. Inventors and innovators experiment with various methods to achieve their goals, rarely finding clarity. The process typically involves multiple attempts and setbacks necessary for refining and improving results. While not every idea proves viable or worth pursuing, those who endure and continue to inspire can evolve into something meaningful. This highlights the importance of persistence and dedication, demonstrating that commitment can transform an idea into a successful reality.

When tending your garden, it's important to value successes and failures equally. Successes offer satisfaction and delight through all the senses, while failures teach valuable lessons and open new possibilities. By embracing both, you can fully appreciate the richness of the experience and understand how triumphs and setbacks shape personal and creative growth. Similarly, we are the architects of our journeys, planting seeds through our choices and actions to shape the landscapes of our lives.

The garden suggests a place where we can meet nature halfway.

~Michael Pollan

Thinning Out

Due to uncertain germination rates, most gardeners sow more seeds than the space can accommodate for proper growth. This often leads to the need for thinning out seedlings—one of the least enjoyable tasks in gardening. Removing healthy but competing seedlings is necessary for cultivating a productive crop. Each plant needs ample space for strong root development, proper branching, good airflow, and efficient nutrient and water uptake. Therefore, the significance of thinning lies in minimizing competition for survival.

After the first set of true leaves appears beyond the initial cotyledons, it's a good idea to check the health of your seedlings. Keep the strongest and healthiest seedlings during thinning and remove the weaker ones. It's best to grow just one seedling per pot or tray cell for indoor sowing unless the crop, like microgreens or sprouts, requires otherwise. When sowing outdoors, follow the spacing guidelines on the seed packet to prevent overcrowding and ensure each plant has enough space and nutrients to grow well.

Poor lighting can cause seedlings to grow long and spindly, weakening them. In contrast, sturdier, bushier seedlings tend to be healthier, especially indoors—particularly for tomato starts. Position indoor grow lights close to the seedlings without touching them to promote vigorous growth.

When all seedlings seem healthy, deciding how to thin them can be challenging. Follow the recommended spacing guidelines and use disinfected scissors or tweezers to remove weaker seedlings. Always disinfect your tools beforehand to prevent the spreading of fungi and pathogens to the root systems of other seedlings. If using scissors, cut as close to the soil surface as possible to minimize disturbance to the roots of healthy seedlings. Alternatively, extra seedlings can be salvaged by gently using tweezers to pull them up at the soil level.

Any viable plants that remain after thinning can be transplanted into pots to share with neighbors and friends. However, be careful when separating roots, as this can often cause more damage than benefit. Thinned edible plants (excluding nightshades like tomatoes, eggplants, chilies, peppers, and potatoes that contain toxins) can be used in salads. Non-edible thinned plants can be composted.

After thinning, take the opportunity to boost growth by applying a mild dose of organic fertilizer. This will nourish the remaining seedlings, supporting strong root development and overall health. Additionally, lightly brushing the tops of the seedlings can simulate natural environmental conditions, encouraging resilience and helping them grow stronger. The added nutrients and gentle stimulation provide comprehensive care, promoting healthy, robust plants.

Young seedlings must move on from their initial containers just as a baby outgrows its crib. Repotting them into slightly larger containers supports continued root development before transferring them to their final growing space. To avoid overcrowding, use wider, shallow containers, which help support healthy growth. Leaving seedlings in their original containers for too long can lead to issues such as girdling roots. It's good to plant smaller seedlings in appropriately sized containers for their development—just as a baby wouldn't transition directly from a crib to a king-size bed. Planting seedlings in large containers carries the risk of excess water retention, which increases the chances of root rot or fungal diseases like damping off.

Use garden cloches, row covers, cardboard, or clear plastic liners and bottles to protect outdoor seedlings from unpredictable weather. These coverings help retain moisture and heat while the seedlings' roots grow and strengthen. Notably, not all seedlings will reach maturity—typically, 20% to 30% may only develop cotyledons and not progress further. As a result, over-seeding is often recommended, especially for outdoor sowing. Thinning becomes necessary once the first true leaves appear, ensuring each plant has enough space to grow and branch out properly.

Hardening Off

Hardening off is the process of gradually acclimating plants, particularly seedlings, to outdoor conditions after being started indoors. This helps them adjust to sunlight, wind, and temperature changes, reducing the risk of shock or damage when transplanted outside. The process involves slowly exposing the plants to their new environment, requiring time and careful attention to ensure proper adaptation. Gradually increasing light exposure builds resilience and prevents burning. This practice ultimately prepares them for successful growth in their new outdoor setting.

Some important practices to follow before transitioning plants to their hardening-off process include exposing seedlings to the outdoors for a short period each day. Start with just an hour or two in a shaded area, and then increase the duration and sun exposure over 7-10 days. Place your seedlings in a sheltered area to protect them from strong winds and harsh midday sun during the initial stages. Slowly introduce them to more direct sunlight to build their resilience as the days progress. Monitor the seedlings carefully, checking for signs of stress, such as wilting, yellowing, or leaf burn, and adjust the exposure accordingly.

On the other hand, don't rush the process. If seedlings are suddenly exposed to harsh outdoor conditions, they may suffer from transplant shock, making it harder to establish themselves. Don't skip the hardening-off phase, even if seedlings appear sturdy; they may not be prepared for the outdoor environment and could be damaged easily. Don't forget to water your seedlings adequately during this time, as they may dry out more quickly outdoors than indoors. Lastly, don't harden off seedlings during extreme weather conditions, such as heavy rain, frost, or extreme heat, as this can stress or damage them before they are fully acclimated. By following these guidelines, you'll help your plants transition smoothly and perform well in their new environment.

Rootbound

Just as plants can become rootbound in their comfort zones, humans can become stagnant. Embracing change is necessary to break free from stagnation and stimulate growth. Indeed, comfort provides safety and predictability; however, excessive comfort can undermine our intentions and hinder progress. Balance is key: too much comfort can jeopardize growth, while discomfort without support can overwhelm us. Our minds and hearts need challenges and new experiences to expand. Without change, we become stagnant, unable to develop or reach our full potential.

The best path forward balances ease and challenge—allowing us to enjoy rest and stability while actively seeking opportunities to expand and evolve. Change and growth occur precisely when we step out of our comfort zone. This process builds resilience and strength, helping us endure life's challenges. Adapting to new circumstances is akin to the hardening off process of plants: we are building resilience and resistance. Gradual exposure to difficulty strengthens us, not by removing the challenge, but by teaching the body and mind to endure it. Plants taken too quickly from the shelter of a greenhouse to the open elements often wither; so, too, do we falter when forced into harsh realities without preparation. True resilience is not avoidance of discomfort, but a steady conditioning—growing stronger, more stable, and more capable with each encounter.

Plants In Pots

A garden offers endless possibilities for design, limited only by imagination. Adding potted plants alongside bedding areas amplifies visual interest and creates a dynamic atmosphere. Container plants are perfect for bursts of color, growing herbs, or managing invasive plants like mint, bamboo, and horseradish that can quickly take over valuable garden space. They also serve as decorative elements, enriching the overall aesthetic of the garden.

However, container plants require more frequent watering than those in bedding areas, especially when placed in direct sunlight. Potted plants can dry out rapidly during hot weather due to evaporation. Soil moisture meters can be used to ensure plants receive adequate moisture. These tools measure the moisture content in the soil of pots and containers, helping gardeners determine when it's time to water.

Growing Up

Space is a highly valuable resource, and how we use it can ignite creativity. To make the most of available space, consider experimenting with vertical growth. Installing trellises, archways, shelves, mounted pots, pallet walls, hanging gardens, hydroponic towers, green walls, and window framing for vertical gardens are all effective ways to grow upwards, maximizing space and abundance. Thinking about expansion in this way encourages creativity and growth, helping to move beyond perceived limitations. Rooftops and shed-top gardens are also great ways to utilize unused space and bring more greenery into your environment.

Even experienced gardeners sometimes regret their choices in space management. Effective planning is key to proper plant placement.

Understanding the mature size of plants helps prevent overcrowding and the need for future transplanting. Planting in an unsuitable spot can cause problems and regrets down the line. Ideally, place each plant where it can grow comfortably without the need for relocation or disruption.

Before planting, consider the growth habits of each plant. Knowing how tall and wide a plant will become helps narrow planting options. Foresight is paramount in this process. Observing the location before planting will reveal whether a plant will eventually obstruct walkways, doorways, gates, lights, water features, or spigots. Thinking ahead and placing plants thoughtfully can avoid costly issues and ensure a more harmonious garden.

Space To Grow

We all need room to grow, where our roots anchor us and our thoughts and creativity expand like branches. Relationships succeed when we respect and allow personal space. It's important to understand the difference between mutualistic and codependent relationships. Mutualism reflects relationships where both parties benefit, each strengthened by the other's presence without losing their integrity. In contrast, codependence describes a dynamic where reliance becomes so great that autonomy weakens, and survival or well-being feels impossible without the other. Where mutualism nurtures resilience, codependence often erodes it.

Flowering plants and pollinators have a mutually beneficial relationship: the transfer of pollen enables plant reproduction, while pollinators feed on nectar. Both species gain from this interaction. A specific example of mutualism is the relationship between ants and peony plants. Ants are attracted to the nectar of peony flowers, and in return, their presence helps deter floral-eating insects. Some even believe that the movement of ants can agitate the flower petals, aiding in their unfurling. However, a peony flower will naturally open over time under optimal conditions.

Mistletoe is an example of a codependent plant relationship with its host trees. In this way, mistletoe is a parasitic plant that attaches itself to tree branches and draws water and nutrients from them. If the host tree is heavily infested with mistletoe, then the tree can weaken over time. This demonstrates a codependent relationship where both organisms are tied together, often with negative consequences for the host.

Codependency in human relationships is quite common. In such dynamics, both partners may struggle to grow individually, leading to stagnation that can impede personal development and make it difficult to adapt to life changes. This pattern can also encourage reliance on unhealthy behaviors to cope with stress or emotional pain, such as substance abuse or other harmful habits.

In codependent relationships, there may be a fear of losing the partner, resulting in clinginess and anxiety, which can create strain. The constant need for giving or receiving support can lead to emotional exhaustion. Individuals might neglect their needs, interests, and friendships, relying solely on their partner for validation and fulfillment. One partner may become overly dependent on the other for emotional support or decision-making, creating an unequal dynamic where one feels more like a caretaker than an equal. Over time, this can lead to increased stress, anxiety, and resentment.

Just as fences help prevent unwanted disturbances, establishing boundaries in our lives by understanding what is acceptable and what is not builds a sense of autonomy. This emphasizes the need for self-awareness, which involves recognizing and understanding our needs, feelings, and behavior patterns. Reflecting on how codependency manifests in our lives is necessary for achieving balance, well-being, and healthy relationships.

We can cultivate independence by nurturing personal interests, hobbies, and friendships. Pursuing our goals and passions strengthens our sense of self and reduces reliance on others. Professional guidance may sometimes be necessary to gain insights and strategies for overcoming codependent behaviors, allowing us to build healthier, more autonomous relationships.

Self-care enables us to prioritize our physical, emotional, and mental well-being. It also offers an opportunity to reframe negative beliefs about ourselves and address feelings of unworthiness. Building a better relationship with ourselves and others requires consistent practice and cultivating the virtuous qualities of grace, patience, and time to develop. By nurturing these qualities, we can cultivate deeper self-acceptance and healthier connections with those around us.

Every person carries the source of their own power. Strengthening and maintaining this power is a vital part of individual character. Often, we lose touch with it early in life, shaped by the expectations of others and the pressures of society. Recognizing the existence of innate power is a crucial step in personal development. In relationships, especially, giving away or temporarily losing connection with our power is easy to do. However, it can never be entirely relinquished; it remains inseparable from who we are. Reclaiming personal power marks a profound return to autonomy. It serves as a means of realigning mind, body, and spirit, restoring the integrity of the whole self.

> **Why live? Life was its own answer. Life was the propagation of more life and the pursuit of living as good a life as possible.**
>
> **~Ray Bradbury**

Propagation Techniques

There are many ways to grow, whether through plants, food, personal character, dreams, or ideas. Established methods can lead to rapid development, but there is also value in experimenting and exploring new possibilities. Finding the best approach to achieving goals is often a personal journey, as different methods can yield varied outcomes. Embracing structure and exploration leads to deeper growth and paths reflecting individual strengths and visions.

There are several plant propagation techniques, each with advantages and suitability for different types of plants. Sowing seeds involves planting them directly into soil or a growing medium, making it ideal for plants that produce many seeds. Cuttings, on the other hand, use plant parts—such as stems, leaves, or roots—to generate new growth. This method is often used for woody plants and houseplants. Layering, a similar technique, is also commonly used for these types of plants. Choosing the correct method depends on the plant type and the desired outcome.

Layering encourages a part of the plant to form roots while still attached to the parent plant, allowing it to establish a new root system before being separated. Grafting involves joining a piece of one plant to the rootstock of another, creating a strong union that can combine desirable traits from both plants. Division splits a plant into smaller sections, each containing its own roots and shoots, allowing for the propagation of multiple plants. Micropropagation, or tissue culture, grows plants from small tissue samples in a sterile environment, often used for mass production. Bulb, tuber, and rhizome propagation relies on underground storage organs to produce new plants. Lastly, offsets and suckers involve removing and replanting young shoots that form around the base of the plant, enabling easy propagation for many species.

Exploring these propagation methods in detail deepens a gardener's understanding and expands knowledge and growth potential. By delving into techniques beyond sowing seeds, gardeners can unlock many possibilities for cultivating new plants. Each method offers unique advantages and challenges, allowing for more control over plant variety, quality, and growth conditions. Mastering these techniques expands a gardener's ability to create a more diverse and thriving garden.

Nature is based on harmony. So if we want to survive and become more like nature, then we have to understand that it's cooperation versus competition.

~Bruce Lipton

Competition

When species compete for the same resources necessary for survival, adaptations often emerge to improve their chances of success. Typically, these adaptations manifest as physical changes to access vital resources. For example, plants compete for light, space, water, air, and minerals and adapt to their environments through physiological, structural, and behavioral changes. These adaptations are critical, enabling them to grow, reproduce, and produce fruit and seeds.

Structural adaptations like spines and thorns on cacti and roses deter grazing animals; these work as defense mechanisms and are nature's way of ensuring survival. Similarly, humans develop psychological defense mechanisms like denial, repression, or rationalization to protect themselves emotionally. These mechanisms act as shields, helping individuals cope with stress, trauma, and challenging situations while preserving their emotional well-being.

These mechanisms support emotional preservation and short-term adaptation, but overreliance on them can create long-term challenges. They may cause avoidance of important issues, resulting in emotional stagnation or even exacerbating the problem. Similarly, plants with overly aggressive defense mechanisms may struggle to attract pollinators or coexist with beneficial organisms. Humans who heavily rely on defense mechanisms risk isolating themselves or missing opportunities for growth and connection. Balancing defense mechanisms with self-reflection and healthy coping strategies helps individuals retain their protective benefits while addressing drawbacks.

Some plants exhibit behavioral changes, such as altering their growth patterns to avoid shading by neighboring plants. Physiologically, plants may develop deeper or more extensive root systems to access water and nutrients more efficiently. They might grow taller or develop larger leaves to outcompete others for sunlight. Additionally, plants can release chemicals into the soil to inhibit the growth of competing species, a phenomenon known as allelopathy.

In competitive environments, plants that can quickly adapt and optimize their resources efficiently tend to flourish and reproduce more successfully. This evolutionary pressure drives the development of traits that increase survival and reproduction, contributing to the diversity of adaptations observed in the plant kingdom. Over time, these adaptations can lead to significant evolutionary changes within species, furthering a dynamic and ever-evolving ecosystem.

Humans have also competed for survival over millennia, often for less logical reasons. Healthy competition can build character and strengthen bonds, but unhealthy competition has led to harm and even fatal consequences. In essence, healthy competition stems from the mindset of self-improvement rather than superiority over others. Psychologists have extensively studied human nature and competitive instinct, revealing that competition exists in various forms and intensities. However, its underlying motivations—from survival and social status to personal achievement—add complexity, making it difficult to fully understand its origins and impact.

Competition between class systems reflects a deeply flawed mindset that views the world as a resource to be exploited for profit and people as tools to be used, manipulated, or discarded. Those in power do not merely seek personal gain; they drive a narrative in which power is defined by control over resources, people, and technology, with no regard for sustainability or ethics.

Inequality runs deep within society, as many social structures are built on scarcity and competition. Capitalism, in particular, enables a select few to manipulate systems for their advantage, maintaining inequality to preserve their status. By monopolizing and concentrating resources in their hands, they secure their power, driven by an inherent fear that sharing too much will lead to their downfall. Rather than using wealth and influence for the greater good, they hoard and invest in sustaining a system that keeps them in elite positions.

When power and wealth become ends in themselves, perception and values become distorted. This fuels self-deceit by becoming trapped in a cycle of consumption, success, and validation, where each victory is fleeting, and the pursuit of more—more control, more influence, more dominance—never ceases. This eventually leads to a grave disconnect from realness and the fundamental humanitarian values of compassion, empathy, and justice.

Over time, elitists lose their moral compass, corrupted by the very systems that sustain them. Conditioned to see themselves as separate from the world, they view their wealth and status as entitlements, with little regard for the ripple effects of their choices on others. The dominant systems—economic, educational, or technological—are structured to keep people focused on surface-level narratives, disconnected from the rhythms of the earth and their inner knowing.

Humanity is witnessing this unfold in real-time as climate shifts expose the fragile relationship between nature and modern society. The system must either be dismantled from within or, better yet, replaced. There is only so much space for one group or power structure to dominate before cracks spread and the foundation beneath them becomes unstable.

Real change will not come from pleading with the elite to act differently but from creating new narratives, systems, and ways of living that do not depend on their approval or participation. When enough people speak the truth, the system's warnings and defenses lose their grip. Transformation becomes inevitable if a critical mass embodies the change they wish to see—living with intention, demonstrating what is possible, and guiding others along the way. Step by step, this shift can free the next seven generations from inheriting the same cycles of ignorance and destruction.

At an individual level, embodying change shifts personal experience and sets an example for others. Self-awareness and moderation allow the benefits of competition to be harnessed while minimizing its harm. Regular self-reflection helps clarify motivations, revealing whether competitive behaviors contribute to growth or reinforce destructive patterns. Striving for a balance between competition and cooperation while considering the broader implications of our actions can lead to healthier and more fulfilling outcomes. Small pockets of change can ripple outward even in a world of contradictions and injustices. Though progress may seem slow, consistent and grounded actions accumulate over time. Focus on personal transformation first—it is necessary.

Cooperation

Competition is a significant ecological force, but cooperation is fundamental to the survival of all life forms. Many species collaborate to support the overall well-being of their ecosystems. For example, ants and bees work together to sustain their colonies, fish move in schools for protection and efficiency, plants form symbiotic relationships with fungi, and wolves coordinate within packs to hunt and protect their territory. Such cooperation among species helps maintain the balance and health of ecosystems, ensuring their resilience and stability.

These interactions often involve mutualism, where both species benefit from the relationship. For example, plants produce oxygen through photosynthesis, supporting the survival of countless organisms. Nature is rich with cooperative relationships that support species survival and strengthen vast ecosystems. Through these collaborative processes, biodiversity is preserved, habitats are sustained, and species can better adapt to changing conditions.

Humanity's real purpose is likely intertwined with stewardship, creation, and transformation. We aren't meant to dominate the earth but to exist in harmony with it as conscious participants in its unfolding. Many ancient cultures understood this—living in reciprocity with the land, honoring the seen and unseen forces at play. Somewhere along the way, that knowledge was fragmented, suppressed, or ridiculed, replaced with an artificial construct that serves only a select few. Those who awaken to consciousness understand that the most profound transformations are not achieved through brute force but through awareness, clarity, and subtlety—through the reawakening of the mind, spirit, and collective heart.

Comparison Is The Thief Of Joy

Our gardens are intended to be pleasant and productive spaces. When comparison and envy creep into our thoughts, the urge to compete clouds the beautiful visions we once embraced. The initial joyful motivation succumbs to the illusory pressure to compete with others, and soon, the love of gardening is overshadowed by the need to compare. Garden envy is real, but it's a noxious weed that strangles the joy of blooms. Instead of focusing on personal growth and the beauty of our gardens, the attention shifts to comparison and competition, leading to a diminished sense of fulfillment and inadequacy.

Constantly comparing our gardens to others creates unnecessary stress and anxiety. The pressure to meet or exceed others' standards can overshadow the peaceful and therapeutic aspects of gardening. Envy breeds resentment and frustration, not only toward others but also towards our own efforts and achievements. When the focus shifts to competing with others, it stifles creativity and innovation. Gardeners become less inclined to experiment and try new things, fearing they won't meet perceived standards. The desire to mimic others' gardens can diminish individuality and uniqueness, depriving the gardener of the personal expression that makes gardening a profoundly creative and individual pursuit.

Redefining success individually, rather than using others as a measure, helps combat jealousy and envy. Instead of measuring success by comparing ourselves to others, we should focus on growth, learning, and enjoyment. These are the true markers of success. Setting personal goals and celebrating achievements keeps our focus on progress. Acknowledging milestones and growth, rather than comparing to others, cultivates a sense of personal accomplishment. One of the best measures of success is how content we feel about ourselves.

Learning from our neighbors and engaging with a gardening community in a spirit of sharing rather than competition can be highly rewarding. Ultimately, we aim to create pleasant spaces, grow food, and enjoy beautiful blooms. Cooperation allows gardeners to gain valuable insights and learn from one another. Seeking advice can lead to meaningful connections, mutual support, and potentially lasting friendships. Participating in community gardening projects or collaborative endeavors can shift the focus from personal competition to collective success, promoting a sense of togetherness and shared purpose.

By embracing a mindset of contentment, gratitude, and individuality, gardeners can transform their gardens into spaces of joy and personal expression, free from the harmful effects of comparison and envy. This shift in perspective can bring a deep sense of fulfillment as we focus on our unique journey and the beauty we create. By taking the time to understand the motivations behind competitive behaviors and striving for a healthy balance, it's possible to leverage competition as a positive force for personal growth and societal progress.

Gardening is learning, learning, learning. That's the fun of them. You're always learning.

~Helen Mirren

Learn As We Grow

Gardening, like any skill, requires continuous learning and improvement. Adopting a strategic approach and setting clear goals are important to achieving success. It's easy to start one task and then jump to others without completing the original goal, which is especially common in gardening. Therefore, creating a focused list of chores or objectives to guide efforts is beneficial. While many other tasks may also need attention, concentrating on the task at hand ensures steady progress.

Foresight is valuable for a gardener, especially when informed by past challenges and setbacks—learning from previous mistakes. Gardening involves constant threats and requires regular adjustments. By taking the time to understand plant life, we can solve current problems and gain insights that improve future planning and results.

Setting goals and developing strategies allow us to direct our course of action. Although we cannot predict the future, we can envision optimal outcomes. We support our growth by focusing on what aligns with our mind, body, and spirit. Just as roots provide stability and nourishment to plants, understanding our core values and what brings us joy significantly contributes to our homeostasis. Cultivating patience is also key, making the growth process more enjoyable. By understanding and anticipating the future effects of our current actions, we reduce problems and improve the garden's overall success and health.

It's important to keep learning while avoiding the need to know everything. Humans aren't meant to know everything, but what we do know can benefit others. Take time to gain perspective and celebrate victories, no matter how small they may seem. Branch out and celebrate the successes of others, too. Regular reflection on progress encourages enjoyment of accomplishments; adjust strategies as needed. Maintaining a growth mindset, where challenges are seen as opportunities for learning, builds resilience and commitment to continuous improvement. Be mindful of the ego; it can undermine our best efforts and take the fun out of life. Balancing ego involves recognizing its role in our lives while remaining open to self-improvement, empathy, and collaboration.

Planting And Transplanting

Like plants in a garden, our ability to grow strong and healthy depends on our environment. To grow and excel, we must recognize what nurtures our well-being and what holds us back. Sometimes, we need to relocate for a more satisfying life. However, just like plants, we may face an adjustment period before we feel settled. Uprooting can be messy and leave a gap, so careful planning and preparation are key to making the relocation smoother and more successful for both plants and people.

Ensure the new location is ready before transplanting. The new space should provide proper spacing, nutrition, and a water source. Once these steps are in place, the transplanting process can begin. It's also important to consider weather conditions; cooler periods are ideal for transplanting because they reduce stress and shock. The quicker the transplant establishes its roots, the better its regenerative growth cycle will be.

Older container plants often benefit from scoring the roots before planting them in the ground. This simple step encourages the roots to spread outward, preventing them from becoming root-bound. Neglecting these basic needs can lead to future problems, potentially requiring another transplant, complete removal, or even the plant's demise. The environment significantly affects plant growth. While it may seem that a perfect setup is necessary, resilience often proves to be equally important.

A person's conviction of will often determines whether they merely survive or truly prosper. Just as some of the most stunning flowers grow well in poor soil or through pavement cracks, people also have the propensity to overcome difficult circumstances and defy great odds. We cannot heal in a harmful environment, but we can reach our true potential by trusting our intuition and making the necessary changes. Allowing ourselves time to adjust to a new environment is integral to the healing process after transplanting.

Love is space. It is developing our capacity for spaciousness within ourselves to allow others to be as they are.

~Kyodo Williams

Garden Space

In garden beds, issues like inadequate spacing and improper planting often result in early plant death, particularly for perennial shrubs and trees. However, kitchen gardens present an opportunity to implement more intensive planting techniques, such as polyculture. Polyculture is a method that mimics natural ecosystems, promoting a diverse and resilient environment. It helps reduce pest and disease problems, improves soil health, and uses resources better. The advantage of polyculture is its ability to yield a varied harvest, increasing nutrition and economic stability. This inspiring gardening approach can turn the garden into a thriving, diverse ecosystem.

When preparing a hole for a plant, envision it as a bed that will nurture its growth and development. Consider how the plant will expand within its environment over the next 3-5 years. Foresee how its growth will impact nearby plants and structures. Ensure the plant has ample space without overshadowing or crowding other plants. Also, consider how its roots might interact with nearby features like sidewalks, foundations, or underground utilities. Being prepared and proactive and planning for a plant's future growth ensures it will grow well without causing problems for its surroundings.

Breaking traditional gardening rules is sometimes practical and necessary, particularly in intensive herb and kitchen gardening. For example, tomatoes are an exception to standard planting practices. Planting them deep into the soil, about two-thirds of the way below the surface and at an angle, encourages adventitious root growth along the stem. Removing the lower branches supports this process. This unconventional method strengthens the root system, improves nutrient absorption, increases drought resistance, and results in a larger plant and more fruitful harvest. It's a testament to the value of experimentation and challenges conventional gardening norms.

Roots need adequate oxygen and space to spread, so a wider planting hole is more beneficial than a deeper one. If possible, scoring the sides of both the plant and the hole encourages better root development. Avoid creating a smooth, bowl-shaped hole, which can cause roots to circle and girdle. Scoring girdled roots helps them integrate more effectively with the soil, promoting healthy expansion and growth. This purposeful disruption strengthens roots, allowing them to establish and spread more efficiently. Together, these techniques ensure the plant is securely anchored and has the optimal conditions for growth.

Planting too deep can cause many problems, especially concerning trees, including root girdling, stunted growth, and poor leaf development. To avoid these issues, mix native soil, nutrient-rich soil, and the recommended amount of organic fertilizer as backfill. Plant trees so the top of the root ball is level with the surrounding ground for the best results.

If a tree or shrub is planted too deeply, it's important to address the issue promptly, as correction may not be feasible later. Gently lifting the root ball and adding backfill soil underneath to achieve the proper ground level helps stimulate healthy root development and reduces plant shock, supporting better growth. For established trees planted too deeply, you can improve their longevity by carefully removing the surrounding soil to expose the tree flare.

Soak the ground with water a day before planting if the soil is compacted and dry. This softens the soil, making digging and preparing the hole easier. Another helpful tip is to moisten the root ball by adding water to the planting hole before covering it with backfill soil. This 'watering-in' technique provides the plant with a reliable water supply as it settles into its new spot, ensuring it receives adequate moisture during establishment. After planting and watering, tamp the soil to eliminate air pockets and ensure good root-to-soil contact. Air pockets can harm the tree's health by disrupting root expansion, leading to poor establishment, desiccation, rot, and weak root systems that limit growth and resilience to environmental stress.

> **Every adversity, every failure, every heartache carries with it a seed of an equal or greater benefit.**
>
> ~Napolean Hill

Growth In Adversity

Recognizing the role of adversity in growth illustrates the parallels between human development and plant growth. Just as people become stronger and more resilient by facing challenges, plant roots strengthen when they adapt to the fluctuations in their environment. Providing the right balance of support and adversity benefits people and plants, leading to hardiness and success.

Comfort alone doesn't always lead to strength and resilience for people or plants. Excessive comfort breeds complacency in people, discouraging risk-taking, skill development, and the ability to face challenges. For plants, it might result in shallow root systems and reduced resilience as they fail to develop the strength needed to adapt to changing conditions. While comfort provides stability, it also impedes progress and adaptability.

Personal development often involves stepping out of comfort zones. Embracing new experiences and confronting fears are needed for growth. These actions help build confidence and encourage a growth mindset. People progress in environments that balance support with challenge, with access to education, mentorship, and opportunities for reflection and improvement.

Constant distractions and interruptions can significantly hinder growth and expansion. Just as people require uninterrupted time and space for self-reflection, focus, and personal development, plant roots also need stability to grow and establish themselves without frequent disturbances. The early stages of root development are especially critical. While facing some challenges can be beneficial, avoid extreme conditions to prevent damage or stunted growth. During these formative stages, it's advantageous to minimize stress by ensuring adequate watering and protection from pests, excessive heat, or frost.

Adversity is instrumental in developing adaptability and flexibility. Challenges often push individuals to discover their strengths and develop effective coping strategies. Similarly, plant roots exposed to moderate stress, such as changes in water or soil conditions, tend to grow more vigorously, produce better yields, and become more resistant to diseases and pests. Proper initial care establishes a strong foundation, allowing the roots to become well-established and better equipped to handle future challenges, ultimately improving the plant's overall health.

Peace in Protection

Garden insect netting provides a strong boundary layer of protection from unwanted pests, making it an excellent tool for preserving the integrity of crops. Row covers and shade clothes are also effective and beneficial additions, especially in raised bed gardens. Insect netting serves as a protective barrier against chewing, piercing and sucking insects that cause plant damage. Bird netting is also beneficial for protecting fruiting shrubs, trellises, and arbors. Netting is best applied before the fruit begins to ripen.

Lapping and siphoning pollinators, like bees and butterflies, need access to food sources. A garden with a diverse perennial selection becomes a banquet for insects. Sacrificial herb crops such as oregano, mint, Echinacea, sage, and embellishing flowering plants serve adequately as food sources for beneficial insects when allowed to flower and go to seed.

Protection is a fundamental aspect of survival. Whether instinctive or intentional, responding to the need for protection creates a sense of immunity and peace, both vital for thriving. There may be no foolproof method or total guarantee of prevention. Sometimes, the luck of a garden gnome or the charm of a leprechaun finds its way in. Until more is observed and instilled, protection remains a meaningful measure. When clear boundaries are established, strength is fortified, and peace has space to grow.

Plants teach in a universal language: food.

~Robin Wall Kimmerer

Companion Planting

Growing certain crops together creates a symbiotic relationship where they benefit each other. This cooperation improves soil quality, more effective pest control, improves pollination, and increases biodiversity and disease resistance. Companion planting is a highly effective strategy for maximizing gardening space, enriching the overall gardening experience, and nurturing a thriving garden while increasing food production.

Companion planting is an effective way to increase diversity in the garden, support the ecosystem, and naturally boost its visual appeal. Companion plants offer several benefits: some attract beneficial insects that aid in pollination and pest control, protecting crops from damage. Plants like tomatoes and basil enhance each other's flavors. Other plants improve nutrient uptake, making essential nutrients available to neighboring plants that might otherwise struggle. Overall, companion plants complement each other's needs and help maintain balance in the garden.

Plant incompatibility can result in issues like blight, competition for nutrients and light, pest infestations, poor fruit flavors, and inadequate root development. Avoiding certain plant combinations—such as tomatoes and potatoes, onions and peas, or cucumbers and melons—can help reduce competition for resources and decrease the risk of disease, pest problems, and cross-pollination.

Three Sisters

The Iroquois Nation practiced a renowned method of companion planting known as the "Three Sisters," which involves growing corn, squash, and beans together. When planted nearby, these plants work well together and benefit each other. Unlike traditional planting in straight rows, the Three Sisters method offers structural support and soil benefits, significantly increasing overall crop productivity.

In this method, the corn stalks serve as natural supports for the climbing bean vines, allowing them to access sunlight and produce fruit. The broad leaves of the squash spread out to act as a living mulch, keeping the soil cool, suppressing weeds, and reducing water evaporation.

Corn requires nitrogen-rich soil, and beans improve soil fertility by fixing nitrogen through nodules on their roots, which house beneficial bacteria. The Three Sisters method exemplifies mutual support and cooperation, benefiting the plants and the people who harvest them.

Robin Wall Kimmerer's culturally significant book, Braiding Sweetgrass, profoundly explores the Three Sisters. She eloquently illustrates the reflective meaning of each plant in human terms: "Respect one another, support one another, bring your gift to the world, and receive the gifts of others, and there will be enough for all" (Kimmerer, 2013, p. 132).

Pondering these principles, we can see the value of having diverse companions in the gardens of our lives. Whether teachers, counselors, firefighters, artists, grocers, bakers, mentors, or other vast contributors to a balanced community, each has a significant role. While perfection is unattainable in any garden, supporting one another helps create a more harmonious and balanced existence for everyone.

Cultural Companionship

The world relies on and benefits from the diversity of its various cultures. Each nation adds a unique contribution to the global community. Cultural diversity enriches and energizes societies by sharing different perspectives, traditions, and backgrounds. Storytelling, a practice known to support thriving Indigenous communities worldwide, highlights the interconnectedness of all beings across our shared planet.

Diverse communities often cultivate a global perspective. Exposure to various viewpoints builds understanding and empathy, improving educational opportunities. This greater understanding supports social cohesion, reduces prejudice, and strengthens unity. Diversity also boosts resilience and adaptability, enabling communities to navigate challenges more effectively as circumstances change. Working together to solve problems allows individuals to share their unique expertise and find practical solutions. At the same time, respecting spiritual practices and traditions is vital for meaningful cultural collaboration.

A diverse garden, with various plants coexisting, reflects the beauty and strength found in a world where people from different backgrounds unite. As companions in the garden of life, each person supports harmony, well-being, adaptability, and resilience within the global community. Native crops from diverse regions unite us through the shared enjoyment of food. Embracing cultural diversity enriches our lives and helps create a more inclusive and harmonious world. By supporting each other's growth and development, we strengthen our collective experience. Friendships and relationships, like varied colors and fragrances, add to the richness of life.

Knowledge From Indigenous Elders

Indigenous Elder of the Americas, Dr. Duke Redbird of the Saugeen Ojibway Nation, speaks of the _Seven Ancestor Teachings_. These are Earth's lessons as experienced in nature. He explains how indigenous ancestors already knew what modern science is now telling us. Redbird speaks about the seven principles of good conduct: love, humility, courage, respect, honesty, truth, and wisdom. He further explains the seven canopies of food found in nature's food forests.

"First canopy: The Canopy of Wisdom- the oldest trees that grow the tallest in the food forests and protect all other plants: the walnut, the chestnut, the beechnut, and the maple trees. From them, we learn wisdom. Walnuts and maple sap provide nutrition for the mind.

Second canopy: The Canopy of Courage- the fruit trees, represented amongst many others by the plum, cherry, apple, and pear trees. Fruit trees are challenged by harsh weather, and still, as fragile as they appear to be, give their fruit representing courage.

Third canopy: The Canopy of Respect– the berry bushes of raspberry, blueberry, thimbleberry, gooseberry, and bearberry are self-fertilizing and self-propagating and grow together amongst each other. They come in different colors, shapes, textures, and flavors, yet they exist and thrive in harmony with one another.

Fourth canopy: The Canopy of Honesty– the food that grows right above the ground, such as squash, pumpkins, cucumbers, cabbages, and lettuce. There is honesty about these foods; the fact that they are trusted and good for you shows in their very existence they are never counterfeit and teach us honesty.

Fifth canopy: The Canopy of Truth- the food found on the ground's surface. Here, we find our medicines. We sort the poison ivies from the good ivies, the poison oaks from the good oaks, the mushrooms from the toadstools. It also includes the strawberry, which represents the earth itself. Unlike every other fruit, the strawberries' seeds are on the fruit's surface, just as we humans occupy the surface of the Earth. The strawberry is also shaped like a heart and is good for your heart. Truth is always in accord with fact and reality, and it is up to us to separate fact from fiction.

Sixth canopy: The Canopy of Humility—We find root vegetables buried under the ground: potatoes, carrots, turnips, and other vegetables. They are not necessarily evident on the surface. We must dig and search for them, often on our knees. In this process, we learn about humility from these foods.

Seventh canopy: The Canopy of Love- these are the creepers and vines that go through the woods and embrace each other, and from them, we learn about love.

Indigenous peoples have guided and practiced these seven ancestor teachings since time immemorial (Redbird, 2023). The Seven Ancestor Teachings, Museum of Toronto presentation, YouTube, September 1, 2023.

Follow The Sun

Another valued aspect of companion planting is understanding the sun's path across the desired growing space and the maximum heights of the plant varieties intended to grow. This information helps to use garden space more effectively, improving overall production. From a practical gardening perspective, taller plants create shade and protect lower, shade-loving varieties, establishing a harmonious companionship. Conversely, shade from taller plants can inhibit the growth of competing varieties.

When laying out raised garden beds, orient them from north to south, especially for low-growing crops. This orientation ensures that each bed receives even sunlight throughout the day as the sun moves across the sky from east to west. It helps all plants get sufficient sunlight, which is necessary for their optimal growth.

Raised east-to-west beds benefit taller vine or trellis crops like cucumbers, peas, pole beans, grapes, and tomatoes. Place the trellis on the north side of an east-to-west raised bed for optimal growth. The most important factor is ensuring the bed receives six or more hours of direct sunlight. Avoid shade from tree branches or shadows cast by structures for sun-loving crops, though these can provide excellent protection for plants that perform well in partial shade.

A garden is always a series of losses set against a few triumphs, like life itself.

~May Sarton

Weather The Storms

While we enjoy choosing seeds for our garden, we quickly learn that we cannot control every aspect of what unfolds. Each garden presents its own set of challenges. Just as we grow consumable food or revel in the seasonal beauty of shrubs and flowers, pests and scavengers inevitably arrive. However, we do control how we confront these challenges. Depending on the extent of the damage, we often cut our losses and start anew. We implement preventative care as the most effective strategy to keep unwanted pests out of our garden spaces.

Our most cherished possessions may succumb to accidents, uncontrollable forces, or unforeseen circumstances in moments of neglect or tragedy. It is precisely during these times that we may falter under the weight of grief, risking the loss of our sense of balance. Yet, within these challenges lie profound opportunities for growth, enabling us to evolve into our most honest and strongest selves. These transformative experiences not only shape our journey but also rigorously test the resilience of our faith and will. They carry gifts that empower us to become better caretakers of our life's gardens, cultivating strength and wisdom amidst the uncertainties.

Removing noxious weeds that strangle nature's blooms takes extra time and attention in the garden. Seizing opportune moments to address issues immediately minimizes their impact and prevents further damage. Allowing problems to persist without addressing them can lead to even more significant complications. By staying proactive and attentive, we can maintain a healthier environment for growth and prevent minor concerns from escalating.

If insects were to vanish, the environment would collapse into chaos.

~E.O. Wilson

Integrated Pest Management

Insects are indispensable in maintaining the balance of ecosystems and supporting biodiversity, emphasizing their importance in sustaining life on Earth. Recognizing their value to soil health heightens our appreciation of their role. Insects actively pollinate many plants, including crops that humans depend on for food, increasing agricultural productivity. They also move and burrow through the soil, leaving behind waste and remains that enrich it as a natural fertilizer. By decomposing animal and plant matter and recycling waste alongside fungi and bacteria, insects contribute significantly to the ecological cycle. Additionally, they are an integral part of the food web, serving as prey for various animals, from birds to mammals. Furthermore, insects help control pest populations naturally, reducing the need for chemical pesticides.

Integrated Pest Management (IPM) offers a thorough and sustainable method for managing pests in agriculture and gardening. It uses a range of strategies to reduce environmental and health risks. It is important to understand that not all pests are harmful; some benefit the ecosystem. For instance, certain spiders and wasps help control the number of damaging pests. Therefore, identifying which insects are problematic is valuable before taking control measures.

The more we observe the plants and wildlife in our gardens and allotments, the better we can support local ecosystems. Sick plants release volatile compounds that signal distress, often attracting insect infestations. Insects are drawn to unhealthy plants as food sources. When a plant begins to die or decay, it emits a different scent that attracts insects looking for food or places to lay eggs. This is a prime example of nature's sensible design.

Other factors contributing to weakened plants include nutrient imbalances, overwatering or underwatering, infections from fungi, bacteria, or viruses, and environmental stress from extreme temperatures, low humidity, or inadequate light. Exposure to toxic chemicals or pollution, as well as damaged roots, can also affect plant health. Addressing these issues promptly can help restore plant vitality and prevent further problems.

Understanding which organisms are present helps us manage pests effectively and maintain the garden's balance. Correct pest identification allows us to implement supportive measures without disrupting the ecosystem. Many insects, bugs, spiders, and wasps help control harmful pests. However, misidentifying these beneficial creatures can lead to unintended harm, undermining our efforts to manage pests and hindering healthy crop growth. This emphasizes the delicate relationship between knowledge and action in cultivating a successful garden.

Coexistence is a measure of intelligence. Before resorting to harsh chemicals to eliminate unwanted pests, take the time to learn about their weaknesses and consider a more organic approach. This protects the soil microbiome and ensures long-term gardening success. When we live in harmony with other species, the entire ecosystem prospers. This isn't always easy or possible, especially when human interests outweigh the needs of the voiceless.

Wasps, for example, show the importance of distinguishing between friends and foes in the garden. There are many types of wasps; some are excellent at patrolling garden beds. Before spraying a wasp nest, identify them first. Paper wasps, for instance, can significantly benefit the garden as they help eliminate pests like aphids, flies, and caterpillars that damage crops. Like most species, they are typically non-aggressive unless provoked. Overcoming unnecessary fear and misconceptions about bugs and insects can differentiate between a harmonious or fruitless garden ecosystem.

When utilizing IPM practices, prevention is the first line of defense. Focus on integrating pest-resistant plant varieties and maintaining proper sanitation. Remove and discard infected plant material to prevent the spreading of disease. Keep these items away from compost piles to prevent the reintroduction of the spores and transmission of disease into growing areas. Regular monitoring, using traps and visual inspections, enables early detection of pest and disease issues.

Introduce other IPM practices depending on the severity of the condition. Biological control of unruly pests involves introducing natural predators or beneficial microorganisms to regulate their populations. Cultural controls modify the environment to deter pests, while mechanical controls use physical methods like traps or barriers. Chemical controls like pesticides are considered a last resort and applied selectively to minimize environmental impact. IPM aims to maintain a balanced and sustainable system, promoting crop health while reducing harm to ecosystems and non-target organisms.

Gardens facing hot and dry conditions are especially susceptible to insect infestations, accentuating the importance of IPM during such periods. Anticipating potential issues, identifying vulnerable areas, and fortifying those most susceptible to imbalance, invasions, or infestations require foresight. Ideally, swiftly addressing these scenarios can reduce infestation thresholds and keep damage to a minimum. Delaying intervention may worsen conditions. Knowing when to seek external assistance may be a lesson in humility, especially when the potential loss outweighs the possible gain.

In the garden, as in life, guarantees are elusive, and everything has an expiration date. Our primary focus is to nurture plants with care, ensuring they grow in a healthy and abundant environment. We build sturdy structures, integrate complementary plants, and attract beneficial insects to sustain fertility. Consistent and proper watering practices, regular soil enrichment, and judicious pruning further help to mitigate disruptions caused by pests and diseases. Stressed plants weaken the garden's defenses and require prompt attention.

In summary, the first step in IPM is prevention, which involves implementing healthy practices like crop rotation, using pest-resistant plant varieties, and maintaining proper sanitation. Next, regularly monitor and inspect for pests to avoid unnecessary treatments. Establish pest thresholds to determine when intervention is needed. Prioritize cultural, mechanical, or biological control methods before resorting to chemical controls. Finally, evaluate and adjust strategies to ensure their effectiveness and sustainability.

Integrated Personal Management

Just as we apply Integrated Pest Management (IPM) practices in our gardens and greenhouses, we can use similar principles in our lives.

This begins with prevention through self-reflection to identify imbalances and their origins. Next, we monitor our behaviors and choices, seeking guidance from trusted sources, including our intuition, to take actions that restore harmony. We then define thresholds that protect our peace and well-being. We implement strategies such as meditation, journaling, physical activity, therapy, and holistic medicine to support our journey. Finally, we evaluate our progress without judgment, maintaining an ongoing commitment to self-improvement and balance in our personal lives and cultivated spaces.

Adopting a holistic approach to our well-being enables us to reconnect with the wisdom that has supported humanity for hundreds of thousands of years before the advent of modern technology. Many cultures have survived and thrived despite challenges we may never fully understand. These communities often lived in harmony with nature, embracing a holistic way of life that allowed them to learn from their environment without causing harm.

However, industry has caused significant damage over the past few hundred years, jeopardizing the future of humanity. The contrast between historical resilience and current environmental challenges emphasizes the need to revisit holistic practices for achieving a balanced and sustainable coexistence with our planet. The attentive gardener must skillfully navigate this dynamic, recognizing that various factors contribute to the complex interplay of growth and resilience in our lives. This journey of understanding and aligning with these elements is a vital aspect of our ongoing personal development.

Stress and imbalance signal misaligned actions and direction. With its formidable force, life nurtures growth from the ashes of despair or topples those at the peak of power. It is dynamic—a continuous balancing act of vibrations and frequencies converging harmoniously. Every action triggers an energetic reaction, and nature, working beyond our sight and understanding, constantly strives to restore equilibrium. This enduring mystery of life reveals a world in constant change, organizing energies with a complexity that often eludes our comprehension.

One of our greatest strengths lies in letting go of anything that doesn't align with our needs, standards, or desires. Striving for personal growth requires a mindset different from settling for less. Ultimately, we are responsible for our choices. When we gather the courage to release what keeps us stuck in a cycle of dissatisfaction, we create space for more of what we truly want. Establishing equanimity in the garden of our lives requires consistent practices of self-reflection, self-care, and self-improvement. Prioritize nurturing personal peace and happiness.

A weed is but an unloved flower.

~Ella Wheeler Wilcox

A Place Of Belonging

Have you ever felt unloved, as if you were invisible to kind eyes, or perhaps felt trampled by the words and actions of others? Maybe you've experienced a sense of being overlooked and undervalued. Like a weed in a flower garden, there are times when we find ourselves in places where we don't seem to fit in. Some people and environments may never fully recognize our true worth for various reasons. However, remember, it's not our job to prove our value to those who don't see it.

Weeds are often seen as the enemy of gardeners and farmers, and for good reasons. They can grow uncontrollably and threaten the health and appearance of cultivated plants. A plant is often labeled a weed based on its location— for example, a rose in a cornfield might be seen as a weed, but that doesn't make it any less beautiful. No matter where a rose blooms, it simply lives within its beauty.

Weeds have a notable role in maintaining the ecological balance of the Earth. Resilient plants that do well on barren land help protect the environment unless the land is sterilized or exposed to chemical treatments. Weeds can spread quickly, forming a layer shielding topsoil from erosion, nutrient loss, and weathering. Their adaptability and growth contribute significantly to the health and sustainability of ecosystems.

Despite their ecological role, human preferences—often driven by the convenience of chemicals and a lack of awareness—have fueled the intense pursuit of perfect gardens. While we can alter the land for specific benefits, excessive interference with nature can lead to severe consequences, potentially threatening the health of the environment.

It's important to recognize that the natural world revolves around growth and survival, with weeds serving a significant role in this process. Understanding their function and the delicate balance within ecosystems can lead us to more sustainable and harmonious gardening practices, helping us appreciate the complex relationship between cultivated plants and the resilience of so-called "weeds."

A Humble Weed

Weeds contribute significantly to the land by attracting pollinators and microorganisms. Pollinators, in turn, strengthen the local habitat by feeding other creatures and supporting the proliferation of weed populations. Microorganisms help stabilize and make nutrients available, thereby improving soil quality. Some weeds also aid in controlling harmful nematodes. Additionally, the roots of weeds contribute to aeration and soil structure. Soil improvements may take time, as nature operates on a seemingly endless timescale, while humans function within a far more limited one.

Nature does not overlook or waste anything; every element helps maintain a delicate balance. This balance emphasizes the interconnectedness of all living things, creating a harmonious system where each participant has a role to fulfill. Disruptions to this balance often stem from external disturbances or human interference. Although usually seen as unattractive in urban areas, weeds are a natural resource that supports wildlife. Wildlands are critical for animal survival, offering places to forage, nest, hide, and rest. The significance of these natural habitats is profound, and within these ecosystems, many weeds have roles that are not immediately visible to us.

Intriguingly, some weeds extend their importance beyond the wild, leaving a mark on human history. Certain varieties are not only edible but have also been integral to the traditional practices of indigenous cultures for centuries. Passed down through generations, these weeds possess valuable medicinal properties, highlighting the deep connection between humans and the natural world.

The humble weed, often dismissed as a nuisance in manicured landscapes, reveals itself as a multifaceted ally in nature's grand narrative. It showcases the remarkable ways every element of the natural world contributes to the delicate balance that sustains life.

Suggesting alternatives to traditional chemical-based crop maintenance may raise concerns among gardeners and farmers. However, we cannot ignore the environmental damage—often overlooked since the mid-twentieth century when pesticide companies began targeting farmers.

The widespread adoption of mono-cropping, golf courses, and manicured lawns in colonized lands has significantly disrupted ecological balances and altered weather patterns.

Adopting a different approach to weed management requires temperance and moderation. Instead of quickly labeling a weed as a nuisance, it is more prudent to consider its potential benefits to other species and the environment. For example, early spring dandelions provide a vital food source for bees emerging from winter dormancy. Sumacs nourish numerous songbirds, deer, and rabbits, while migratory birds benefit from the antioxidant-rich berries of Virginia creeper.

The threatened Monarch butterfly population depends entirely on milkweed for survival. Milkweed, often mistakenly regarded as a weed by those unfamiliar with its role, is the only plant on which Monarch butterflies lay their eggs; it is the host plant for their caterpillar larvae. Planting a milkweed species native to a region helps ensure successful migration and reproduction. Despite this, many milkweed species are toxic and may be considered invasive in garden settings. It's important to remember that numerous plants, including common ones, can be poisonous if ingested by humans or animals. However, toxicity doesn't necessarily mean a plant should be avoided altogether. Knowing what to grow can help mitigate potential risks.

Just as we carefully handle the thorns of a rose, we should also exercise caution with certain plant saps, like those of rue or Bishop's weed, which may cause adverse reactions. Fortunately, planting milkweed seeds benefits Monarchs and other important insects. Researching and selecting the right milkweed species for your region is worthwhile to ensure a successful and beneficial relationship between plants and pollinators.

Watering Weeds

Gardeners know that maintaining a healthy garden requires routine, with proper watering being a fundamental part of care. Similarly, just as we avoid watering weeds to prevent them from spreading, we should be mindful not to "water" the weeds of worry in our lives. By paying close attention and observing daily, we can identify areas where worries might grow. Monitoring these concerns helps us avoid actions that might make them worse. These mental "weeds" only gain power when we actively feed them with our attention.

Overthinking is a prime example of giving attention and resources to something unproductive or harmful. Unchecked mental habits misdirect our efforts, negatively affecting our psychological and physical health. To address overthinking, it's helpful to develop strategies for managing and redirecting thoughts. Techniques such as breathwork, mindfulness, cognitive-behavioral therapy, setting clear goals, limiting information intake, and practicing self-compassion can reduce the impact of overthinking and improve personal success.

Feeling fear, self-doubt, and negative thoughts is a normal part of being human. However, when these patterns persist and become unproductive, they can create significant inner turmoil and conflict. Developing mental strength and resilience is key to maintaining inner peace. We often "water" mental weeds by imagining worst-case scenarios, which distorts reality and leads to unrealistic projections.

As many wise individuals have noted, most problems exist only in our minds. We nurture these mental troubles when we fixate on repetitive negative thoughts and anticipated outcomes. Shifting our focus to the present moment and letting go of the desire to control outcomes is an effective way to restore mental neutrality. Embracing the present helps us release the need to foresee the unknown and trust in our ability to navigate life's challenges. Often, our fears and projections are worse than reality.

We all face various problems. To manage them effectively, we can avoid adding to them, accept help when needed, and redirect our focus toward self-improvement to maintain perspective. Dwelling on guilt and shame with "would've," "could've," and "should've" thinking can undermine self-esteem and contribute to feelings of hopelessness and depression.

Many strategies can alleviate mental distress. Mindfulness, meditation, exercise, and intentional living are natural barriers to mental weeds. By observing our thoughts without becoming attached to them, we can break the cycle of repetitive thinking. Instead of being controlled by our thoughts, acting as a witness to our mind enables us to manage them more effectively. We can overcome negativity by removing negative influences and redirecting our focus toward positive, constructive thoughts. This mental maintenance creates space for healthier perspectives and a more balanced inner landscape. Additionally, interrupting negative thoughts with uplifting ideas or even song lyrics can help relieve overthinking.

Perspective is a powerful remedy for shifting us away from fear-based thinking. A helpful grounding exercise is to gaze at the night sky and recognize how our problems pale to the vast expanse of the universe. Acknowledging that we all live within a brief moment of existence and accepting that we inherently make mistakes keeps us humble and aware of our place in the world. Everything, including our perceived problems, has a temporary existence. Changing our viewpoint helps diminish the intensity of our fears, revealing that our issues are just a small part of a much larger picture. This broader perspective allows us to manage our worries and navigate life more clearly and gracefully.

Many effective ways exist to manage mental clutter and reconnect with our truths. By adopting a flexible mindset, using positive affirmations, practicing mindfulness and gratitude, and embracing self-compassion, we water the flowers of personal development and well-being in our gardens. Daily journaling and meditation allow us to observe and reflect, which helps maintain the health of our life's garden.

Brain-challenging activities build mental strength and cognitive conditions that stimulate effective learning and critical thinking. Activities such as reading, solving puzzles, playing strategy games, or learning a new language or instrument engage the mind in meaningful ways. The time and effort invested in these activities gradually transform them into constructive routines.

Weed It And Reap

Living with some weeds is usually tolerable until they become a problem, a common experience for every gardener. The best time to remove weeds is early in their development before they flower and spread seeds. Boiling water offers a simple and environmentally friendly method to manage weeds, although it may require a few applications. The high temperature of the water bursts plant cells, causing the weed to die. Pour the boiling water directly onto the weeds, thoroughly covering the leaves and stems. This method works well for small patches of weeds or in specific garden areas. Avoid surrounding plants, as boiling water can harm any vegetation it touches. Additionally, boiling water can raise soil temperature, potentially affecting nearby seeds or plants.

Weeds have widespread negative impacts in gardens, as they reduce yields and occupy space meant for desired plants. They compete for water, nutrients, and sunlight, hindering the growth of garden crops. Additionally, weeds can disrupt air circulation, increase humidity, and create conditions favorable to pathogens and diseases. Some weeds attract problematic pests and contribute to crop diseases, while others replace native vegetation. Farmers, in particular, can attest to the damage weeds cause in their fields.

Weeds naturally seed and spread as part of the environment, but you can control their growth with various practices and efforts. Effective weed management requires preventive measures, monitoring, and control strategies to minimize their impact and protect plant health and productivity. Techniques for managing weeds include applying thick layers of mulch, using woodchips on cardboard in large areas, solarization, and planting densely to reduce the space available for weeds to grow. Tools like string trimmers can be helpful, but they often only cut weeds above ground, leaving the roots intact and allowing weeds to regenerate. Additionally, string trimmers can destroy critter habitats and harm the animals themselves.

When overwhelmed by mental weeds or other challenges, we may need help to find our way and make necessary changes. Seeking assistance requires both humility and strength. We can address past neglect and commit to new growth with the proper support and guidance. Building discipline involves establishing helpful daily practices and making mindful observations. This transformation sets the stage for future growth, bringing the rewarding fruits of our labor, extending inner peace, and laying the foundation for equilibrium.

Engaging with our mental, physical, and spiritual landscapes reminds us of the continuous nature of change and impermanence. Recognizing our limits and knowing when to seek help can be one of our bravest actions. Achieving peace within our garden stands as the ideal triumph for any gardener. By clearing sacred space for the seeds of joy to take root, we discover empowerment and a rejuvenated spirit, cultivating an environment ripe for new possibilities.

Most plants taste better when they've had to suffer a little.

~Diana Kennedy

Fertilizing Needs

Plants benefit from a certain amount of stress to build resilience. However, fertilizers supply essential nutrients that plants require for growth, such as nitrogen, phosphorus, and potassium. These nutrients support various functions, including root development, flowering, and fruit production, which can significantly increase crop yields. Fertilizers boost plant growth and vigor by providing these necessary nutrients, resulting in healthier and more productive plants. Additionally, healthy plants can better resist diseases and pests, and fertilizers can bolster their defenses, making them less susceptible to various threats.

Timing is important when fertilizing a garden. Applying fertilizer too early can lead to waste and runoff, potentially contaminating nearby waterways if it doesn't reach the roots effectively. Fertilizing during hot, dry months can cause plant burn and death. Ideally, fertilization should be done at the start of the plant's growth season, when new growth is visible in spring. Nitrogen, a key nutrient, is especially important during this period as it stimulates growth when plants emerge from dormancy. Early spring crops benefit from an all-purpose fertilizer applied during this time.

For many plants, a second application around mid-season can help maintain healthy growth. This is especially true for crops or plants with a long growing season, which need additional nutrients to support continued development. When preparing a new garden bed or planting new plants, mix fertilizer into the soil to give the plants a strong start. Watering the root zone before fertilizing can help incorporate the material and prevent root burn. It's best to avoid fertilizing at the end of the growing season as this can encourage late growth that may be damaged by frost or reduce the plant's winter hardiness. Proper timing of fertilization ensures effective nutrient uptake and reduces the risk of harming plant health and the environment.

Dedicated annual flower and vegetable beds benefit from fertilization before planting to ensure the soil is enriched with nutrients. After planting, it's good to water the plants immediately to help them establish and absorb these nutrients effectively. Adding humus and manure in the fall prepares the soil for spring planting.

Some plants, like irises, have different dormancy periods than other plants. Irises are dormant during the summer and begin growing in the autumn, so they should be fertilized during their active growing season in the fall. In contrast, shrubs and trees generally do not need fertilization in the fall but benefit from it when they start their active growth phase in the spring.

Slow-release fertilizers are convenient because they provide nutrients gradually throughout the growing season, requiring only one application. By understanding the specific needs of different plants and timing fertilization appropriately, gardeners can support optimal growth and health throughout the year.

Foliar fertilizer is a nutrient solution applied directly to the leaves of plants, allowing for rapid absorption of nutrients through the leaf surfaces. This method effectively addresses nutrient deficiencies and promotes growth. It is best to apply foliar fertilizers during the plant's active growing season, typically in spring and early summer, when nutrient uptake is at its peak. Foliar feeding is especially beneficial just before flowering or fruiting, as it supports reproductive growth. It can also be helpful after transplanting to reduce transplant shock and encourage quick establishment.

Following the recommended dilution rates and application guidelines to avoid over-fertilization when using foliar fertilizers. Apply during cooler parts of the day, such as early morning or late afternoon, to minimize evaporation and prevent leaf burn. It's advisable to avoid application during extremely hot or windy conditions.

Organic And Synthetic

Understanding the soil's composition is important for effective fertilization. Factors such as soil texture, organic matter content, and pH affect how well nutrients are available to plants. A soil test offers valuable insights into these elements and helps to make informed choices about fertilization. Analyzing the soil test results allows for adjustments to fertilization, addressing deficiencies or imbalances, which facilitates better plant growth and improves yields. Soil tests often provide specific recommendations for the types and amounts of fertilizers needed, ensuring the best results while reducing waste and minimizing environmental impact.

Prioritizing soil health is a necessary proponent for successful gardening. Incorporating organic materials like compost, untreated grass clippings, and cover crops enriches the soil with essential nutrients and improves its structure, promoting better water retention, aeration, and microbial activity. This approach aligns with the principles of permaculture, which emphasize working with natural processes to create sustainable and resilient gardening systems. Feeding the soil and nurturing its microbiome creates a fertile environment where plants blossom. This approach reduces the need for synthetic fertilizers and pesticides. Ultimately, healthy soil forms the foundation of a productive and eco-friendly garden.

While synthetic fertilizers can deliver nutrients to plants quickly and in concentrated amounts, they often have environmental consequences. Their water-soluble forms can easily leach into groundwater, leading to pollution and damaging ecosystems. Additionally, their high salt content can disrupt the balance of soil microorganisms over time, which may diminish the soil's long-term fertility and resilience.

In contrast, organic fertilizers, such as compost, manure, and bone meal, offer a more sustainable approach to feeding plants. These materials release nutrients slowly as they decompose, promoting healthy soil structure and microbial activity. Organic fertilizers also improve soil moisture retention and reduce the risk of nutrient runoff, thereby supporting overall environmental health.

Gardeners can develop balanced ecosystems that benefit plants and the environment using organic fertilizers and soil-building practices. This approach supports sustainability and responsible stewardship, ensuring the long-term health and productivity of our gardens and surrounding ecosystems. As gardeners and environmental stewards, we must recognize that everything is interconnected through the soil, which is vital to the health of all living things. The soil is, in fact, alive.

Alfalfa meal is a versatile and beneficial amendment for organic gardening. Its nutrient-rich composition supports plant growth and improves soil health, making it an ideal choice for eco-conscious gardeners. Triacontanol, a natural growth hormone found in alfalfa meal, amplifies its effectiveness by promoting vigorous growth and increased plant fruit production. Moreover, alfalfa meal's content of trace minerals contributes to soil fertility and overall plant health. The presence of saponins adds another benefit by acting as a natural pest repellent, thus reducing the need for chemical pesticides and aligning with sustainable gardening practices.

Integrated Pest Management (IPM) practitioners can benefit by incorporating alfalfa meal into gardening routines. This approach stimulates plant health, improves soil structure, and naturally deters pests, supporting a balanced ecosystem in the garden. However, too much of anything is not necessarily a good thing. Excessive use of alfalfa meal can lead to nutrient imbalances or soil saturation, potentially harming plant health. It is considered slow-release; thus, it is best applied in spring for maximum benefit.

Know Your Nutrients

While plants require 17 essential nutrients for healthy growth, the six most important for their health are Nitrogen (N), Phosphorus (P), Potassium (K), Calcium (Ca), Magnesium (Mg), and Sulfur (S). Among these, the primary macronutrients encompass Nitrogen, Phosphorus, and Potassium (potash), commonly indicated by the N-P-K values on fertilizer labels. The remaining trio—Calcium, Magnesium, and Sulfur—are classified as secondary macronutrients, as they are not needed in substantial quantities for plant health. Micronutrients such as Copper (Cu) and Iron (Fe) are required in smaller amounts, along with Boron (B), Manganese (Mn), Molybdenum (Mo), Chlorine (Cl), Nickel (Ni), and Zinc (Zn). Carbon (C), Oxygen (O), and Hydrogen (H) are obtained through the air and water.

Nutrient Deficiency

Just as the human body exhibits signs and symptoms of nutrient deficiencies, plants communicate their needs through observable symptoms. It is important to note that plants may also show signs of excesses in certain elements. A thorough examination of the plant, neighboring plants, and the environment is necessary for assessing and evaluating potential issues.

Although not the only indicator, plant leaves reveal telltale signs of underlying issues. Chlorosis, commonly recognized by yellowing leaves, is one such symptom. The inability to produce chlorophyll in the leaves can be attributed to pathogens or nutrient deficiencies. Typically, chlorosis manifests due to a shortage of nitrogen or excess water. Prolonged excessive watering drowns the plant, commonly resulting in root rot and ultimately leading to necrosis (death of plant tissue). Therefore, examining the surroundings and environment of the plant is as necessary as observing the plant itself. Understanding the cause is much more important than just trying to remedy the symptoms.

Another symptom that may be seen in plant leaves, similar to nitrogen deficiency, is inadequate levels of sulfur, which can result in yellowing leaves, particularly affecting young leaves. Potassium deficiencies often manifest as yellowing or browning along the edges or margins of the leaves. In older leaves, interveinal chlorosis, or yellowing between the veins, indicates a lack of magnesium.

Iron deficiency symptoms resemble those of magnesium deficiency but primarily affect younger leaves. Calcium deficiency is evident when new leaves die off, develop 'tip burn', or when fruits like tomatoes show blossom end rot. However, calcium deficiencies are often not due to low soil calcium but result from uneven watering, excessive soil moisture, or root damage. Phosphorus deficiency may appear as dark green or purplish leaves, along with reduced flowering and fruit production. By regularly observing plants, conducting soil tests, and understanding the specific needs of different plants, gardeners can identify and address nutrient deficiencies effectively.

Universal Healthcare

Nutritional health is paramount to an individual's overall well-being, just as healthy soil supports plant growth. The human body and the soil rely on balanced biomes to function optimally. Maintaining a healthy gut biome is similar to the necessity of having healthy soil. Exploring health models beyond Western medicine can provide valuable insights into holistic approaches to well-being. While Western medicine often focuses on treating symptoms, holistic health models consider the interconnectedness of various factors contributing to health imbalances and sickness.

Factors such as diet, lifestyle, environmental influences, stress levels, emotional equilibrium, and genetics all play significant roles in human health. By addressing these factors holistically, individuals can promote overall well-being and prevent illness before it occurs. Holistic health models recognize that the mind, body, and spirit are interconnected and that imbalances in one area can affect other aspects. Therefore, effective treatment involves considering all facets of a person's health, including mental, cognitive, emotional, spiritual, and physical well-being, addressing root causes rather than just symptoms.

One of the oldest systems of medicine is Ayurveda, which originated in India over 5,000 years ago. 'Ayurveda' is derived from Sanskrit, with 'Ayur' meaning life and 'Veda' meaning knowledge or science. Ayurveda is often referred to as the science of life or the science of longevity. Central to Ayurveda is balance, harmony, and the interconnectedness of the body, mind, and spirit. It emphasizes the importance of preventive measures for overall well-being rather than just treating symptoms or illnesses after they occur.

Ayurveda offers a holistic approach to healthy living by incorporating elements such as diet, lifestyle, herbal remedies, yoga, meditation, and cleansing practices to support balance and harmony within the individual. It recognizes that each person is unique, with health influenced by a combination of factors, including physical constitution (dosha), mental and emotional state, diet, environment, and lifestyle. By understanding and addressing these factors, Ayurveda aims to restore and maintain balance, leading to optimal health and well-being. It provides valuable insights and practices that can complement Western medicine, contributing to a more comprehensive approach to health and wellness.

Beyond Ayurveda, several other traditions deserve exploration, such as Traditional Chinese Medicine, African Traditional Medicine, Holistic Native American Health, Unani Medicine, Maori Health, and Reiki, a Japanese form of energy healing.

Incorporating holistic approaches to health, such as focusing on nutrition, stress management, mindfulness, exercise, and emotional well-being, can help individuals achieve greater health and vitality.

Let food be thy medicine and medicine be thy food.

~Hippocrates

Herb Gardens

Plants provide food and medicine, both of which are fundamental to life. Herb gardens offer a wealth of culinary and healing benefits. By exploring the medicinal properties of herbs, a garden design can meet specific health needs and interests. However, it's important to be cautious when growing potentially toxic plants, particularly near food-growing areas. Thoughtful planning and placement can help mitigate risks, ensuring a safe and enjoyable gardening experience.

Herbs can be used in many forms, including therapeutic tinctures, salves, aromatic soaps, and flavorful spices. Cultivating a diverse herb garden effectively creates an easily accessible library of holistic wellness resources. Each herb is a beneficial tool for promoting physical health, mental clarity, and emotional balance, significantly contributing to overall well-being.

Herbs are indispensable companions in any garden, offering numerous benefits beyond their culinary and medicinal uses. In addition to enhancing the flavors of meals and serving as natural remedies, herbs play pivotal roles in garden ecosystems. Some herbs improve soil health, benefiting the growth and flavor of nearby vegetables. Their flowers attract pollinators like bees and butterflies, which are vital for plant reproduction, while their strong scents deter pests naturally, reducing the need for chemical interventions.

Harvest most herbs just before they start to flower or during early bloom, when their flavor and essential oil content peak. Harvest herbs in the morning, after the dew has dried, before the sun fully heats the plants. Pick the young, tender leaves for herbs like basil, mint, and parsley, as older leaves tend to be tougher and less flavorful. For fast-growing herbs like mint, oregano, or thyme, regular harvesting encourages new growth and keeps the plant healthy.

Herbs add diverse textures and colors to garden aesthetics, especially when they flower and go to seed. They fill gaps between other plants, reduce weed growth, and create a lush, productive environment. This mutualistic relationship among herbs and other garden plants sustains a balance where each species supports the health and resilience of the whole garden.

Rosemary and lavender are renowned for their culinary and aromatic qualities and ability to naturally repel certain insects in the garden. These herbs emit fragrances that mosquitoes find displeasing, making them effective natural deterrents when planted near outdoor seating areas or windows. Lavender, in particular, is known to repel moths, with dried lavender often used in sachets to protect clothes from moth damage in closets and drawers. Due to their pungent scents, these herbs can also help deter flies, including houseflies and fruit flies.

Like lavender, rosemary also repels moth larvae that target stored grains and fabrics. While not a comprehensive solution for pest control, incorporating rosemary and lavender into garden design benefits the landscape aesthetically and contributes to a more pest-resistant environment. This approach aligns with natural gardening principles that minimize reliance on synthetic pesticides.

Studies have shown that rosemary's invigorating scent improves cognitive function and memory retention, making it a promising herb for mental clarity and focus. Traditionally, rosemary has been used in herbal medicine for its various health benefits. It is believed to have antioxidant and anti-inflammatory properties and has been used to help digestion. Rosemary can enhance the flavor of root vegetables like potatoes and carrots, providing a robust, pine-like taste.

Rosemary is often planted in gardens for its ornamental beauty, culinary applications, and ability to attract beneficial insects such as bees, ladybugs, lacewings, and hoverflies. These insects help maintain a balanced garden ecosystem by supporting pollination and controlling pests.

Rosemary can be grown as a hedge, in containers, or as a fragrant addition to herb gardens and landscapes. Several cultivars of rosemary have different growth habits and flavors. Some popular varieties include 'Arp,' 'Tuscan Blue,' and 'Prostratus' (creeping rosemary). Due to their wide-spreading habit, most rosemary cultivars need ample growth space. Consider this before planting to avoid interfering with other plants or structures.

The best time to transplant rosemary is in the spring or early fall when extreme temperatures don't stress the plant. Avoid transplanting during the heat of summer or the frost of winter. Rosemary has a deep root system, so it's important to keep the root ball intact to minimize stress. Gently loosen the roots if they are compacted. Rosemary prefers well-drained, slightly acidic to neutral soil. After transplanting, water the plant well, but avoid overwatering, as rosemary is drought-tolerant and prefers dry conditions once established.

Peppermint and chamomile are also common garden herbs that offer many health benefits beyond their culinary uses. Peppermint is well-known for easing digestive discomfort and promoting digestion when brewed into a soothing tea. Its natural menthol content helps to relax muscles in the digestive tract, alleviating symptoms like bloating and gas. Mint is considered a mental stimulant and is best ingested earlier in the day rather than before bedtime. It is sometimes used to alleviate mental fatigue and improve focus. When planting nearby, the mint can add a refreshing, slightly sweet flavor to peas and cucumbers. Due to its vigorous and often invasive rhizome runners, mint is best grown in containers. When planted directly in the ground, mint can quickly take over a garden bed or yard, outcompeting other plants.

Chamomile, on the other hand, is revered for its calming properties. A cup of chamomile tea before bedtime can induce relaxation, ease stress, and support restful sleep, making it a popular choice for winding down at the end of the day. Chamomile prefers well-drained soil with moderate fertility. It performs well in full sun to partial shade. It is relatively tolerant of drought once established but benefits from regular watering during dry spells, especially in hotter climates. In cooler climates, it may behave as an annual, while in milder climates, it can persist as a perennial, especially if protected from harsh winter conditions.

Basil, cilantro, thyme, and oregano are highly favorable additions to any herb garden. These herbs can also complement particular fruit and vegetable flavor profiles and be effective companion plants. Basil pairs well with tomatoes, peppers, and zucchini, adding a fresh, aromatic flavor. Cilantro enhances the taste of corn, tomatoes, and peppers with its bright, citrusy notes. Thyme complements a wide range of vegetables, including carrots, potatoes, and tomatoes, with its earthy, slightly sweet flavor. Oregano boosts the taste of vegetables like tomatoes and peppers with bold, savory notes.

Ginger, turmeric, and cinnamon, although usually not grown in temperate climates, possess potent anti-inflammatory properties and aid digestion. They can help alleviate chronic inflammation in the body. These herbs and spices also support digestion by stimulating enzymes that increase nutrient absorption and promote gut health.

Incorporating these herbs and spices into daily routines, whether through teas, culinary applications, or aromatherapy, not only adds delightful flavors and scents but also contributes to overall well-being and health maintenance. Their natural properties offer a holistic approach to supporting various physical and mental health aspects, making them valuable additions to a healthy lifestyle and the garden.

Echinacea (Coneflower) is valued for its medicinal benefits and vibrant blooms. It provides immune support, especially during cold and flu season, and may reduce the duration and severity of respiratory infections. Topical preparations of echinacea can help heal minor cuts, scrapes, and burns due to its anti-inflammatory properties. Additionally, it has been studied for its ability to reduce inflammation, which can benefit conditions like arthritis. Thanks to its soothing effects, echinacea can also be used in creams or ointments to address skin conditions such as eczema or psoriasis. Some people turn to echinacea for its calming properties, which may help alleviate mild anxiety and stress.

We can consume echinacea in various forms, including teas, tinctures, capsules, and extracts. To harvest, gather the flowers and leaves during peak bloom. This plant grows well in full sun but can tolerate partial shade, and it is drought-tolerant once established. Ensuring good air circulation around the plants helps prevent fungal diseases.

St. John's Wort (Hypericum perforatum) is commonly used as a natural treatment for mild to moderate depression and anxiety. Many people find it effective for improving mood and emotional well-being. The plant contains hypericin and hyperforin, compounds believed to have antidepressant effects by influencing neurotransmitters in the brain.

Due to its anti-inflammatory properties, topical applications of St.

John's Wort oil may heal minor wounds, burns, and skin irritations. Some people also use it to relieve nerve pain, including conditions like sciatica or neuropathy. It may also help alleviate symptoms associated with menopause, such as mood swings and irritability, and can be beneficial for sleep disturbances related to anxiety or depression.

The best time to harvest St. John's Wort is when the flowers are in full bloom, typically in mid-summer, when the plant's active compounds are most concentrated. Use clean, sharp scissors or pruning shears to cut the flowering tops, and aim to harvest in the morning after the dew has dried for optimal quality. To avoid overharvesting, take only a portion from each plant to allow for continued growth and maintain the plant's health.

After harvesting, spread the flowers and leaves in a single layer on a clean, dry surface away from direct sunlight. Allow them to dry completely, which may take several days to a week. Once dried, store the herbs in an airtight container in a cool, dark place to preserve their potency.

Always consult with a healthcare professional before using any herbs for medicinal purposes, especially when taking other medications, as they can interact with various pharmaceuticals.

Ashwagandha is a potent perennial herb used for thousands of years to treat various conditions, including anxiety, male infertility, inflammation, minor aches and pains, stress, depression, and insomnia. Numerous studies have shown positive effects on athletic performance, vitality, and strength. Additionally, ashwagandha helps regulate blood sugar levels and acts as an adaptogen, aiding the body in managing stress and restoring balance.

This herb grows in warm, dry, sunny climates with well-draining soil and a pH between 7.5 and 8. As a nightshade, it can be grown from seed and propagated by taking root cuttings from established plants. The plants are ready for harvest after at least six months of growth.

Dandelion is a hardy perennial herb that often grows effortlessly, commonly appearing as a weed in many landscapes. It offers numerous health benefits, including supporting liver health, aiding detoxification, and improving digestion. You can harvest and eat dandelions, but avoid collecting them from public lands due to potential exposure to chemical sprays and animal waste.

Dandelion is known for its astringent and bitter taste, particularly in older leaves. However, young, tender leaves are more palatable and can be washed and added to salads. The leaves can be steamed for a cooked dish or dried in teas and tinctures. Additionally, dandelion flowers are edible and can be incorporated into cooking and baking recipes. Be sure to clean the flowers thoroughly, as insects may be present in the petals.

Gardening adds years to your life and life to your years.

~Anonymous

Nurtured by Nature

The initial costs of building a garden are modest compared to the long-term returns on investment. The benefits and rewards of having a functioning garden are extensive and diverse. In addition to the tangible rewards of harvesting fruits, vegetables, and herbs, gardening offers numerous intangible advantages. It provides significant therapeutic benefits, supporting healing and holistic wellness and increasing physical health and longevity. Gardening also improves local ecology and strengthens meaningful connections to nature. Successfully cultivating plants from seeds or cuttings to maturity brings a deep sense of accomplishment and joy. Gardening is not just a hobby but a way of life, offering an ongoing journey of learning and skill-building and constantly expanding our knowledge and capabilities.

Garden life requires some toughness and grit to be successful, and that kind of perseverance is often hard-won. Losing crops before they mature is painful, but losing them after they've matured carries a deep sense of disappointment that is hard to shake. Yet, every gardener experiences setbacks and will taste the bitter to relish the sweet. When distractions in modern life divert our focus from our goals, we risk missing out on opportunities we've worked hard to cultivate. Life may bring uncertainties that require adaptation; however, self-sabotage, such as becoming careless or neglecting the fruits of our labor, leads to waste and often regret.

Embracing setbacks with accountability transforms them into lessons rather than failures, promoting a mindset focused on growth and learning. However, stubbornness and blind spots in our behavior can lead us to repeat mistakes and hinder progress. We must self-reflect and adjust our approach based on our learning to move forward. Understanding our missteps is necessary for integrating those lessons and avoiding repetition. By doing so, we can make more thoughtful decisions and create a path toward meaningful progress. Consistently practicing appreciation, observation, meditation, cultivation, and active participation aligns us with greater abundance. Inconsistency kills.

Blind Spots

Personal "blind spots" refer to areas where we lack self-awareness or insight, making it difficult to recognize certain truths about ourselves or our behaviors. For example, if you see yourself as honest but frequently attract deceitful individuals, you might wonder why this pattern keeps occurring. This is a cue to engage in self-reflection and explore your blind spots. In this case, one blind spot could be not setting clear boundaries, which makes you vulnerable to those who exploit your openness. You might also ignore your intuition and go along with others, even when you know it's not right for you.

Additionally, you might trust others too easily or overlook warning signs, which can stem from a tendency to assume that everyone shares your morals and values. This positive projection can cloud your judgment. Your self-perception may also be influenced by seeking validation from external sources, causing you to overlook dishonesty in favor of emotional fulfillment, ultimately leading to unhealthy relationships. You might find yourself unconsciously drawn to people who reflect unresolved issues from your past, such as a desire to "fix" someone or recreate familiar dynamics from earlier relationships.

Identifying these blind spots requires self-reflection, seeking feedback from trusted friends, mentors, or a therapist, and being open to exploring why certain patterns keep recurring in your relationships. Examine and challenge your assumptions about trust and honesty to become more discerning in your interactions. This awareness will empower you to make more intentional choices moving forward.

Practice compassion by being gentle with yourself throughout this process. Recognizing blind spots can be uncomfortable, so it's important to acknowledge your efforts toward growth and change. With increased awareness, you can act intentionally and make conscious choices in your relationships. This might involve being more selective about who you allow into your life or pausing to assess your feelings and instincts before committing to a new relationship. Give yourself permission to reject anything or anyone that doesn't align with your values. This is essentially how you cultivate self-realization and embody radical self-love.

Doubt and hesitation can also act as blind spots because they often cloud our judgment and prevent us from taking action or making decisions that align with our true desires. Our actions today shape our future, and by cultivating harmony, we project positivity toward future developments. Building self-confidence, trusting our instincts, and adopting a more positive mindset can help us overcome these barriers and make choices that reflect our true selves. Letting go of doubt while embracing trust and faith in life's purpose while co-creating our desires with universal forces nurtures a genuine sense of wholeness within.

Self-sabotage is a blind spot because it often operates unconsciously, making it difficult to recognize the behaviors or patterns that undermine our goals and well-being. People may engage in self-sabotaging actions, such as procrastination, negative self-talk, or setting unrealistic expectations without realizing it. A scarcity mindset—thinking "I don't have what it takes" or "I'm not enough" —keeps us stuck in a self-sabotaging loop of misalignment. Interrupt this scarcity thinking by cultivating an abundant mindset. Shift your internal dialogue to affirmations like "I can" and "I am."

Self-sabotage can also undermine relationships. For example, if you borrow money from others without the intention of repaying it, you erode trust and respect in those connections. This can result in isolation and strained relationships, ultimately affecting your support system. Ignoring the responsibility to repay borrowed money reflects a tendency to avoid accountability. This avoidance can hinder personal growth and prevent developing important life skills, such as financial management and building meaningful relationships. Hoping others will forget about the debt indicates a fear of confrontation. This pattern of avoidance can extend to other areas of your life, limiting your ability to address issues directly and leading to further self-sabotaging behaviors. Additionally, this behavior can create feelings of guilt and anxiety, which may manifest as stress or shame.

Overall, this pattern undermines your goals for financial stability and healthy relationships, illustrating how self-sabotage can have broader implications for your life. Engaging in self-sabotaging behaviors can reinforce negative beliefs about yourself, creating a cycle that is difficult to break.

Our life's garden is constantly evolving through cycles of life and death. The journey of deep healing often begins with radical change, introspection, self-care, and recognizing the need for external support. This acknowledgment is an important step that opens the door to seeking assistance in cultivating wholeness. Acceptance is part of this process; by embracing our need for help, we allow ourselves to receive the support and guidance necessary for our healing journey.

Just as a garden requires time and active maintenance, personal growth also needs patience and nurturing. It's important to extend grace to ourselves and others, allowing growth to occur at its own pace. By cultivating an honest relationship with ourselves and adopting a mindset of trust, faith, acceptance, and grace, we create a supportive environment for healing and transformation. This journey of self-discovery leads to greater fulfillment, wholeness, and alignment with our true selves.

Create Sacred Space

In contemporary society, there's often a disconnect from the ancient reverence for the land and nature as sacred entities. Ancient traditions, especially among Indigenous peoples, emphasize a profound respect for natural resources and advocate for mindful, sustainable practices. They understand the delicate balance between human needs and environmental preservation, respectfully taking only what is necessary and ensuring reciprocity by giving back to the Earth in various ways.

Central to these traditions are ceremonies and healing practices that honor the interconnectedness of all living beings with the environment. Indigenous peoples carefully harvest specific herbs, flowers, and vines and use them in sacred healing rituals, acknowledging their spiritual and medicinal significance. These practices support and nurture physical and spiritual landscapes, creating a harmonious relationship between people and the natural world.

However, modern society often overlooks or disregards these principles. Rapid industrialization and urbanization have led to widespread exploitation of natural resources, often without regard for sustainability or conservation. This exploitation disrupts ecosystems and erodes the cultural and spiritual connections that once guided a harmonious coexistence with nature.

Misusing or overusing natural substances, whether recreational or medicinal, weakens the sacred connection between humans, nature, and the self. What starts as a potential path for healing and spiritual growth can turn into a harmful habit, distancing individuals from their true selves and diminishing their respect for the natural world. Indigenous traditions exemplify the balance, reverence, and intentionality required to sustain a deep and harmonious relationship with nature.

Reconnecting with these ancient principles means rekindling a sense of reverence and responsibility toward the Earth. It requires adopting practices that emphasize sustainability, respect for biodiversity, and mindful consumption of natural resources. By embracing these values, we honor the wisdom of our ancestors and pave the way for a more balanced and sustainable future where humans and nature coexist harmoniously. The well-being of future generations depends on the changes and practices we implement today.

The shift toward revering nature as sacred may seem daunting on a global scale, yet individuals have the power to nurture this mindset in their everyday lives. Creating sacred spaces like gardens and integrating small yet intentional mindfulness and gratitude practices can strengthen our connection with the natural world and align us with its rhythms and gifts.

Creating personal space is a way of honoring oneself. Decluttering and removing unnecessary items that no longer serve a purpose or hold sentimental value reflects personal growth and clears a path for new possibilities. Detoxifying physically, mentally, and digitally creates distance from thoughts, emotional issues, and mental projections, allowing these feelings to exist independently. Shifting perspective, practicing breathing exercises, and using grounding techniques help create space between thoughts. Emotions can be felt and processed without judgment, and negative or fearful thoughts can be replaced with positive ones.

Conscious awareness in our daily activities can take many forms. It might involve taking a moment to appreciate the beauty of a sunrise or sunset, acknowledging the nourishment provided by a meal made from locally grown produce, or simply pausing to breathe in the fresh air during a nature walk. These moments of awareness help us recognize the interconnectedness between ourselves and the earth, nurturing a more profound sense of reverence.

Expressing gratitude for the harvests we receive—whether from our gardens, local farmers, or the natural environment—creates an energetic exchange of appreciation and reciprocity with the land. This practice acknowledges the Earth's abundance and instills a responsibility to care for and protect it. When we act locally, we generate energy that is perpetuated throughout society globally. This is why healing ourselves is so vital to healing the world. It all starts with the care we provide in our immediate environment. If, ideally, everyone contributed to their local communities, the global community could heal and repair rapidly.

Conscious efforts to honor nature as sacred contribute to a collective movement toward environmental stewardship and sustainability. By integrating these practices into our daily lives, we recognize the Earth as a precious gift that sustains all life, motivating us to align with its natural rhythms. In doing so, peace is found in the garden of life.

> I've always felt that having a garden is like having a good and loyal friend.
>
> ~C Z Guest

Let Nature Be Your Guide

A garden thrives on relationships—a continuous dance among various insects, critters, and elemental forces. As stewards and nurturers, we collaborate to support life, yielding a harvest of wonder, joy, beauty, freedom, and creative expression. Similarly, our relationships flourish through mutual understanding, care, and attention. An aligned gardener recognizes the importance of cultivating the art of surrender, allowance, reciprocity, and support. It's an art because these skills require daily practice and focus. Maintaining healthy and vibrant relationships, including the one with ourselves, involves investing time, energy, and care to create safe spaces where love, empathy, and kindness can develop.

Growing a garden, like building a life, is a privilege that offers countless opportunities for discernment and choice. Each decision—whether selecting plant varieties or choosing beneficial companions—empowers us to create spaces that reflect our preferences, values, and aspirations. Opting for organic foods and flowers establishes a healthier environment and prioritizes the well-being of our soil, plants, and, ultimately, ourselves.

Inviting favorable companions, such as pollinators, beneficial insects, and companion plants, further enriches the garden's ecosystem and contributes to its vitality and resilience. By promoting symbiotic relationships and creating habitats for these allies, we cultivate a harmonious and balanced environment where all living beings can proliferate.

Similar to any relationship, certain factors contribute to growth and sustainability. The most important part of caring for a garden is daily maintenance. Surprisingly, it doesn't demand much once established, but consistency is key. Once you've laid the groundwork and set up a healthy foundation for your garden, you can step back and let nature take its course. Often, less interference is better, as nature doesn't need to be micromanaged. Gardeners excel at supporting life rather than controlling it. Even a small amount of daily attention can greatly affect plant health and growth.

Gardening involves more than just growing plants. It's about co-creating successful relationships in spaces that resonate with our values, support our well-being, and honor the beauty and abundance of nature. It's important to remember that gardening is a journey, not a destination. Growth cannot be rushed. Embrace the ever-evolving process, and find joy in every stage of development and transformation. Each day presents an opportunity to learn, experiment, and connect with nature, enriching our lives in ways that extend far beyond the garden itself. Cultivating relationships is a central part of the process.

No matter how far we stray from living in a space of love, it remains a constant within our soul. We can always return to love. Once we shift from a mindset of needing love to that of being love, the entire trajectory of growth transforms. This is especially true within our relationships with ourselves and others. Becoming love is the path to authenticity and nurtures the seeds of effortless awareness.

The true essence of a gardener lies in the journey of becoming our natural selves. Gardening uniquely transforms us from the inside out. It helps us connect with the rhythms of nature, encouraging mindfulness and presence while deepening our appreciation for the beauty around us and within us. Embrace the journey, enjoy the process, and celebrate the endless possibilities that gardening offers.

> **Gardening is full of mistakes; almost all are pleasant, and some are instructive.**
>
> ~Henry Mitchell

Work, Rest, Repeat

Engaging in seasonal and daily tasks is part of maintaining a healthy and abundant garden. These tasks include seed sowing, propagating, planting, watering, weeding, fertilizing, pest control, harvesting, saving seeds, preserving, pruning, composting, mulching, and cleaning bedding areas. While there is always something to be done in the garden, it's equally important to recognize the need for rest. However, finding moments of relaxation amidst the fruits of our labor can provide a deep sense of satisfaction and rejuvenation. These moments fuel us to continue our tasks with renewed energy and enthusiasm.

In both the garden and life, we inevitably make mistakes. These blunders are a natural part of the learning process, and we must allow ourselves the space to make them. However, our growth depends on how we respond to these errors. Fatigue often leads to mistakes, as tiredness clouds judgment and reduces focus. Although we can create magnificent works, we also hold the potential to destroy them. As the saying goes, if we fail to learn from our mistakes, we will repeat them. By equipping ourselves with knowledge and resources, we can avoid unnecessary anguish and invest time in thorough research, which paves the path to success.

Shape Up

Life provides many opportunities to prune and correct misguided thoughts and behaviors. However, people often live habitually rather than consciously due to their stubborn nature. Numerous examples demonstrate how to improve mental, physical, or spiritual well-being. Athletes focus on strength and performance, adjusting their diets and exercise routines as needed to improve. In the same way, we must consciously train specific aspects of ourselves to achieve our desired results and reach new levels.

Training the mind is fundamental to developing the discipline needed for progress. Redirecting thoughts is a key practice that strengthens awareness and supports personal growth. Mindfulness—staying present and aware of thoughts without judgment—effectively stabilizes the mind. Reframing negative thoughts into positive ones challenges and changes unproductive thinking patterns and facilitates solution-focused thinking. Additionally, using positive affirmations rewires the brain, reinforcing a more positive and resilient outlook.

As discussed, meditation, journaling, breathwork, visualization, and practicing gratitude effectively strengthen, rewire, and train the mind. These practices cultivate clarity and optimism. Setting clear intentions sharpens focus and reduces distractions. Training the mind and maintaining peace requires time and consistent effort. Over time, these practices significantly improve mental well-being, emotional control, and personal satisfaction.

Effective Pruning

Understanding pruning principles—its methods, purposes, and timing—is critical for avoiding unnecessary plant fatalities. Pruning goes beyond cutting branches; it involves strategically boosting plant vigor, controlling growth, and encouraging flowering and fruiting. We can make informed decisions that save time and resources with proper knowledge.

Numerous available resources delve into various pruning techniques tailored to different plant species. It is highly advisable to consult multiple sources and acquire comprehensive knowledge beforehand. This approach allows gardeners to grasp the nuances of each plant's response to pruning tools and timing, ensuring that the process is carried out effectively and safely.

Even though some plants are resilient enough to recover from inexperienced pruning, each variety reacts differently. Correct information allows gardeners to make informed decisions, leading to healthier plants and more successful gardens.

Pruning is a nuanced skill that demands years of practice, patience, and knowledge, yet even seasoned practitioners may make mistakes. Often, gardeners and arborists approach pruning intending to exert control over plants. However, it's important to understand that nature lives without human intervention, and attempts to regulate it can yield varied results. While specific pruning methods can improve plant health and longevity, others may precipitate rapid decline or even plant death. Acknowledging and honoring this delicate balance is necessary for maintaining a harmonious relationship between human interaction and nature's innate resilience.

Expert professional pruners are a rare breed, capable of seeing and listening attentively to the needs of plants and allowing the plant itself to become their teacher. Regrettably, many individuals tend to chop and hack away at plants in pursuit of a desired size, often without fully grasping the potentially detrimental consequences. Improper pruning can exacerbate minor issues, turning them into significant problems. Albeit judicious pruning is usually necessary for practical reasons and compliance with homeowner association rules, nature possesses its own language that humans seldom hear or acknowledge. As gardeners, we aim to encourage the success of both new and established plantings.

Each plant necessitates a tailored approach to pruning. Conducting prior research into the requirements of each variety is advisable before engaging in any cutting. Disregarding specific pruning protocols may lead to unnecessary waste and expenses. Certain shrubs and trees provide habitats for endangered wildlife, and the overdevelopment of land threatens their survival by removing these critical habitats. A prime example is the importance of dead palm tree fronds. If left undisturbed, these hanging fronds act as nesting havens for Great Horned Owls, birds of prey, bats, lizards, squirrels, and other wildlife. Leaving dead fronds unpruned is critical to the survival of many threatened species.

When done correctly, pruning provides more than just size management. It promotes healthy growth and stimulates flower and fruit production. Some pruning techniques encourage growth and fruiting, while others may limit development. Understanding these nuances for specific varieties is critical to the plant's health. This understanding is particularly vital when pruning fruit trees, as improper cuts can lead to many problems in the future.

Proper pruning practices help to improve air circulation and control the spread of disease. Thinning out and removing dead, damaged, or infected parts, always with appropriate, sterile tools, creates better sunlight penetration and reduces the risk of blights and other fungal diseases. Maintaining the desired shape and structure of ornamental plants and topiaries contributes to their artistic aesthetic and enhances their overall appearance.

Pruning Techniques

Proper branch cutting with hand pruners ensures the cutting blade is positioned above the branch, cutting ¼" above the bud and sloping away from it. This technique prevents sap from suffocating the bud. A general rule for seasonal pruning is to cut no more than one-third of the plant's size.

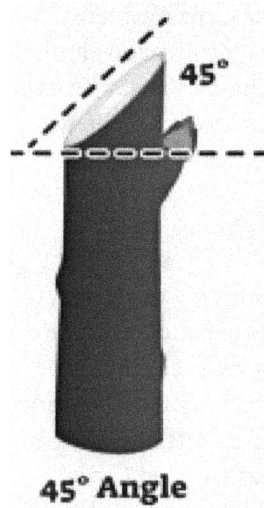

45° Angle

For larger branches requiring a handsaw, follow the three-step cut method:

1. Make an undercut one-third of the way through the branch's diameter to prevent the bark from tearing.
2. Make a top cut to remove the limb.
3. Finish by removing the stub with a perpendicular cut above the limb collar.

(Source: West Virginia Extension Services, "Facts about Pruning," April 2019, p. 5.)

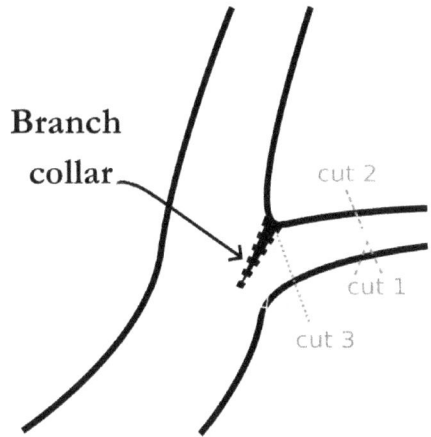

Deadheading or pinching involves removing spent flower heads, which can stimulate further flowering. Pinching is also utilized to encourage lateral branching by removing the tips of new shoots. This action prompts the plant to send two new lateral stems, increasing foliage and flower production. Basil is a prime example of a plant that benefits from pinching.

Thinning or removal cuts involve removing entire branches at their point of origin, typically at the trunk or base. These selective cuts help improve airflow, increase light penetration, and open the canopy. During this process, no more than one-third of the plant's total size must be removed. However, certain perennials, like delphiniums and daisies, tend to produce a second bloom if cut back after the first bloom fades.

Heading or topping involves removing the young tips and shoots of trees or shrubs to stimulate more branching growth. It's important to note that heading cuts should not be made on wood older than one year. Additionally, topping older trees is not recommended, as it can compromise their structural integrity, expose bare wood to disease insect infestations, and eventually kill them.

Shearing is a method used to quickly reduce the size of a plant to achieve a desired shape. When shearing, it's crucial to cut the sides at a slight angle so that the base is slightly wider than the top, like a bell shape. This helps avoid common pruning errors like the lollipop or lion's tail look.

Training plants to grow for a particular aesthetic or function involves numerous methods. Gardeners often prune, stake, trellis, cage, espalier, bend, graft, pin, pinch, and remove buds to effectively grow plants in limited spaces. Proper training encourages greater yields and healthier plants. It supports plants structurally and reduces the risk of disease by keeping them lifted from the ground and improving airflow.

Timing Is Everything

Consideration of timing is important before engaging in pruning activities, as it can significantly impact the health of plants and the quality of the blossoms or fruit they yield. For summer and fall flowering shrubs, it's best to prune them after bloom or before the next season's vegetation begins to grow. Fall can be a good time for pruning many deciduous trees and shrubs. For instance, pruning trees like oak, maple, and birch in late fall, after they've dropped their leaves, can help them recover more quickly in spring. However, heavy tree pruning should be avoided in late summer or early autumn in regions with severe winters. Broadleaf evergreens like Magnolias, Madrones, and Oaks should never be pruned if the wood is frozen; spring is the best time for heavy pruning. While pruning during late winter dormancy or early spring is most common, summer pruning is undertaken to reduce shading and growth reduction.

Achieving a balance in pruning is key to maintaining raspberry, blackberry, and blueberry shrubs. This balance is necessary due to their different growth patterns. Consult multiple credible resources before determining the best approach to pruning. Understanding the growth habits of different berries is a must, as some plants flower and fruit on new wood while others on old wood.

Raspberries come in two growth patterns: Everbearing (Fall-bearing) and Summer-bearing raspberries. Everbearing produces fruit on new canes (primocanes) in late summer or fall. They typically yield a crop in their first year. After harvest, cut back the entire plant to ground level. This encourages new canes to grow and produce fruit the following year. Pruning in late fall or early winter is usually fine in colder climates, but avoid it during freezing weather.

Summer-bearing varieties produce fruit on canes that grew the previous year (floricanes). They yield fruit in mid-summer. These raspberry canes can be cut back to ground level after being fruited. This helps to improve airflow and reduce disease. Leave the new canes that will produce fruit the following summer. Thin out weak or crowded canes to about 4-6 per foot of row for better fruit quality and air circulation.

Blackberries have two growth patterns: trailing and erect. Trailing plants usually need support for their long, arching canes, and they produce fruit on second-year canes. After the harvest, cut back the spent canes to ground level. This helps manage the plant's size and encourages vigorous growth in the new canes. New canes should be tied to a support system and spaced out to ensure good airflow and light penetration.

Erect blackberry varieties have a more upright growth habit and don't need support. They can be either summer-bearing or everbearing. Like trailing varieties, remove old fruiting canes to ground level after harvest. For those with a more upright habit, cut back any weak or excessive canes to maintain plant health and productivity. Thin the canes to ensure proper spacing and to improve fruit quality. Avoid over-pruning by removing too many canes with both varieties, as this can reduce yield.

Blueberries have specific growth habits; pruning is necessary to maintain plant health and optimize fruit production. Four main types of blueberry bushes exist: highland, half-high, lowbush, and rabbiteye. The common highland varieties can grow 4-6 feet tall and are grown in many regions. Half-high blueberries are a 2'-4' hybrid of highbush and lowbush varieties, preferring colder climates. Lowbush varieties stay much smaller, typically grown in colder climates and often found in wild settings. Rabbiteye blueberries are larger and more tolerant of heat and drought environments.

Blueberries produce fruit on wood that is at least one year old, so proper pruning maintains a balance between old and new wood. Prune during late winter or early spring before new growth begins. For blueberries in colder regions, pruning should be done after the coldest part of winter but before buds begin to swell. Thinning increases fruit size and quality by reducing overcrowding and allowing more light and air to reach the plant's interior. Thin out weak or overcrowded canes, maintaining a well-spaced structure with 6-8 main canes. Remove any small or spindly shoots.

Dead, diseased, and overcrowded canes should be removed during dormancy to encourage healthy growth and fruit production. Also, remove any branches that cross each other or grow inward. Maintain an open center to allow sunlight to reach all plant parts and facilitate harvesting. Trim back the top of the plant and any overly tall or leggy branches to maintain a manageable size and shape. Promote vigorous new growth and balance old and new wood for consistent fruit production. Remove older, less productive branches (usually more than 4-5 years old) to make way for younger, more productive canes. Aim to balance old and new wood; ideally, the plant should have a mix of 1-, 2-, and 3-year-old canes.

Never shear blueberry shrubs, as their flowering and fruiting buds are located on the tips of the stem growth. Understanding the most effective practices to encourage optimal fruit production for fruiting varieties can make the difference between an abundant harvest and a failed crop.

Fruit tree pruning varies by type—deciduous trees (those that lose their leaves seasonally), stone fruits (such as cherries and peaches), and evergreens (including citrus, olive, and avocado). It's best to prune for optimal fruit production during the tree's dormant season, typically in late winter to early spring, before new growth begins. Timing is critical because fruit trees have specific dormancy and growth periods that align with their pruning needs. Pruning too late in the season can disrupt their growth cycle, significantly reducing their ability to produce fruit that year.

Fruit trees typically undergo a natural cycle, forming buds for the next season's fruit shortly after the current year's harvest or during late summer and early fall. If pruning occurs late in this cycle, there's a risk of removing these significant buds needed for the following year's fruit production. Pruning stimulates new growth. When done late in the season, this can divert the tree's energy from developing and maturing fruit buds. Instead, the tree may allocate resources towards producing new shoots, reducing the likelihood of a fruitful yield in the upcoming season.

Deciduous trees are best pruned in late winter or early spring, just before new growth begins. This helps avoid exposing new cuts to harsh winter conditions. Stone fruit trees are pruned in late summer after harvest to prevent the spreading of diseases. Remove some older branches to encourage new growth and fruiting. Evergreens should be pruned in late winter or early spring before new growth starts. Always cut out any dead, diseased, or damaged branches and remove branches that cross each other or grow inward. To stimulate new growth and fruiting, cut back the tips of branches to encourage lateral growth. Aim to maintain a balanced, open structure.

Boxwoods are versatile and can be shaped into formal or natural hedges. They are typically pruned with hand pruners for optimal results, but this may not always align with time or budget constraints. Many pruners resort to using power shears, which can be more cost-effective. However, it's important to note that this isn't always the best approach.

Fundamental knowledge lies in understanding what's best for the plant, especially regarding timing. Using power shears when temperatures are too cold can cause boxwoods to turn grey, while shearing during warmer months may result in burning and browning. Early summer maintenance pruning should be done with hand pruners to avoid browning. The optimal times to use power shears on boxwoods are typically early to mid-spring (April) and mid-autumn (October) in the Northern Hemisphere.

Boxwood requires formative maintenance and sometimes rejuvenation pruning. Formative pruning establishes the desired shape and size and begins when the shrubs are young. Trim back the tips of the branches to encourage dense, compact growth. Maintenance pruning keeps the shape and size of established boxwoods. Lightly shear the outer branches to keep the hedge or plant looking neat. Avoid cutting into old, bare wood, as boxwoods do not readily regrow from old wood. Rejuvenation pruning is a severe approach to revitalize older boxwoods that have become overgrown or misshapen. Reduce the size by cutting back up to one-third of the plant's height and width. This should be done in stages, over a few years if necessary, to avoid stressing the plant. Always cut to a point where there are healthy leaves or buds to encourage new growth.

Let It Be

Leaving certain plants to overwinter without pruning or deadheading can be beneficial. This practice allows plants to conserve energy and facilitates healthier growth in the spring. Additionally, they add visual interest to a dormant garden and provide food and shelter for wildlife, including beneficial insects and birds, contributing to the ecosystem's overall health.

Leaving plants in place helps stabilize soil and prevent erosion during winter storms or heavy rains, protecting the landscape. Allowing certain plants to go to seed can increase biodiversity in the garden, as self-seeding plants can spread and create a more varied ecosystem. By thoughtfully choosing which plants to leave overwinter, gardeners can support ecological balance and improve the overall health of their gardens.

Shrubs with features like berries, colorful stems, or interesting seed heads add winter interest, and pruning them prematurely can remove these valuable features. Some examples include ornamental grasses, red-twig dogwoods, and winterberry holly.

Garden Tools and Safety

Using garden tools safely helps prevent injury and ensures efficient work. Always inspect tools before use to ensure they are in good condition, with no loose parts or rust. Approach each plant with clean, disinfected tools, particularly when pruning different species. Without proper sanitation, pathogens like blight, fungus, or diseases can transfer from one plant to another, leading to contamination. After pruning each plant, clean the blades with a disinfectant such as ethanol, isopropyl alcohol, hydrogen peroxide, or a diluted bleach solution. This practice helps maintain plant health and prevents the spread of diseases.

Sharp tools are as necessary as clean ones. Incorporate sharpening stones into your toolkit and keep lubricants handy for moving parts and mechanisms. When pruning, choosing the right tool for the job is key. Anvil pruners cut through dead wood with precision and ease. Bypass pruners are ideal for live wood, as they make clean cuts that preserve the integrity of the remaining wood, unlike anvil pruners, which can crush or damage it. Choose the tool that matches the wood's diameter to achieve the best results.

Every task requires the right tool, and our effectiveness relies on having the appropriate equipment. It's not about having the fanciest or most expensive tools but choosing the ones best suited to the task. Experienced gardeners often use unconventional tools to get the job done. Whether it's a spoon or a shovel, the key is to select the most precise and functional tool for the job.

Personal safety in the garden is as important as using the right tools. Always wear Personal Protective Equipment (PPE) to prevent injuries and illnesses. Gloves protect hands from cuts, scrapes, and punctures caused by sharp tools and thorny plants. Wearing long sleeves, masks, and gloves when applying chemicals or fertilizers reduces the risk of harmful exposure. Sturdy shoes or boots protect feet and help prevent slipping. By prioritizing safety with the right protective gear, we can work in the garden confidently and reduce the risk of accidents.

Work Smarter, Not Harder

Doing hard work does not mean working hard. Hard work often implies long hours or physical exertion, but it doesn't always equate to achieving meaningful results. It's possible to work intensely and expend energy without being productive or effective. Hard work focuses on tasks that matter, applying deliberate effort to achieve goals. It involves strategy, managing time wisely, and working smart. True hard work centers on consistency, discipline, and emphasizing quality over quantity. In this sense, hard work is not about how hard or how long we work, but about the value and outcomes of our work.

Health is one of life's most valuable assets. When we're in good health, we can enjoy experiences beyond monetary wealth and fully engage in activities easily. To prevent strain and injury while gardening, consider using ergonomic tools. These tools are designed to reduce physical stress and make tasks easier. Positioning oneself comfortably in the workspace helps avoid overreaching and improves tasks more efficiently. Whenever possible, use the legs for lifting by squatting rather than bending. Be mindful of movements and approach tasks with care and ease.

Raised garden beds can also make gardening more accessible by reducing the need for bending. They can be built at a height that allows for comfortable work. Some raised beds even come with built-in benches, which help minimize stress on the knees and back while planting or weeding. Additionally, mobile or stationary gardening benches offer convenient alternatives for comfortable gardening.

Taking regular breaks can help prevent fatigue. Use these moments to stretch and move around to keep muscles flexible. Staying hydrated and stretching before and after gardening can also reduce muscle cramps and fatigue. Keep tools and equipment organized and ensure clear pathways to maintain a safe and efficient environment.

Before starting gardening, create a plan to manage time and workload effectively. If additional tasks arise, add them to the bottom of the list while sticking to the original plan. Working in sections ensures steady progress without feeling overwhelmed or overworked.

Life Tools

Each person holds a core responsibility for their own life, and numerous tools are available to support success. The primary duty lies with oneself. Regularly reflecting on thoughts and feelings helps identify when to focus on personal growth, enabling full engagement with each moment. The mind should not be a weapon against us; instead, it can be honed and sharpened into a powerful tool. By utilizing available resources, we refine mental clarity, much like a stone sharpens a blade. Without these tools, we risk becoming dull and ineffective. Daily practice maintains mental sharpness, helping us reduce distractions that hinder productivity and engagement.

Simple tools like quiet reflection, journaling, and breathwork prove effective when practiced consistently. Meditation balances well-being, while exercise and dancing ground and connect us to our bodies. Proper nutrition supports physical and mental health, and engaging in music—whether singing or playing an instrument—unleashes creativity. Just as learning a foreign language builds connections, mastering another language, including music, builds confidence and self-expression.

Many healing practitioners teach, use, and share tools that help reconnect us to source energy. Tune in to messages and practices that resonate. Apply shared wisdom to nurture personal growth and healing. Share experiences openly when the time and space are right. Growth, learning, and healing unfold together in life's garden.

Our effectiveness depends on our chosen tools, so using them wisely and recognizing their value is important. Doing so allows us to improve our lives and share our strengths with others. Neglecting our well-being limits our ability to support others. When prioritizing health and happiness, we can contribute more effectively and enjoy life more fully. Tools hold value only when we use them; without action, their potential—and ours—remains untapped. Using these tools to their fullest shows respect for ourselves and nurtures our growth.

Pruning Relationships

Just as plants need selective pruning to grow well, we must evaluate and refine our social circles to support personal and emotional growth. Personal development and evolving relationships require intentional decisions about where we direct our energy. Recognizing when a relationship no longer serves our greater good and prioritizing our mental well-being are necessary steps. Letting go of connections that once held meaning but have become stagnant or harmful requires self-respect, courage, and introspection—and remains a natural part of our evolution.

Sometimes, we outgrow relationships—whether with childhood friends, former partners, colleagues, or even family members. Letting go of connections that have fulfilled their purpose is a natural part of tending to our life's garden. Relationships often exist for a reason, a season, or a lifetime, and understanding their temporary nature can help us navigate this process with grace. Finding the inner strength to release connections that no longer bring positivity allows us to cultivate a healthier, more fulfilling life. By honoring past lessons and experiences without judgment, we open ourselves to the present and create space for new, meaningful relationships to bloom.

Radical changes are sometimes necessary to start fresh—both in the garden of our lives and our physical gardens. Well-being and progress should guide these transformations. When a plant has suffered significant neglect or damage, regenerative pruning may be the best solution, involving a severe cutback, sometimes to ground level. While many established roots are strong enough to support new growth, not all plants can survive such drastic measures. Similarly, radical change may benefit our personal lives, but not everyone can navigate it without support. In such situations, seeking professional help is wise. Starting over demands grit, determination, and an unwavering belief in oneself.

As part of our maintenance routine, it's helpful to prune away influences, opinions, and thoughts from others that may cloud our judgment. Cultivating the ability to think and speak independently is vital for building individuality and self-empowerment. Although our environment will always impact us, learning to respond thoughtfully to external opinions can significantly influence our growth. Integrating practices of self-reflection, observation, and the stillness of meditation into our daily lives can substantially aid in this discernment process. Pruning relationships and influences create space for new connections that better align with our current values, goals, and aspirations. This natural process of personal growth leads to deeper fulfillment on our life journey.

> Everything that slows us down, forces patience, and sets us back into the slow circles of nature is a help. Gardening is an instrument of grace.
>
> ~May Sarton

<u>Integrity Matters</u>

Beauty often emerges as a feeling that authentically shines when rooted in sincerity and integrity. Gardens can become healing spaces and sanctuaries where grace and peace nurture the body, mind, and spirit. This experience goes beyond simple desires and aesthetics, providing deep, multifaceted nourishment. Recovery and renewal are important aspects of the beauty that unfolds through the grace found within these spaces. The garden is a reflective space, helping us recognize what needs adjustment, pruning, or removal. It provides a place where we can contemplate life's journey, learn from experiences, and envision future paths. This transformative journey requires a sincere and mindful approach, inviting us to be present in each moment and embrace our essence rather than simply focusing on actions.

Nurturing personal integrity is fundamental on our ascending path of self-development. Maintaining a healthy sense of self and integrity is a valuable asset to our character, serving as a meaningful gift to the world. Self-awareness involves upholding this integrity in our daily choices and actions. Without it, we risk becoming like a tree yielding only unripe or spoiled fruit, spreading discord within the mind and body and unsettling the spirit.

A tree with sturdy branches weathers storms and remains firmly rooted; in the same way, personal integrity helps us navigate unexpected challenges with resilience and grace. Maintaining integrity requires careful self-awareness and commitment to resist the weeds of deceit or dishonesty. Every choice we make is like planting a seed, contributing to the cultivation of a strong character. This growth, in turn, offers the world the fruits of sincerity, trustworthiness, and a peaceful, liberated spirit.

Building character with integrity is an internal process that establishes the groundwork for personal success. Each misalignment between our choices and values can create vulnerabilities in our overall well-being and growth. The encouraging part of this journey is that we can address these vulnerabilities once we recognize them. Living with integrity means understanding the impact of our actions on others, making choices that align with our values, and contributing positively to the broader community.

Trusting our choices encourages significant growth spurts. The hope for humanity to cultivate a more just and verdant world begins with each individual. However, some may resist embracing integrity because it challenges their self-awareness, a facet they may be reluctant to explore. Achieving profound personal change demands honesty, determination, accountability, and discipline to uphold personal honor and truth.

Life presents significant opportunities as gates in a garden. Opening these gates requires courage; beyond them lie new adventures and growth. Each day offers a fresh chance to sow and cultivate seeds of tomorrow's aspirations. We receive seeds of inspiration from many sources—messages, thoughts, dreams, and ideas. While we may overlook some, we gather others and store them for future planting. Some we integrate into our lives immediately. Trusting our intuition, instincts, and impulses sets us in motion, fostering the potential for abundant growth.

The ability to receive more than expected is rooted in the trust we build within ourselves. By tending to the garden of our lives with mindfulness and openness, we increase the potential for unexpected rewards. This process mirrors the relationship between a dedicated gardener and a thriving garden: thoughtful care and investment lead to a vibrant, fruitful life.

Our garden aims to nurture what we wish to grow—dreams, goals, or personal development. We have the potential to realize our fullest selves, but this often requires focused attention and additional resources. Growth may involve seeking knowledge and guidance from those with experience. Fellow gardeners can offer valuable insights that enrich our lives in ways we might not have recognized ourselves. By sharing our abundance, we benefit ourselves and support and inspire others to prosper.

Life's garden path is often challenging, particularly when facing difficult circumstances. Yet, remarkable transformations occur when people unite with compassion and steadfast integrity. This collective power demonstrates that even the most demanding situations can lead to positive, profound change when efforts are rooted in empathy and honesty.

> I am your moon and your moonlight, too. I am your flower garden and your water, too. I have come all this way, eager for you. Without shoes or shawl, I want you to laugh, kill all your worries, love you, and nourish you.
>
> ~ Rumi

Planting By The Moon

Sunlight isn't the only celestial body that contributes to a bountiful harvest; the moon also plays an important role in crop germination and root development. Aligning gardening activities with the phases of the moon is an ancient practice. There are 13 lunar months in a year, each starting with a new moon and ending with a full moon. Many cultures have traditionally named these months based on natural events or seasonal changes. Some people adopt the 13-moon cycle system to emphasize natural rhythms and holistic living.

A helpful guideline for planting during specific moon phases is to focus on crops that grow above ground—such as leafy greens, brassicas, corn, tomatoes, melons, and zucchini—during the waxing moon. This is especially effective when the moon's illumination increases during the 1st and 2nd quarters. Annuals are also ideal for planting at this time. Harvesting and storing crops is generally most effective just before the full moon in the second quarter when the crops reach their peak ripeness.

The first quarter moon is an excellent time to plant crops with seeds outside their fruit, such as corn and strawberries. It is also a favorable period for planting leeks, asparagus, celery, broccoli, gourds, squash, and leafy greens. Grains and cereals grow well during this phase, too. Cucumbers can be successfully planted during the waxing moon's first or second quarter. The moon's gravitational pull influences water, and as explained in The Farmer's Almanac, "during the new and full moon phases, seeds are believed to absorb the most water due to heightened tides" (*Why Do We Garden By the Moon?* by Jaime McLeod, December 19, 2023).

During the 3rd and 4th quarters of the moon, when the illumination is awakening. By facing the darkness within us with courage and compassion, we can emerge stronger, wiser, and more resilient.

We cannot rush or force the emergence or development of our becoming; it requires temperance and compassion. Much like a seed slowly unfurling its tender shoots and leaves toward the light, we gradually unfold into new levels of awareness, understanding, and self-realization. With patience, care, and trust, we journey through the soul's darkness, emerging gracefully into the light of our true nature.

Diversity creates harmony, and harmony creates beauty, balance, bounty, and peace in nature and society, in agriculture and culture, in science, and politics.

~Vandana Shiva

Masculine And Feminine

In astrology, each zodiac sign and classic element embodies masculine or feminine qualities. Masculine energy is associated with traits such as action, logic, and strength, while feminine energy is characterized by intuition, nurturing, and creativity. Signs aligned with the air and fire elements typically exhibit masculine traits, known for their dynamism and assertiveness. Conversely, earth and water elements are linked with feminine qualities, symbolizing receptivity and emotional depth. This perspective encourages us to embrace all facets of ourselves, understanding that true wholeness arises from integrating and balancing these diverse qualities. The ethereal spirit, however, transcends gender, as it is all-encompassing, whole, and complete.

The personification of Earth and Nature as the divine feminine, often revered as 'Mother,' holds profound significance in many cultures and spiritual traditions. Just as a mammalian mother nourishes her young with breast milk, the Earth has consistently sustained life by providing abundant nourishment throughout history. This nurturing role is intricately connected to its relationship with celestial bodies, particularly the Sun and Moon.

In many spiritual and cultural traditions, the Sun is often associated with masculine energy, while the Moon is linked to feminine energy. The sun is a symbol of strength, vitality, and action. It represents qualities such as power, clarity, and assertiveness. The Sun is personified in various mythologies as a god or hero who brings light and warmth. The Moon is a feminine energy associated with intuition, emotion, and nurturance. It represents cycles, reflection, and the subconscious. Many cultures personify the Moon as a goddess, emphasizing its connection to the rhythms of nature and feminine wisdom.

The Earth is often seen as a representation of the divine feminine, embodying fertility, nourishment, and life-sustaining qualities. It serves as both a mother figure and a metaphorical womb, providing the nurturing environment from which life arises. Rain, a vital natural element, nurtures seeds until the right conditions for germination are met. The sun's warmth and light support photosynthesis and encourage plant development, while soil and water nourish and anchor the roots. Wind promotes upward growth and branching, while strong roots provide stability during turbulent weather. Water sustains cells during extreme heat. Each element of nature interacts with the others, balancing to maintain harmony, each playing an equally vital role in sustaining life.

Many spiritual traditions encourage aligning with nature's rhythms and the universe's cycles to nourish the spirit and strengthen the connection to the divine feminine. Practices like meditative mindfulness help individuals attune to the natural world and harness the nurturing energy of the universal mother. By engaging in these practices, we draw from the Earth's wisdom, deepen our understanding of our interconnectedness with all living beings and the cosmos, and honor the sacredness of the Earth. This alignment cultivates respect and reverence for the natural world and our place within it.

The cyclical nature of the feminine emphasizes the importance of rhythm, renewal, and interconnectedness in both personal and ecological systems. This cyclical approach facilitates a holistic understanding of life, emphasizing the value of rest and regeneration alongside action and productivity. The female biological cycle exemplifies this concept, with the menstrual cycle reflecting renewal, growth, and transformation phases, much like the moon's cycles. Women's life stages—the maiden, mother, and crone—represent a journey of cyclical growth, nurturing, and wisdom. Each stage carries its unique significance and contributes to the broader cycle of life.

The masculine represents the strength found in nature, such as sturdy mountains, strong trees, and mighty rivers. This strength provides a sense of stability and endurance. The divine masculine embodies the protective forces in nature, safeguarding ecosystems and ensuring balance within them. It is associated with the active forces in nature, driving growth and development. This includes processes like pollination, seed dispersal, and the nurturing actions of animals. The masculine also defines boundaries, as seen in natural phenomena like mountain ranges or riverbanks delineating spaces.

Mother Nature operates in cycles, much like a garden. Feminine energies are fluid, round, and cyclical, while masculine energies are rigid, structured, and linear. These qualities are reflected in human consciousness as well. By embracing the fluidity of the feminine and the stability of the masculine, we create an environment where both nature and ourselves can grow. This balance enables us to navigate life's complexities, cultivating a holistic approach to well-being and nurturing our connections to the world around us.

Humans embody masculine and feminine qualities that contribute to our wholeness as individuals. Our life's task is to maintain a dynamic balance between these aspects. Just as an excess of any single element can harm organisms in a garden, an imbalance between feminine and masculine energies can disrupt the natural flow of life, hindering personal and collective development. Healing is the union of the feminine and masculine within each individual and, ultimately, within the collective—guiding intuition and emotion with purpose, clarity, and self-respect.

When masculine energy becomes dominant, it can manifest as aggression, rigidity, or an overemphasis on structure and control. Conversely, an overabundance of feminine energy can lead to passivity, indecision, or excessive emotional sensitivity, potentially making it harder to take decisive action. Therefore, cultivating awareness of these qualities and integrating them within ourselves is necessary for achieving greater harmony, balance, and fulfillment. By honoring both energies, we can create greater equanimity and enriching experiences, allowing for growth and connection in all areas of our lives.

In all its forms, pollution disrupts the sacred balance necessary for life to flourish, whether through environmental harm to ecosystems or internal disharmony within ourselves. Restoring this balance is central to healing the damage caused by ignorance and carelessness. By aligning with Mother Nature's cycles and nurturing harmony between feminine and masculine energies, we can create environments—within and around us—that support growth, abundance, and accord for all beings. Intentional cultivation of balance allows us to engage more deeply with life and facilitates a more sustainable existence for present and future generations.

Seasons Change

The four seasons reflect masculine and feminine energies related to nature's cycles. The masculine energy is present during the Vernal Equinox, a time of action, growth, and renewal. This leads to the Summer Solstice, representing fullness, strength, and outward expression. This period emphasizes growth and abundance.

The Autumn Equinox marks the start of the feminine aspects of nature, focusing on reflection, gratitude, and release. It's a time to gather the harvest and prepare for the quieter months ahead. This theme continues through the Winter Solstice, characterized by rest, introspection, and nurturing. This season encourages inner work and contemplation, promoting rejuvenation and renewal.

Seasonal clean-ups in the garden, particularly in spring and autumn, are common practices to prepare for changing seasons. While this is an effective way to maintain the garden, it's also beneficial for local ecosystems to leave some plants intact rather than cutting them back. Migrating birds and wildlife rely on these plants for food and shelter, making gardens valuable refuges that support local biodiversity.

Native plants provide significant benefits, especially during the winter months. While most life remains dormant in the cold, local wildlife finds shelter in evergreen trees, perennial shrubs, and grasses. Birds can access seeds, berries, and insects from these vital food sources. Additionally, leaf debris and trees provide habitats for various butterfly larvae throughout the winter. Gardens sustain nature year-round.

To support wildlife habitats during fall clean-up, avoid cutting back the following plants:

- Deciduous trees and spring-flowering shrubs, such as quince, spirea, forsythia, and lilacs, provide necessary shelter.
- Butterfly bush, ornamental grasses, grass meadows, and wildflower meadows offer valuable habitats.
- Milkweed, stonecrop (sedums), rudbeckia, sunflowers, and agastache support pollinators and wildlife.
- Echinacea (coneflower), lavender, sages (salvia), yarrow, heuchera, and hellebores provide food and shelter for local wildlife.

Landscape Design

The interplay between masculine and feminine energies is clearly reflected in landscape design, offering valuable insights into our relationship with the natural world. Traditional farming techniques, like planting crops in neat rows, epitomize a structured and linear approach typically associated with masculine energies. This method emphasizes organization and efficiency, reflecting human efforts to impose control and order on the land.

In contrast, nature unfolds with an organic, fluid aesthetic, embodying feminine qualities that often appear spontaneous and ethereal to human perception. Embracing the wild beauty inherent in natural landscapes inspires a harmonious balance between structured design and the untamed essence of nature. This approach celebrates the diversity and resilience of natural ecosystems, acknowledging their intrinsic ability to grow without rigid human intervention. Nature exists with intentionality, often beyond the full grasp of human comprehension.

Professional landscape design balances hardscapes and natural elements to create functional and visually appealing outdoor spaces. The masculine aspects of hardscapes, such as pathways, fences, raised beds, and support structures, provide stability and organization while serving practical and artistic purposes. These elements help define spaces, improve accessibility, and harmonize with the natural environment. However, hardscapes must compliment the natural surroundings, not overwhelm them. The goal is to achieve a harmonious integration where hardscapes improve the aesthetic and functionality of the outdoor space without disrupting or dominating the natural flow.

Incorporating creativity into landscape design allows for artistic expression and flair. A garden becomes a canvas for personal expression, offering opportunities for innovative design features. Elements like seating areas, water features, or sculptures can be aesthetic enhancements and interactive components that enrich the garden experience. These features invite people to engage with the space, encouraging moments of contemplation, relaxation, or social interaction amidst the natural beauty of the surroundings.

By infusing creativity into landscape design, gardeners and designers transform outdoor spaces into dynamic environments that reflect individuality and nurture meaningful connections between people and nature. This approach adds to the visual appeal of gardens, creating memorable and inviting spaces that inspire and delight those who experience them.

Natural Beauty

Maintaining a garden involves nurturing and aligning with nature's innate unpredictability rather than seeking to control it. Embracing this unpredictability and working in sync with the natural rhythms of the environment allows gardeners to cultivate beautiful and sustainable landscapes. Naturalized spaces exemplify this approach, allowing plants to grow and evolve freely. This method showcases nature's adaptability and intelligence. Over time, these areas undergo transformation and vigorous growth, reflecting the dynamic cycles of life and change inherent in the natural world. By collaborating with nature's rhythms, gardeners create healthier ecosystems and landscapes that evolve harmoniously over time.

Some may characterize lawns and meticulously manicured landscapes as embodying masculine energies, emphasizing order, control, and structure. Lawns may be visually appealing to some, but they are one of the least sustainable landscape uses due to their significant adverse environmental consequences. Lawns contribute to biodiversity loss by creating monocultures that limit habitats for diverse plant and animal species. Additionally, the maintenance of lawns requires large amounts of water, which can strain local water resources, especially in regions facing water scarcity.

Furthermore, using chemical fertilizers and pesticides in lawn care poses severe environmental and human health risks. These chemicals can leach into groundwater, pollute water bodies through runoff, and harm marine life. They can also adversely affect neighboring wildlife and domesticated animals, contributing to insect population decline and other ecological imbalances.

Rethinking outdoor spaces and moving away from the traditional lawn-centric landscaping approach is a necessary transformation for societal evolution. Adopting more sustainable and environmentally friendly landscaping practices, such as incorporating native plants, creating wildlife habitats, and reducing chemical inputs, can mitigate the harmful effects of conventional lawn care while promoting biodiversity and ecological resilience. By reimagining our outdoor spaces in alignment with nature, we can create landscapes that enhance the beauty of our surroundings and support the health of our ecosystems and communities. This shift represents a vital step towards building a more sustainable and resilient future for life on Earth.

A garden's ephemeral growth often aligns with feminine energies, emphasizing nurturing and organic expression. Unlike lawns, which offer a rigid structure, gardens provide a dynamic and ever-changing landscape reflecting the natural cycles of growth and renewal. Rewilding natural spaces can restore ecological balance, rebuild soil, improve water health— particularly in wetlands—and mitigate the effects of overdevelopment and urbanization.

By recognizing and honoring masculine and feminine energies in landscape design, we can create outdoor spaces that appeal to the senses and invite a deeper connection with the natural world. This balance allows for the coexistence of structure and spontaneity, resulting in aesthetically pleasing and harmonious landscapes.

Natural beauty prevails in its raw, unaltered state, free from artificial enhancement. Likewise, love, in its purest form, is simple and inherently beautiful. By living mindfully and returning to love, we reconnect with the essence of natural beauty.

Equanimity

The historical imbalance between masculine and feminine energies in society and humanity's relationship with nature poses a significant challenge. The suppression or devaluation of feminine qualities has often resulted in harmful consequences. Accepting and honoring these qualities is a decisive step towards holistic well-being and spiritual growth for individuals and the planet.

Masculine and feminine energies are intrinsic to the human experience, embodying unique strengths and merits. Achieving a balance between these forces is fundamental for human evolution. Throughout history, humanity has often misunderstood, feared, and subjugated the feminine aspects of nature, allowing predominantly destructive masculine forces to dominate. As a result, we have reached a critical juncture in human history.

Acknowledging the complementary nature of masculine and feminine energies is necessary for achieving balance and equanimity. Embracing, integrating, and honoring both aspects allows us to acutely identify with our wholeness and true nature. Recognizing and respecting these energies across all areas of life—relationships, work, and environmental stewardship—cultivates greater harmony and cooperation within society and with the natural world. This produces a more sustainable, compassionate, and harmonious world for ourselves and future generations.

Three To One

The concept of the sacred trinity—masculine, feminine, and spirit—offers a framework for understanding how these energies are interconnected and their roles in our spiritual evolution. By acknowledging and accepting this trinity within, we access our core essence and begin to live in alignment with our personal truth. Connecting with our inner spirit and aligning with our inherent duality enables us to develop deeper self-awareness. Alignment work cultivates a sense of internal wholeness and harmony as we recognize and integrate the masculine and feminine aspects as integral parts of our spiritual being.

Releasing control, we trust our internal sacred union, unlocking infinite possibilities for growth and transformation. Surrendering the need for dominance, we allow our inner spirit to guide us with wisdom and clarity. Letting go of the pain of holding on, we deepen our connection with ourselves and the universe. Through this alignment, we create peace and balance, transcend the separateness of our being, and harmonize with the greater whole. The garden teaches humanity to recognize and witness our wholeness and divinity through its transformative process of creation.

The spirit transcends gender and represents our true essence beyond physical form. When the sacred masculine and feminine energies unite within this essence, they create a powerful integration of complementary forces. This union catalyzes conscious evolution and spiritual growth, allowing us to transcend limitations and move toward higher levels of consciousness, self-actualization, and enlightenment.

Recognizing the interconnectedness between ourselves and the universe is a pivotal step in the journey of self-awareness and empowerment. This awareness guides us towards equilibrium of the mind, body, and spirit, establishing a solid foundation for a purposeful, harmonious, and fulfilling life. It serves as a powerful reminder of our inherent potential to create a meaningful and authentic life in the simplicity of our being.

We are responsible for cultivating a worthwhile life experience, including self-awareness, while engaging in practices that assist in grounding us in the present moment. To affect meaningful change in our reality, we must collectively raise our consciousness and address the internal imbalances and destructive tendencies within ourselves. Each individual prioritizing personal growth and healing is foundational; only then can we collectively contribute to healing our planet and generating positive global change.

By addressing and reconciling imbalances within ourselves—whether mental, emotional, or spiritual—we initiate a process of healing that extends beyond personal transformation. This introspective journey addresses the root causes of issues and sets the stage for broader societal and environmental transformation.

It is important to understand that perfection is an elusive goal, but we can make meaningful progress through consistent daily practice and incremental improvements. Every step we take to cultivate self-awareness and pursue personal growth contributes to the collective evolution of humanity and the planet.

There is peace in the garden. Peace and results.

~Ruth Stout

Balance And Harmony

Every aspect of life is interconnected, from the smallest microorganisms to the vast expanses of the cosmos. When these elements are in harmony, life expands, expressing itself to its fullest potential. Creativity is an example of this alignment. However, any disruption to this balance can lead to ripple effects that impact the entire system. Nature provides us with both awe-inspiring beauty and stark reminders of its power. The gentle flutter of a butterfly's wings and the relentless force of a hurricane illustrate the natural world's delicate equilibrium and inherent resilience.

Similarly, we need to maintain balance in our physical, emotional, and spiritual health. When we prioritize one aspect in favor of another, such as work over rest, material pursuits over spiritual growth, or individual gain over collective well-being, we risk destabilizing the harmony that sustains us. In essence, balance is not just a state to be achieved but an ongoing adjustment and alignment process. As we strive for balance in our lives, we contribute to the greater harmony of the world, embodying the interconnectedness and beauty of all existence.

The Earth is grappling with ecological imbalance, a stark reality reflected in erratic weather patterns and alarming threatened species and extinction rates. Resource extraction, urbanization, and human activity are the primary catalysts for these imbalances, driving the degradation of our planet's delicate ecosystems. We must refrain from willfully ignoring the pressing issues, including escalating pollution levels, ocean acidification, overfishing, overhunting species, rampant logging, factory farming, waste generation, and other ecological disturbances.

The alarming decline of insect populations worldwide starkly reflects the growing imbalance between nature and human activity. Old-growth forests are rapidly disappearing, with less than 36% remaining on Earth. This number will decrease by the time you finish reading this. Humans have destroyed entire ecosystems by replacing native vegetation with non-native, hybridized species, creating artificial, controlled landscapes. This imbalance threatens the survival of all species, pushing humanity to a severe ecological tipping point. We stand at a critical juncture in our evolution as a species, compelled to awaken to the reality of the impending consequences.

Restoring equilibrium is not only a societal necessity; it's a critical imperative for the well-being of our planet and all its inhabitants. This journey toward restoration begins with each individual committing to radical self-care—a transformative practice that transcends personal boundaries and empowers us to make a difference. By prioritizing personal care and well-being, we naturally become more attuned to our environment, cultivating empathy, compassion, and a sense of responsibility toward the Earth and its inhabitants. This ripple effect can spark positive shifts and transformative changes on personal, societal, and global levels. If we want to see positive changes, we must be the change.

When our intention is infused with love and attention, we make more aligned and thoughtful choices, becoming catalysts for profound growth. Love and care inspire us to take action, advocate for change, and work toward a more sustainable and harmonious relationship between humanity and nature. Eventually, our deep connection to these values enables us to navigate life's challenges while maintaining balance. By embracing deep self-care and extending that care to others and the planet, we help restore equilibrium and promote the well-being of all life on Earth.

Raise Your Standards

Garden spaces naturally evolve through seasonal changes, and it's worthwhile to incorporate these shifts into every gardening plan. Focusing on improvements such as accessibility, bedding areas, hardscapes, watering systems, and overall aesthetics contributes to increased productivity and enjoyment. Ideas naturally evolve, and learning new methods for refining garden tasks is part of the journey. Creative and practical adjustments enrich the gardening experience, leading to greater satisfaction. Although these transformations take time, practicing patience as you cultivate your space leads to lasting and rewarding results.

Our bodies are our true home, and we experience each moment from within the vessel of our being. Raising our standards for mental, emotional, and physical health as a daily priority allows us to set intentions for active growth. We can gradually move toward a sustainable sense of wholeness by prioritizing how we feel, independent of others' thoughts, words, and actions. Embracing and accepting the fullness of our entire being enables us to live honestly from our heart space. There is immense satisfaction in connecting with the love that is at the core of our lives.

Intentions are key to cultivating homeostasis and stability. Establishing consistent routines and aligning our actions with our goals opens pathways for progress and growth. A well-structured routine helps us to use our time effectively while remaining adaptable, allowing our creativity to emerge. However, routines must also be flexible, as sticking rigidly to them can lead to stagnation and monotony. The creative force flows through us but requires our ability to respond; this is an integral part of the human experience. In every moment, we have choices, and our feelings guide us in recognizing whether those choices are beneficial. While we can ignore our moral truths and indulge our ego, this often leads to superficial and unsustainable satisfaction. Aligned intentions help maintain balance, support personal development, and inspire meaningful actions.

Our daily affirmations and intentions can be simple yet impactful, setting a baseline mood on which to build. Incorporating activities like body movement, meditation, stress reduction, leisure, socializing, and playtime are all practical components of self-care that contribute to maintaining equilibrium. By incorporating these practices into our daily lives, we counteract stagnancy and confusion, cultivating equanimity and inner peace.

At times, distancing ourselves from individuals, environments, or situations that disturb our inner peace may be necessary. Practicing self-respect is an act of self-care rooted in love, and it involves recognizing our worth, needs, and boundaries. Accepting and appreciating the lessons offered by adversity helps us move beyond stuck emotions and repetitive patterns. Allowing others to be who they are without trying to change or control them creates internal space to expand our awareness. Answers often emerge naturally when we approach life from a place of detachment, letting things unfold as they are.

The consequences of our actions ripple through time, affecting not only our own lives but also the experiences of others. Living in harmony today helps cultivate balance for the future. Nurturing inner peace contributes to the collective consciousness and supports inner and worldly harmony. We radiate positivity and attract similar vibrations when we align with loving, supportive universal energy. Therefore, being mindful of the energy we project is important, as it shapes future manifestations and experiences.

Constantly reacting to life from a place of survival mode keeps us in a cycle of stress and tension. Many of us fall into this way of living because we were raised in environments where survival instincts were prioritized, and over time, it becomes a habitual way of being. However, understanding the difference between survival and thriving mindsets is key to shifting our approach to life. Survival mode is driven by fear, scarcity, and the need to protect ourselves, whereas thriving is rooted in growth, balance, and alignment with our true potential. Recognizing which mode we're in allows us to shift toward a more harmonious, fulfilling existence, one where we can succeed rather than merely survive.

Our inner state influences our external experiences, and intentionally cultivating personal peace helps restore inner balance over time. By letting go of external expectations and societal pressures, we are able to reignite the path to personal fulfillment and soul satisfaction. When we live in alignment with our true nature, we create a sacred space for energy to flow freely, allowing life's magic to unfold and miracles to happen.

> ... in gardens, beauty is a by-product.
> The main business is sex and death ...
>
> ~Sam Llewelyn

Sexual And Asexual Reproduction

Biodiversity is critical in maintaining ecological balance and supporting all life forms on Earth. Cross-pollination and self-pollination are fundamental processes in plant reproduction, facilitating the transfer of pollen between flowers and ovules. Some plants exhibit hermaphroditism, with male and female reproductive organs within the same flower, known as complete or bisexual flowers. In contrast, some plants have separate male and female reproductive organs, resulting in incomplete or unisexual flowers.

This diversity in floral structures contributes to the richness of plant life and provides opportunities for specialized pollination mechanisms to evolve. It emphasizes nature's adaptability and complexity, with each species serving a particular role in the ecosystem. Biodiversity, which includes the variety of life forms and ecosystems on Earth, is necessary for the health and resilience of our planet. Healthy ecosystems rely on the interactions among diverse organisms, from soil bacteria and pollinators to marine life and migrating animals.

Many plant and tree varieties—such as certain blueberries, apples, pears, plums, almonds, and some cherries—require cross-pollination and must be planted with at least one compatible variety to produce fruit. For effective pollination and optimal yields, these varieties should bloom at the same time and be located within 50 to 100 feet of each other to allow beneficial insects to transfer pollen efficiently. Self-pollinators, however, can fertilize themselves because they have both male and female reproductive parts. This means they can set fruit without needing pollen from another variety. Examples include peaches, apricots, quince, some cherries and blueberries. While they can produce fruit independently, yields are sometimes improved with other nearby pollinators.

Asexual reproduction, a captivating aspect of plant biology, is a testament to the adaptability and resilience of plant species. This method allows many species to propagate without pollinators or seeds, resulting in offspring genetically identical to the parent plant, known as clones. The various mechanisms of vegetative reproduction, such as corms, tubers, rhizomes, bulbs, stolons, adventitious roots, and taproots, further underscore the adaptability of plant species. Examples of plants that reproduce vegetatively include garlic, potatoes, daffodils, ginger, mint, ivy, and strawberries.

Apomixis is a mechanism of asexual reproduction in plants. Apomixis is a process where plants can produce seeds without fertilization. This means that the seeds are genetically identical to the parent plant. Plants that reproduce through apomixis include blackberries, asters, meadow grasses, and dandelions. This method allows for efficient reproduction and colonization without the need for pollination.

Fragmentation is another form of asexual reproduction in which new plants grow from small, separated parts of the parent plant. This can occur naturally by breaking off plant parts or artificially through techniques like plant propagation from cuttings. Plants that reproduce through fragmentation include mushrooms, mosses, and potatoes. Both apomixis and fragmentation are valuable strategies for plants to propagate and spread in various environments. They allow for rapid reproduction and expansion of populations, contributing to the resilience and success of many plant species. These mechanisms of asexual reproduction allow plants to efficiently propagate and colonize new habitats, contributing to their success and diversity in various ecosystems.

Parthenogenesis, meaning "virgin creation," is a form of female asexual reproduction observed in various organisms across the animal kingdom. While parthenogenesis doesn't occur naturally in mammals, it is common in other taxa, such as plants, reptiles, insects, fish, and birds. In parthenogenesis, offspring develop from unfertilized eggs, with the offspring being genetic clones of the parent.

Species capable of parthenogenesis typically reproduce through sexual means. However, parthenogenesis may occur under specific environmental conditions or as a response to reproductive challenges. This asexual reproductive strategy increases the survival and propagation of organisms. Parthenogenesis can sometimes lead to rapid population growth, particularly in environments where mates may be scarce, or conditions are favorable for asexual reproduction. However, sexual reproduction remains central to maintaining genetic diversity and adapting to changing environments. Overall, parthenogenesis demonstrates the remarkable diversity of natural reproductive strategies and emphasizes the adaptability of living organisms to different ecological challenges.

Every organism upholds ecological equilibrium, no matter how small or seemingly insignificant. By preserving biodiversity and protecting the delicate balance of ecosystems, we ensure the preservation and diversification of life for future generations. The interconnectedness of all life forms and the importance of ecological balance are potent reminders of our responsibility to steward and protect the natural world. Through collective efforts to conserve biodiversity and promote sustainable practices, we can safeguard the integrity of our planet and ensure a thriving future for all beings.

Human Sexuality

Discussions about reproduction often serve as an introduction to human sexuality, but it's important to recognize that sexuality is complex and multifaceted. While reproduction is one aspect, it is not the sole focus for many individuals. Human sexuality encompasses a wide range of behaviors, desires, identities, and expressions, influenced by biological, psychological, social, and cultural factors. This diversity reflects the profoundly personal nature of each individual's experience, shaped by complex sensory and cognitive abilities, allowing varied interpretations of the world.

As conscious beings, we have the ability to explore and express our sexuality in diverse ways, encompassing not just physical acts but also emotional connections, intimacy, pleasure, and personal identity.

Recognizing and embracing the complexity and diversity of human sexuality is an integral aspect of building an inclusive society that respects all experiences and identities. By understanding the various facets of sexuality, we can cultivate a culture that celebrates diversity and upholds people's right to express their innate selves, as they are. Respecting personal choices, protecting, and prioritizing consent, regardless of age, benefits society as a whole. We must also protect those who have lost their power or voice, especially youth, ensuring their safety and agency. As long as there is no harm or self-harm, everyone deserves the opportunity to be themselves freely, without oppression or restriction.

Expression

Gene expression in plants is the process through which information from a gene is used to produce functional products like proteins. Several factors influence this expression, including epigenetics, hormones, and environmental conditions. For instance, nutrient levels and stress factors—like drought—can significantly impact how genes are expressed, enabling plants to adapt to their environment. Additionally, during specific stages of development, certain genes are activated. Chemical modifications to DNA, like DNA methylation, can also alter gene expression, allowing plants to respond more effectively to changing conditions. In drought conditions, these modifications help activate stress-related genes, enabling the plant to conserve water and adapt to the new environment.

Just as in nature, humans can be born with varied sexual organs and sexual expressions. Whereas humans cannot self-fertilize, they can be born with male and female gonads, a condition known as intersex or hermaphroditism. Sexual orientation, including bisexuality, asexuality, homosexuality, and heterosexuality, refers to the sexual attraction—or lack thereof—to others. Humans can experience and identify with more than one sexuality throughout their lives, as sexuality exists on a spectrum and can evolve over time.

Human sexuality is a normal and natural aspect of being human, and people can and do explore their sexuality in various ways. The criticisms and judgments imposed by society, religion, institutions, and governments can often suppress this exploration and creative expression, hindering the natural evolution of human sexuality.

The notion that any form of sexuality other than heterosexuality threatens human existence is illogical, as queer individuals can reproduce through various means if they choose. The diversity of human sexuality should be embraced, as it does not pose a real threat to the population.

By acknowledging and embracing the diversity of human sexuality, we can build a more inclusive and supportive society where individuals are free to explore and express their sexuality without fear of discrimination or stigma. Celebrating diversity enriches our collective experience and cultivates a more compassionate, safe, and understanding world.

Medical News Today. (2023, October 16). What are the different types of sexuality? https://www.medicalnewstoday.com/articles/types-of-sexuality)

Be not afraid of growing slowly; Be afraid only of standing still.

~Rachel Austin

Late Bloomers

In nature, everything blooms in its own time. Some plants bloom early, while others take longer to reach their full potential later in the season. Including late bloomers in the garden offers many benefits and is an excellent approach to seasonal gardening. Late-blooming plants like goldenrod, asters, and chrysanthemums enrich the garden's beauty from summer to fall, ensuring that something is always in bloom.

Late bloomers are excellent additions to maintaining the ecosystem's health by attracting pollinators when food sources are typically scarce. By providing flowers later in the season, these plants offer habitat and food for wildlife, including beneficial insects that aid in pest control. Early bloomers, like daffodils, hellebores, primrose, and dandelions, are vital food sources for bees and other pollinators. The garden's balanced mix of early and late bloomers establishes ecological resilience. Different plants blossom under varying environmental conditions, ensuring the garden remains vibrant and healthy even if some species struggle. Late bloomers often prevail in less-than-ideal conditions, such as poor soil or partial shade, making them versatile additions to various garden settings.

Some people who take longer to reach their potential are often called late bloomers. They may need time to discover their true path, and exploring different options allows them to acquire various skills and knowledge. This makes them versatile and resourceful, enabling them to navigate different situations effectively. Late bloomers frequently engage in self-reflection and personal growth, leading to a deeper understanding of themselves. This self-awareness can improve decision-making and develop interpersonal relationships.

We often place unnecessary stress on ourselves by believing we should have everything figured out by a certain age. This mindset can create irrational expectations and illusions that lead to stress and anxiety, fueling negative self-talk. Late bloomers are role models, showing that it's never too late to pursue passions or make significant life changes. Their stories can inspire others to embrace their unique paths and timelines.

The understanding and perception of time is primarily a human construct shaped by the various calendars created by different cultures. Each person's experience of time is subjective; some may feel it passes quickly, while others find it drags on. In the garden, plants adapt to changes and bloom accordingly. Context plays a significant role in shaping our perception of time. Late bloomers contribute depth and diversity to human experiences, demonstrating that success and fulfillment can be achieved at any age or stage of life. Their journeys remind us of the importance of patience, resilience, and the ongoing pursuit of personal growth, enriching their lives and those around them.

The law of harvest is to reap more than you sow. Sow an act, and you reap a habit. Sow a habit, and you reap a character. Sow a character, and you reap a destiny.

~James Allen

The Right Time

Harvest time is critical for maximizing the benefits of plants, particularly regarding their medicinal properties and overall yield. Recognizing when crops are at their peak ripeness is paramount to gardening success, as overripe fruits can spoil quickly. Harvesting at the right time ensures that plants contain the highest concentration of beneficial compounds. Timing affects flavor, texture, and nutritional content in culinary herbs and vegetables. Each plant has its growth cycle, so understanding when it reaches maturity benefits gardeners and farmers. Harvesting too early may result in underdeveloped flavors or medicinal properties, while waiting too long can lead to overripening and a decline in quality.

When planning harvest time, consider the weather conditions. Dry days are ideal for many plants, as excess moisture can lead to spoilage during storage. Avoid harvesting in wet conditions, as this can introduce mold and shorten shelf life. Additionally, plant health must be monitored to determine the right time to harvest. Check for signs of pests or diseases and address any damaged produce promptly to prevent the spread of issues. If pests or diseases are prevalent, it may be wise to harvest sooner to protect investments and avoid losing the entire crop.

Harvesting in the morning or early evening is ideal, as crops are cooler and more hydrated during these times. Avoid harvesting during the hottest part of the day, as produce can wilt or experience heat stress. Certain crops, such as leafy greens and herbs, tend to taste better when picked early in the day, while others, like tomatoes and melons, may develop richer flavors if harvested later. Avoid heavy watering before harvesting root crops like potatoes and carrots to prevent the soil from becoming too muddy. However, make sure the plants are not overly decreasing, focus on planting crops that grow well in this declining light. In particular, the third quarter is a good time to plant root vegetables, onions, and tubers. It's also suitable for cane berries, strawberries, artichokes, grapes, perennials, trees, and shrubs. Planting is generally not recommended in the fourth quarter, as this is when the earth's water table is believed to be receding. Instead, use this time for weeding and improving the soil with compost and mulch.

It's advisable to avoid planting on the first day of the new moon and during the moon's transitions between quarters. These periods are better suited for garden maintenance tasks. However, an old gardening adage suggests planting potatoes during the dark of the moon. This phase, often linked with rest and regeneration, is ideal for preparing the garden for future growth rather than engaging in active planting.

Understanding the regional plant hardiness zone and average frost dates is important for maximizing seed germination and achieving successful yields. Timing is critical, as sowing seeds too early can lead to withering and rot, while frost after germination can result in early plant death. Knowing what to sow and when is paramount for achieving high yields. Although a controlled indoor greenhouse environment is ideal for seed propagation, sowing directly in garden soil requires attention to moon phases and weather patterns to increase yields and improve garden management.

The Moon And The Stars

Our ancestors carefully observed their crops and tested different plots to determine which thrived in their environments. They passed this knowledge down through generations, helping to maintain the balance of life and to recognize the interconnectedness of all our relations between the heavens and Earth. They used star constellations to guide their daily activities and closely monitored the sky to forecast weather, animal behaviors, fertility, and migration patterns. This understanding helped improve food production and ensure survival.

The moon's position within various constellations has helped our understanding of star patterns, leading to detailed mapping and planting. Many gardeners and farmers follow the moon's placement within each zodiac sign, as each sign has specific effects on gardening. For instance, the moon in Cancer is considered ideal for grafting, planting, and transplanting due to its highly fruitful nature. When the moon is in Scorpio, it is best for planting vine crops like cucumbers and pole beans. Capricorn is favorable for root crops and tubers. Taurus benefits most crops, whether they grow above or below ground. Pisces supports strong root development, which is necessary for nearly all plants. Therefore, sowing seeds is generally most effective when the moon is in Cancer, Scorpio, or Pisces.

Certain astrological constellations, including Leo, Virgo, Aquarius, and Gemini, are considered barren signs unsuitable for planting. Focusing on tasks like weeding and controlling pests during these periods is better. The waxing moon in the Fire signs—Aries, Leo, and Sagittarius—is recommended for pruning, as it encourages growth. Conversely, pruning during the waning moon in these Fire signs hinders growth.

Biodynamic farming considers the farm a whole organism, where all elements—plants, animals, soil, and humans—are interconnected and influence each other. It emphasizes biodiversity and the creation of a balanced, self-sustaining ecosystem. An uncommon aspect of biodynamic farming is its consideration of cosmic rhythms and celestial influences on agricultural activities. It considers lunar cycles, planetary movements, and zodiac signs when scheduling planting, cultivating, and harvesting. It integrates spiritual and ethical considerations into agricultural practices, emphasizing the farmer's role as a land steward.

Dark Moon Phase

The journey of personal development often reflects the cyclical nature of the moon, with its phases of waxing and waning, light and darkness. Just as the moon goes through periods of darkness during the new moon phase, we also face times of difficulty and introspection in our lives. These dark nights of the soul are moments of deep introspection, where we confront our innermost fears, wounds, and uncertainties. During such times, unforeseen challenges and tragedies can profoundly affect us, testing our sense of identity, purpose, and belonging.

Nurturing healing and strengthening inner guidance is necessary amid challenges. This process involves practicing self-compassion, seeking support from loved ones or professionals, and engaging in healing practices like therapy, meditation, or creative expression. Although these periods of vulnerability can be incredibly difficult, they also offer significant opportunities for growth, transformation, and spiritual stressed or dry, as this can affect the quality of the produce.

When harvesting perennial plants, it's important to consider their ability to regrow and perform well in future seasons. Overharvesting can deplete the plant's energy reserves and hinder its regrowth, potentially reducing future yields. Harvest only a portion of its growth to ensure the plant remains healthy and productive, leaving enough behind for the plant to continue flourishing. For instance, when harvesting leaves from an herb like oregano, trim only a few sprigs while leaving the plant's core intact. By cutting only a third of the plant at most allows the remaining leaves to continue growing, ensuring that the plant will regenerate and produce fresh leaves in the coming weeks. Overharvesting oregano, however, by cutting too much at once, can weaken the plant and reduce its ability to proliferate and produce in the future. By practicing mindful harvesting, the plant's long-term vitality is maintained, ensuring it will continue to provide bountiful harvests for years to come.

Additionally, be aware of regional seasonal variations, which can influence plant growth and quality. Knowledge of the Plant Hardiness Zone and Climate Zones helps gardeners and farmers select the right plants and practices for their specific environments, ultimately increasing productivity and sustainability. Understanding these factors aids in determining the best time to plant and harvest.

Waste Not, Want Not

An abundant harvest can be both a blessing and a challenge for a gardener who may not be prepared to manage the bounty. Although careful planning can help, even the best-laid plans are not always foolproof. For example, a bumper crop—such as an unexpectedly large harvest of zucchini—can leave a gardener struggling to salvage the produce before it spoils. Sharing the surplus is an effective solution. With excess produce, gardeners can donate to food banks, soup kitchens, and shelters, ensuring the harvest benefits others.

Harvest season is an ideal time for garden parties and community gatherings. Neighbors can host potluck events or participate in food swaps, sharing and exchanging surplus items. Another creative option is to set up a food stand for neighbors and passersby to enjoy fresh produce. A vendor booth at a local farmer's market offers an excellent opportunity for those looking to generate income. With the proper licenses, selling prepared foods can also be profitable. Harvest season becomes not only a time of abundance but also a time for community connection and entrepreneurial ventures.

We can use fallen fruit from trees and vines as feed for pets or livestock. Establishing relationships with local farmers can also strengthen community ties. Understanding which types of produce are suitable for specific animals helps establish connections with the right farmers. A greenhouse provides the opportunity to save pits from stone fruits and regrow them into new trees, offering potential profits. Another benefit of recycling the Earth's bounty comes through composting. Fruit scraps, such as peels, cores, and overripe pieces, can be added to a compost pile to create nutrient-rich compost for the garden. Incorporating these practices into a routine can significantly reduce food waste while positively impacting the community and the environment.

Make Do And Mend

Just as a garden yields a harvest, life experiences cultivate wisdom over time. Each day, we awaken to the gifts of life, presence, and the opportunity to use our skills and talents for the greater good. Wasting these gifts leads to stagnation rather than fulfillment. When we apply our skills to improve life, we align our energies with purpose. Living with intention, making the most of our time, and focusing on meaningful pursuits are needed to create a rewarding life.

Wasting talent, time, and life affects the individual and the broader community. Failing to fulfill our potential breeds frustration and regret. When talent goes unused, personal and professional growth stagnates. Neglecting to nurture skills stifles progress and causes missed opportunities for development. Talented individuals inspire others to pursue their passions and expand their abilities. Wasting talent forfeits the chance to motivate and uplift others, limiting the ability to make a positive impact. Untapped potential leads to personal stagnation, preventing a fulfilling life.

We all experience good days and those when staying in bed feels like the best option. Sometimes, deep rest is exactly what we need to recharge and find motivation for tomorrow. The key lies in the difference between repetition and continuity. Repeating a behavior forms a habit, while maintaining continuity keeps us active and engaged. This enables us to establish healthy routines rather than fall into bad habits. Rest and relaxation refresh every part of our being and bring clarity. When we're ready, we take an idea, turn it into a plan, and put it into action. This is how we break free from dull, repetitive behaviors. Becoming our best selves requires taking the necessary steps to get there.

> Preserve and treat food as you would your body, remembering that in time, food will be your body.
>
> ~B. W. Richardson

Preservation And Storage

If history has taught us anything about the evolution of civilization, it is the critical importance of food preservation. Throughout millennia, civilizations worldwide have developed and refined methods to store and preserve food to ensure survival during times of scarcity and sustain communities through harsh winters or prolonged periods without fresh harvests.

Ancient civilizations such as the Egyptians, Greeks, Romans, and Chinese employed methods like drying, salting, smoking, and fermenting to extend the shelf life of food. These practices prevented spoilage and enabled societies to trade and transport food over long distances, facilitating cultural exchange and economic development.

In medieval times, food preservation became even more sophisticated with techniques like pickling, curing, and using sugar and spices. These methods preserved food and transformed culinary traditions and diets, influencing cultural identities and global cuisine. Technological advancements and food science further revolutionized food preservation during the Industrial Revolution. Canning, pioneered by French chef Nicolas Appert in the early 19th century, and later developments in refrigeration and freezing enabled mass production and distribution of preserved foods on a global scale.

Purpose Of Preservation

Food preservation is important today for ensuring food security, reducing waste, and addressing modern challenges such as climate change and global supply chain issues. Preserving food through various methods such as canning, freezing, drying/dehydrating, fermenting, pickling, smoking, salting/curing, sugaring, vacuum sealing, root cellaring, refrigeration, jellying, and oil preservation serves multiple valuable purposes in our daily lives and broader society.

Preservation helps minimize food waste by extending the shelf life of perishable items like fruits, vegetables, and herbs. This waste reduction conserves resources and addresses food insecurity by ensuring that edible produce doesn't go unused. Food preservation also extends the availability of seasonal foods beyond their harvest times, allowing us to enjoy diverse flavors and nutritional benefits throughout the year.

Food storage and preservation also help save money by preserving a surplus of in-season produce, lowering grocery bills, and reducing the need for expensive out-of-season items. Properly preserved foods retain their vitamins, minerals, and antioxidants, providing a healthy alternative when fresh options are scarce or costly. Additionally, learning food preservation techniques builds self-sufficiency and empowers individuals to take control of their food supply, creating resilience during uncertain times.

Food preservation contributes to environmental sustainability by decreasing dependence on commercially processed foods and supporting local agriculture. It also minimizes transportation emissions and packaging waste. Essentially, preserving food is a practical skill that supports sustainability, increases food security, facilitates healthy eating habits, and strengthens community resilience in the face of economic and environmental challenges.

Once we realize and identify the value of our space, we are more apt to protect it and keep it sacred. Plants are a sacred offering from nature. However, food engineering has hijacked nature, reducing the nutritional content and altering the nutritional compounds. This gives greater impetus to grow and preserve as much food and heirloom varieties as possible for maximum nutrition and health benefits.

Plan Ahead

If we are what we eat, then we embody the essence of our gardens. There's an unparalleled sense of fulfillment and joy when savoring fruits of labor, especially when those ripe, succulent fruits come straight from the vine. Harvest time isn't just the end of the growing season; it's the culmination of our hard work and dedication. This moment of reaping our rewards also signals the start of new efforts—the real work in the garden continues as we prepare for preservation, planning, and nurturing for the next season.

Planning preservation methods before planting allows gardeners to choose crop selections that align with their preservation goals and available garden space. For example, growing high-yield tomatoes specifically for canning or cultivating herbs like basil for freezing pesto ensures a practical and focused garden approach. Additionally, designing the garden layout to accommodate preservation needs, such as dedicated space for drying racks, cold storage, or freezer storage, optimizes efficiency, ease, and enjoyment throughout the gardening season.

Ensuring the integrity of the harvested yield is necessary for maximizing the full benefits of gardening. Proper handling, storage, and preservation techniques help maintain the quality and nutritional value of the produce, allowing gardeners to enjoy the fruits of their labor for an extended period. This attention to detail and commitment to sustainability contribute to long-term gardening success and overall satisfaction with the process.

Preservation Prep

Preparing for harvest season goes beyond gathering the yield—it requires understanding and applying effective preservation techniques to maximize the use and longevity of homegrown produce. Start by recording the details of your harvest, including dates, quantities, and quality. This information helps plan future planting and harvesting strategies. Label jars or bags with the crop type and date to ensure you use the oldest produce first. Preparing recipes for jams, jellies, sauces, or fermented products also helps make the most of your time. Have canning equipment and supplies ready: jars, lids, freezer bags, etc., and a dehydrator or drying rack. Ensure harvesting tools like pruners, shears, and knives are sharp and clean to avoid damaging plants. Gather baskets, crates, or buckets that allow air circulation to prevent damage and spoilage. Ensure they're clean to avoid contaminating the harvested produce.

Storage

Some crops, like garlic, onions, shallots, sweet potatoes, pumpkins, and winter squash, require curing before consumption. Cure them in a warm, dry, well-ventilated area for about two weeks. Curing toughens skins and rinds, improving flavor and extending shelf life. Having proper curing areas ready during harvest increases efficiency. These processes are needed for long-term storage and significantly improve the quality of crops, especially those kept through the winter or for future use.

Store potatoes in a cool, dark, well-ventilated space to prevent spoilage. Light exposure causes potatoes to turn green and produce chlorophyll and the toxin solanine. While the green color itself is harmless, solanine can be toxic in large amounts, causing nausea and other symptoms. To avoid this, remove any green areas before eating and discard completely green or sprouted potatoes.

Some types of produce, like potatoes and onions, should not be stored together due to the release of ethylene gas—a natural hormone that accelerates ripening and causes nearby fruits and vegetables to spoil more quickly. Apples, for instance, emit high levels of ethylene, which can lead to wilting, bitterness, and premature spoilage in leafy greens, carrots, berries, avocados, and broccoli. To extend their shelf life, store apples separately from other produce.

Bananas also emit ethylene, which can cause other fruits to ripen too quickly, leading to overripe or spoiled produce. Store bananas separately from fast-ripening fruits like avocados, tomatoes, and peaches, all of which are best kept at room temperature.

Tomatoes and cucumbers are sensitive to temperature changes and should be stored separately. Storing them together can cause faster spoilage due to their differing moisture levels and ethylene sensitivity. Cucumbers do well in cooler refrigerated conditions, while tomatoes are best kept at room temperature.

Preservation Practices

Drying and dehydrating foods are traditional methods where moisture is removed from fruits, vegetables, and herbs, preserving them for long-term storage. Air Drying is a simple method of laying or hanging foods in a well-ventilated area, protected from moisture. It is often used for herbs, beans, some fruits, and vegetables. Ensure good airflow around the vegetables to prevent mold and spoilage. Store dried vegetables in airtight containers in cool, dark places to maintain quality. Other methods include freeze-drying, oven-drying, sun-drying, and smoking.

Dehydration is another cost-effective way to preserve foods. Dehydrated foods do not require added preservatives, which can be advantageous for avoiding chemicals and additives. Both methods extend shelf life, enhance flavor concentration, and create lightweight, portable snacks. It is also ideal for herbs like rosemary and thyme and fruits like apples and berries. Whether you air-dry herbs, sun-dry tomatoes, or use a modern dehydrator for fruits and vegetables, the process revolves around achieving the desired level of moisture removal to maintain quality and longevity.

Dehydrated foods are versatile—they can be rehydrated for cooking, enjoyed as snacks, or ground into powders for seasoning mixes. This preservation method reduces food waste by allowing home gardeners to preserve excess produce at peak freshness.

All preservation methods lead to gradual nutrient loss over time, with vitamins A, C, and E being especially susceptible. While dehydration does cause some nutrient loss, it preserves a significant amount of the food's vitamins, minerals, and enzymes compared to heat-intensive methods like canning, which result in more substantial nutrient degradation. Freezing and fermentation tend to retain the most nutrients, especially when done effectively.

Freezing involves either flash-freezing produce or using freezer bags and airtight containers to maintain freshness and nutritional value. This method is excellent for berries, green beans, and other vegetables. When freezing produce, preparing it properly to maintain quality is critical. This often involves washing, trimming, and sometimes blanching to preserve color and texture. Additionally, using freezer-safe containers or bags and labeling with the date helps keep track of freshness. Properly frozen produce can last several months and provides a convenient way to enjoy seasonal flavors anytime.

Fresh herbs like parsley, basil, cilantro, and dill can be chopped and frozen in ice-cube trays with water or olive oil for easy portioning and use in cooking. Many vegetables, such as green beans, peas, corn, broccoli, cauliflower, and carrots, can be blanched (briefly boiled and then cooled in ice water) before freezing to preserve color, flavor, and nutrients. Tomatoes can be frozen whole or chopped for later use in sauces, stews, or soups. Some varieties may require peeling before freezing, or they may peel more easily after freezing. Leafy greens like spinach, kale, and Swiss chard can be blanched and frozen for later use in smoothies, soups, or cooked dishes.

Citrus fruits such as lemons, limes, and oranges can be juiced and frozen in ice cube trays or zested and frozen for later use in recipes. For convenience, stone fruits like peaches, plums, cherries, and apricots can be pitted, sliced, and frozen. Fruits like apples, pears, plums, peaches, and apricots may benefit from a quick blanching before freezing to help retain their color and texture. Strawberries, blueberries, raspberries, and blackberries also freeze well. Wash them, remove any stems or hulls, and spread them in a single layer on a baking sheet to freeze individually before transferring them to appropriately labeled freezer bags or containers.

Canning—whether through water bath, steam, or pressure methods—is used to preserve foods in jars, creating a vacuum seal that helps prevent spoilage. Water bath canning is used for high-acid foods, typically those with a pH of 4.6 or lower. The process involves submerging jars filled with food in a large pot of boiling water and processing them at a specific temperature for a set amount of time. This method is commonly used for fruits, jams, jellies, pickles, and high-acid tomatoes.

Steam canning generates steam surrounding the jars, heating them and their contents to eliminate bacteria, yeast, and molds. Jars filled with food—typically fruits, tomatoes, or other high-acid foods—are placed in the canner equipped with a lid and steam vent. However, steam canning is not recommended for low-acid foods, such as vegetables or meats, as the temperatures may not be sufficient to destroy harmful bacteria safely.

Pressure canning is necessary for low-acid foods with a pH level above 4.6. These foods require higher temperatures to destroy harmful bacteria such as Clostridium botulinum spores. Pressure canners are specialized equipment that creates a high-pressure environment, allowing foods to reach temperatures above the boiling point of water. Foods suitable for pressure canning include vegetables, meats, poultry, seafood, and soups.

Each method follows similar basic steps: preparing the food, filling sterilized jars, sealing them with lids and bands, processing them in boiling water, steam, or a pressure canner, and cooling them to create a vacuum seal. The choice between water bath, steam, and pressure canning depends on the food's acidity level, ensuring safe storage and long-term shelf stability.

Traditional and steam canning are time-tested food preservation methods that significantly benefit individuals and communities. One of its primary advantages is the extended shelf life, allowing foods to be safely stored at room temperature for extended periods, often up to several years. This capability ensures a steady supply of nutritious foods beyond their natural growing seasons and helps reduce food waste by preserving surplus produce from gardens or local farms. From a practical standpoint, canned foods offer convenience and versatility in meal preparation, providing ready-to-eat or easy-to-prepare options that require minimal effort.

Fermentation harnesses beneficial bacteria to preserve foods, such as cabbage in sauerkraut or cucumbers in pickles while enhancing their flavor, texture, and nutritional content. This transformative process has been used for centuries to preserve food and enrich its flavor and nutritional profile.

This natural method involves beneficial microorganisms breaking down sugars and carbohydrates in foods, producing acids or alcohol that act as natural preservatives. Beyond preservation, fermentation increases the bioavailability of nutrients such as vitamins and minerals, making them more easily absorbed by the body. It also introduces probiotics and enzymes that aid in digestive health and overall vitality. Some fermented foods are easier to digest because the fermentation process breaks down certain components (like lactose in yogurt).

Fermentation transforms diverse foods and beverages, from cheese and tempeh to sourdough bread, kimchi, kombucha, beer, and wine. It imbues foods with distinct flavors, from the tangy complexity of sauerkraut to the probiotic richness of yogurt and the umami depth of miso and soy sauce. Fermented foods span a wide range of culinary traditions worldwide.

This ancient technique reduces food waste by extending shelf life without refrigeration and effectively supports sustainability by utilizing local and seasonal ingredients. Culturally, fermented foods are indispensable, reflecting diverse regional flavors and culinary heritage. As modern diets focus more on gut health and sustainable practices, fermentation is valuable for enhancing flavors, boosting nutritional content, and reconnecting us with age-old culinary traditions.

Fermentation Quick Guide

What You'll Need:

- Fresh vegetables (e.g., cabbage, carrots, cucumbers, etc.)
- Non-iodized salt (sea salt or kosher salt)
- Water (preferably filtered, without chlorine)
- Jars or containers (glass is ideal)
- A weight (optional, to keep food submerged)
- Airlock lids or clean cloth and rubber bands (for covering the jars)

Basic Steps for Vegetable Fermentation:

Prepare the Vegetables:
Wash the vegetables thoroughly.
Chop, shred, or slice them as desired. For example, cabbage is typically shredded for sauerkraut, while cucumbers might be left whole for pickles.

Salt the Vegetables:

Toss the vegetables with non-iodized salt. The general ratio is 1-3 tablespoons of salt per quart of vegetables.

The salt draws water out of the vegetables and creates a brine, which helps preserve the food and prevents harmful bacteria from growing.

Massage the Vegetables:

If making sauerkraut or kimchi, massage the salted vegetables for 5-10 minutes until they release enough liquid to cover themselves in the brine.

Pack the Vegetables into a Jar:

Firmly pack the vegetables into a clean jar, ensuring no air pockets.

If the vegetables don't have enough liquid to cover them completely, add a brine (dissolve 1 tablespoon of salt in 1 cup of water) until submerged.

Weigh Down the Vegetables (optional):

Submerge the vegetables under the brine with a fermentation weight or a clean jar to prevent mold from forming.

Cover and Ferment:

Cover the jar with an airlock lid (which allows gases to escape while keeping air out) or a clean cloth secured with a rubber band.

Store the jar at room temperature (65-75°F) away from direct sunlight.

Fermentation time varies: sauerkraut may take 1-4 weeks, while pickles might take a few days to a week.

Taste and Store:

After a few days, start tasting the ferment to see if it has reached your desired level of sourness. Once it's fermented to your liking, transfer the jar to the refrigerator to slow down the fermentation process.

The fermented vegetables are now ready to eat and will keep in the fridge for months.

Enjoy!

Seed: That which arises from itself again and again and again.

~ Vandana Shiva

Saving Seed

The practice of saving seeds as gardeners is an investment in the future. Whether growing herbs, flowers, or fruits, viable seeds hold the potential to nourish future generations. It's a practice that sustains biodiversity by safeguarding traditional and heirloom plant varieties that might otherwise disappear due to the dominance of high-yield hybridized commercial crops. By saving seeds, we reduce dependency on external sources and gain the ability to grow our own food, ensuring food security during uncertain times. Moreover, saving seeds helps with economic savings and supports sustainable agricultural practices, making it a strategic approach with long-term benefits.

By saving seeds from our garden, we can preserve our favorite varieties, gain a deeper understanding of plant life cycles, and ensure a sustainable source of future plants for the garden or community. From a practical standpoint, saving seeds can significantly reduce costs for farmers and gardeners. When we save enough seeds, we can share them. We can save money and become more self-sufficient by not having to purchase seeds each planting season. This practice also allows for adaptation to local growing conditions over time, as seeds saved from plants that thrive in a particular area are likely to produce offspring better suited to those conditions.

Saving hybrid seeds can be problematic for several reasons. Hybrid seeds result from crossbreeding two different plant varieties to achieve specific traits, such as higher yields or disease resistance. However, when gardeners save seeds from hybrid plants, the next generation often doesn't exhibit the same characteristics as the original hybrid. Instead, the seeds may revert to the traits of one or both parent plants, resulting in unpredictable growth and performance. This instability reduces crop yields and weaker resistance to pests or diseases. Some hybrid seeds are also patented, and saving or replanting them may violate intellectual property laws. Over-reliance on hybrid seeds can also reduce genetic diversity in crops, which is indispensable for long-term food security. Unlike hybrid seeds, open-pollinated and heirloom varieties allow consistent and reliable seed saving.

Heirloom Seeds

Heirloom plants contribute to genetic diversity, a necessary and valuable component for maintaining resilient ecosystems. These varieties are often more adaptable to regional conditions and may possess unique traits valuable in the face of environmental changes. Known for their rich flavors and high-quality characteristics, heirloom varieties are often superior to hybrids and commercial crops, selected for taste, texture, and nutrition. Many heirlooms have been passed down through generations, preserving agricultural traditions and cultural heritage.

Growing heirloom varieties allows gardeners to save seeds yearly, adopting a sense of independence and reducing reliance on commercial seed companies. This seed-saving practice contributes to sustainability by conserving seeds that may be better suited to local conditions. Over time, some heirlooms have naturally developed resistance to pests, diseases, and harsh climates, reducing the need for chemical inputs and improving agricultural sustainability. By supporting heirloom varieties, gardeners help protect biodiversity and preserve plant species that might otherwise be lost due to the dominance of hybridized high-yield crops.

Dry Seed Saving

For plants such as corn, beans, grains, peas, and sunflowers, start by choosing healthy, mature plants with desirable traits for seed saving. Allow these plants to mature and produce seeds fully. Hand harvest seeds when ripe, often indicated by color changes or when seed heads dry out. Use a fine mesh sieve to separate small seeds from chaff. Dry seed plants can also be cut down and dried by hanging for future seed collection. Spread seeds in a single layer on a screen, paper towel, or newspaper in a cool, dry place. Ensure they are completely dry to prevent mold during storage.

Wet Seed Saving

For wet-seed saving, choose the best, fully ripened fruits. The seeds will have the highest chance of germination if harvested from healthy, mature produce. For wet-seeded plants like tomatoes and cucumbers with a gelatinous membrane around the seeds, remove them with gel coating from the fruit and place them in a jar or bowl with a little non-chlorinated water. Allow them to ferment for a few days in indirect sunlight, stirring occasionally.

After fermentation, discard any floating seeds, mold, or pulp from the top. The viable seeds will settle at the bottom. Pour out as much liquid as possible while retaining the viable seeds. Add clean water to help separate the seeds, allowing the viable seeds to gather at the bottom again. Repeat this process as necessary.

Once the seeds are clean, pour them into a mesh strainer and rinse thoroughly. Allow the seeds to dry at room temperature, out of direct sunlight, for a few days. Finally, store the seeds in an airtight container or envelope with a silica packet. Label them with the harvest date, plant variety, and other pertinent information. Keep the seeds in a cool, dark, and dry place to maintain their viability until it's time to plant them again.

Seed Storage

It has been said that growing your own food is like printing money. Investing time and energy into food preservation and seed saving offers a significant return on investment. Taking the necessary precautions and handling your goods carefully is the best strategy for maximizing this return. Storing seeds for future use requires organization to set yourself up for success.

Store them in airtight containers in cool, dark, and dry places to preserve seed viability. Regularly inspect seeds for signs of moisture or mold. Though not essential for all seed types, adding silica packets can help reduce humidity and extend seed longevity. Silica packets are especially useful in humid environments, as they absorb excess moisture and help maintain low humidity levels for long-term storage.

When stored properly, dry seeds, such as beans and grains, are less likely to experience moisture issues. However, they can attract pests. Freezing beans and grains before long-term storage kills any potential pests and eggs, helping to preserve their quality. Additionally, roasting beans in the oven can eliminate pests, larvae, or eggs, making it especially useful for extended storage. This process ensures long-term preservation by killing any bugs that may be present.

Preheat the oven to 160-180°F (70-82°C), a temperature range high enough to eliminate pests but low enough to avoid cooking or burning the beans. Spread the beans in a single layer on a baking sheet, ensuring not to overcrowd them to allow for even heat circulation. Roast the beans for about 20-30 minutes, stirring occasionally to ensure uniform heating. You may hear a slight crackling or popping sound, which is normal. After roasting, check the beans to ensure they are dry, free of visible pests, and smell fresh—not burnt. The heat should have effectively eliminated any pests or eggs present. Once roasted, allow the beans to cool completely before storing them in an airtight container in a cool, dry, and dark place. Roasting can also enhance the flavor, imparting a subtle nutty taste to the beans.

Saving herb seeds is a simple and rewarding process that lets gardeners continue growing their favorite herbs season after season. Begin by selecting healthy, vigorous plants with desirable flavor and growth habits. Allow these plants to mature fully, letting them go through their natural flowering and seeding stages. As the seeds develop, keep a close eye on the plants. Harvest the seeds when the seed heads or pods are dry and beginning to open or when they shed seeds easily.

For herbs like cilantro or dill, cut the entire seed head when it turns brown and dry. Then, extract the seeds by gently crushing or rubbing the seed heads to release them. Alternatively, shake the seeds from the pods or seed heads into a container. After extraction, spread the seeds in a single layer on a paper towel or fine mesh screen to air dry in a warm, well-ventilated area. Stir or shake them occasionally to ensure even drying. Once completely dry, store the seeds in labeled envelopes or small containers in a cool, dry place away from direct sunlight. Proper storage keeps herb seeds viable for one to several years, allowing you to grow your favorite herbs year after year.

The importance of saving seeds is multifaceted and fosters a deeper connection to the land and a sense of stewardship over food supply. Saving heirloom varieties, in particular, preserves food heritage. Seed saving is a key factor in becoming self-sufficient. It also encourages learning about plant life cycles, pollination processes, and the importance of healthy soils, building a greater appreciation for the natural world and sustainable practices. Additionally, it empowers communities to share knowledge and resources, contributing to a more resilient and supportive local food system.

Plant Life Cycles

Annual plants complete their life cycle in one growing season and do not overwinter. Some annual crops include corn, tomatoes, peppers, beans, lettuce, cucumbers, wheat, and rice. Annual flowering plants are the same. Their life cycle comprises germination, vegetative growth, flowering, seed production, and death.

Biennials like carrots, beets, cabbage, and parsley require two growing seasons to complete their life cycle. In the first year, they germinate and have vegetative growth (roots and leaves). In the second year, they flower, produce seed, and die.

Perennials require a dedicated space and regrow each season, living for over two years. Blueberries, rhubarb, and artichokes are examples. In the first year, they germinate and grow vegetatively. In subsequent years, they go dormant in the winter, regrow during spring, flower, and produce seed. Asparagus needs three years to grow before it can be harvested.

Self-Seeders are plants that drop seeds germinating in the same area, often leading to new plants each year. Examples include wildflowers, pansies, cosmos, chervil, oregano, and sunflowers. They are similar to annuals but often persist due to their self-seeding nature.

> **Do not measure success by today's harvest. Measure success by the seeds you plant today.**
>
> ~Robert Louis Stevenson

Saving Seeds Of Thought

Just as gardeners save seeds to grow new plants, we can preserve valuable thoughts and experiences that have the potential to blossom into personal growth or creativity. Nurturing ideas, insights, or lessons can lead to something meaningful later. Journaling or using a sketchbook are great ways to cultivate creativity.

Digital and audio notes allow for easy access and organization. Creating physical or digital mood boards also helps to visually collect images, colors, and textures that inspire creative works. The same is valid for photography. Taking photos of interesting scenes, textures, or subjects can serve as a reference for future projects.

Collaborating and engaging in discussions with others can help refine and expand creative vision, opening up new directions. Participating in workshops allows you to learn new techniques and gather fresh ideas from peers and instructors. Experimenting with different materials or methods can lead to unexpected discoveries, sparking further creativity. Additionally, reflecting on your completed work helps you recognize what resonates, guiding future projects.

Just like planning future garden crops requires time and preparation, reflecting on your thoughts, jotting down insights, and revisiting them when the time is right to create inspiration and wisdom to help navigate challenges and pursue goals. A garden requires care and attention, and the seeds of thought must be nurtured through contemplation, discussion, and application.

> Nature herself does not distinguish between what seed it receives. It grows whatever seed is planted; this is the way life works. Be mindful of the seeds you plant today, as they will become the crop you harvest.
>
> ~Mary Morrissey

Mindful Cultivation

The garden may often feel like it demands endless work, but in time, it becomes clear that it has a life of its own—and we are its stewards, guiding its growth and evolution. Similarly, in life, there's always something demanding our attention: responsibilities, goals, and challenges. Yet, as we immerse ourselves in the garden—or life—we understand that we are not the sole creators or controllers of its growth. The garden, like life, follows its own rhythm, unfolding through processes of growth and change.

The most fulfilling moments arise when we pause to appreciate what has grown and bloomed as a result of our efforts. Whether witnessing flowers blossom, seeing children grow into healthy adults, or achieving personal milestones, taking time to savor these moments nourishes our being and becoming. It reminds us that while goals and results matter, the journey itself—the learning, the growth, the experiences—is equally valuable. Enjoying the process and finding fulfillment in the journey is as important as achieving any result. In the end, the garden—and our lives—are dynamic and ever-evolving. Embracing this and finding joy in both the process and the outcomes inspires us to cultivate a more profound sense of fulfillment and connection with the world.

As the garden becomes established and matures, we often notice that it blooms with less effort on our part. This is a testament to the power of patience, nurturance, and allowing nature to unfold at its own pace. By creating the right conditions and offering consistent care, we set the stage for abundant growth and prosperity. Moreover, periods of inactivity and rest allow us to recharge and replenish our energy reserves, leading to increased productivity and creativity in the long run. Rest is not a luxury but a necessity for sustaining our well-being and creativity. Acknowledging the importance of rest can make us feel more valued and respected.

Being fully present in the moment allows us to observe our garden, which reflects our efforts and intentions. We can see what is reflected without attachment when we remain still and present as observers. This practice nurtures stability and acceptance of what is, free from judgment. Through mindful cultivation, we nurture a garden—both within and around us—seeing things as they are and understanding the value of our actions. Only in stillness can we hear our truth clearly. These moments of clarity are valuable growth indicators, offering feedback and illuminating the path forward. This feedback loop provides insight into realignment, improvement, and growth.

When we can witness the interconnectedness of each being contributing to the entire ecosystem, we gain a deeper appreciation for our role within the complexity of the whole. Each plant plays a distinct role—some provide nutrients and support other plants, some attract pollinators or deter pests. Similarly, various aspects of our lives, including relationships, work, and hobbies, contribute to our growth and fulfillment. In life, intentional actions and mindful decisions shape our experiences. When we cultivate and nurture this space, we become more capable of accepting disappointments with wisdom and grace, recognizing that everything is temporary by nature.

Simply being present in any given moment and appreciating the beauty and abundance surrounding us can bring a new sense of joy. A well-tended garden integrates various elements harmoniously. Holistic growth involves balancing physical, emotional, mental, and spiritual well-being. Each aspect requires focused attention and care, just as each part of the garden needs nurturance to grow. When we tend to all areas of our lives with mindfulness, we cultivate a deeper sense of health and happiness, creating a more integrated and fulfilling existence.

Essentially, tending to our life's garden is a delicate balance of action and stillness, work and rest. By embracing this balance and finding joy in both the process and the outcome, we can cultivate a rich, fulfilling life in harmony with the natural rhythms of existence. The daily aspects of the journey shape and enrich our experiences, creating a more profound sense of satisfaction and contentment.

Sustainable gardening practices—such as growing organically, enriching the soil, and conserving water—demonstrate a profound respect for and understanding of nature's intricate cycles. In the same way, sustainable living practices—like cultivating a healthy relationship with oneself and others, managing stress, and nurturing creativity—are important for cultivating long-term well-being. Both approaches require conscious effort and alignment with natural processes, ensuring immediate growth, lasting vitality, and harmony.

Nature holds remarkable power to heal and restore our health on multiple levels. It calms our minds, soothes our spirits, and alleviates our anxieties. Immersing ourselves in nature, whether by observing a body of water, hiking in the mountains, or simply spending time in our garden, allows us to deeply connect with the earth and its elements. Inhaling the fresh air and releasing our stale thoughts, we release tension and negativity, making space for rejuvenation and renewal.

Nature provides us with a space to quiet the noise of our busy minds, offering a sense of peace and solace that can be difficult to find elsewhere. In this peaceful environment, we often experience shifts in perspective and clarity, gaining insights and understanding that elude us in the hustle and bustle of everyday life. Whether it's the gentle rustle of leaves in the wind, the soothing sounds of running water, or the vibrant colors of flowers in bloom, nature speaks to us in a language that transcends words, inviting us to slow down, breathe deeply, and reconnect with ourselves by observing the world around us without attachment to it. As with any worthwhile endeavor, this takes practice.

As we nurture our relationship with the natural world, our garden becomes more than just a place of beauty—it becomes a sacred space where we can commune with the earth, replenish our spirit, and find renewal in its abundance. It is a reminder that we are not separate from nature but rather an integral part of it, and by honoring and nurturing this connection, we can cultivate a more harmonious and fulfilling existence for ourselves and future generations.

Playtime

If we remember to play fully, we remember to live fully. Children's play is primary to the health of their daily existence—a time for daydreaming, creativity, and unbridled joy. Through play, we can explore our world, express ourselves freely, and connect meaningfully with others. Play taps into our imaginations and encourages us to embrace the spontaneous, playful spirit within us. It also helps us connect with our inner child. Whether building sandcastles, riding bikes, or watching clouds, playtime offers uninhibited exploration and discovery.

It's easy to lose touch with the playful side of ourselves as the demands of adulthood take over. However, the importance of play in our lives remains just as vital as ever. Play brings us joy and lightness of being and helps us reduce stress, nurture creativity, and strengthen social connections. By making time for play, we can reconnect with that sense of wonder and spontaneity that defined our childhood. By engaging in hobbies, making music, participating in sports, or simply spending time with loved ones, play allows us to fully embrace the present moment and live harmoniously with our inner and outer world.

As children, many of us were told to "go play"; if we were lucky, we could use our imaginations, play pretend, and create games. We would color or scribble on paper or walls, finger-paint, feature our talent show, make mud pies, and play sports because we loved the game. We'd dance with or without music, roller skate, hula hoop, jump rope, hopscotch, and practice magic tricks; rarely were there strict rules or agendas. During playtime, playful ideas came to us as freely as the breeze.

So, what happens? Why do we lose touch with this aspect of our nature? When do we become so serious that we forget to enjoy ourselves? When does the laughter fade? Various factors contribute to this shift, and each person's experience may differ in understanding why it occurs.

One significant factor is societal pressure and expectations, which often prioritize productivity, achievement, and success over leisure and enjoyment. From a young age, we are conditioned to focus on school, work, and other obligations, leaving little room for play and recreation. As we age, we may become more self-conscious and worried about how others perceive us. This can lead us to suppress our playful impulses in favor of conforming to societal norms. The fear of judgment and criticism can inhibit our ability to embrace our playful side and express ourselves freely and fully.

The stresses and pressures of modern life can also diminish our capacity for playfulness. As we juggle work, family, and other responsibilities, it can be easy to overlook the importance of relaxation and leisure. Many of us feel guilty or selfish when we take time for ourselves, so we focus on work and productivity, neglecting our well-being. This shift significantly reduces our enthusiasm for life and enjoyment of simple pleasures.

Most notably, the emotional pain of heartbreak can seriously impact our ability to enjoy life. It often leads to feelings of disconnection, withdrawal, and isolation, along with negative thought patterns, grief, and fear of future relationships. If we do not address these feelings, heartbreak can linger, affecting future relationships and our overall outlook. This can make it harder to find joy and fulfillment.

This is why we dig in the dirt and cultivate new life. Working with the land has the power to rejuvenate the mind, body, and spirit, creating a rewarding and transformative experience. Gardening is not only a physical activity but also offers significant therapeutic benefits. There is joy in nurturing life, which elevates healing and renewal.

Gardening and working with the soil don't have to feel like chores, and there's no need to fear hard work—it can be fun. Leisure time in the garden is also an experience worth its weight in sweat equity. Engaging in playful activities is a form of self-care that brings joy and magic at any age. This mindset opens the door to greater happiness, fulfillment, and well-being. By embracing enjoyment and leisure, we strengthen our connection to purpose, meaning, and our relationship with ourselves and the world around us.

Animals in the wild often make time for play. Elephants splash in water, otters slide down slopes, and crows show off playful antics. Ravens perform aerial acrobatics, seals play tag, and squirrels chase each other. Some birds hang upside down, while monkeys swing from vines and drum with sticks. Penguins toboggan on their bellies, and whales breach, creating spectacular splashes. Play is an integral part of a balanced life.

As adults, it's common to feel uncertain about how to play. We often forget or suppress that playful side of ourselves. Releasing our serious nature allows a light heart to bring levity. Do what feels good, as long as it benefits you and, especially, others. To reconnect with your playful spirit, try skipping stones across a stream, building a fort for a tea party, embarking on a scavenger hunt, making music with anything, dancing, or playing in sand or mud. Stargaze, watch clouds, explore trails, climb rocks, play hide-and-seek, or capture the flag. Create nature art with garden debris or swing at a playground. Engage in activities free from agenda that invite a light-hearted approach to life and rekindle the joy of play.

Despite the challenges, it's important to remember that play is fundamental to human nature and needed for maintaining equilibrium between the mind, body, and spirit. By intentionally setting aside time for play and recreational activities, we can reconnect with our inner child and rediscover the joy, spontaneity, and creativity of embracing our playful spirit. Engaging in play allows us to heal the disconnect that may have developed over time. When we permit ourselves to participate in activities that bring us joy and laughter, we tap into a more profound sense of awareness and genuineness. As we lighten up and let go of seriousness, our disposition naturally softens, aligning us more closely with our true selves. This openness allows us to receive life's gifts and fully embrace the present moment.

Play To Win

In life, we have options for how we approach anything: we can do it well, not do it at all, or do just enough to get by, even if it could be better. This mindset also applies to how we live. Some people play the game of life to win, actively engaging and striving for success. Others disengage, either by not participating or by sabotaging themselves. Then, there are those who do the bare minimum to avoid failure, playing not to lose. This can be seen in many areas, such as work, school, relationships, and personal growth.

By consciously reflecting and aligning with our true intentions, we can shift our energy and elevate ourselves to a higher frequency. This helps us become more engaged and genuinely play to win. At times, though, it is wiser to step away from certain projects or relationships if they aren't the best use of our time and energy. The key is being honest with ourselves about our desires and creating from a place of clarity.

A Place To Grow

Introducing children to gardening is a valuable way to encourage their understanding and development. Creating a space for a kid's garden can be a fun and engaging project for them. Start with easy-to-grow, low-maintenance plants like pole beans, cucumbers, lettuce, herbs, radishes, tomatoes, and flowers like marigolds and zinnias. Watching their plants grow and harvesting the crops makes gardening enjoyable and educational.

Gardening can serve as a rich educational tool, teaching children about responsibility, patience, and the cycles of nature. When children engage with plants, they learn firsthand about the importance of nurturing living things, from planting seeds to caring for them through each growth stage. This process helps build a sense of accomplishment and pride as they see their efforts manifest as healthy plants and harvests.

Creating a dedicated space for a child's garden nurtures their creativity and problem-solving skills. It allows children to decide which plants to grow, how to arrange them, and tackle challenges like pests or weather. This autonomy encourages confidence and teaches them about the cause-and-effect relationship between their actions and the outcomes. Additionally, gardening facilitates sensory development. Children experience the textures of soil, leaves, and flowers while also smelling the scents of herbs or flowers, listening to the rustling of plants in the breeze, and observing the vibrant colors and intricate details of nature. These sensory experiences can help develop a deeper connection to the environment and build their cognitive and emotional growth.

Gardening also provides an excellent opportunity for children to learn about healthy eating. By growing their food, children are more likely to appreciate fresh produce and better understand where their food comes from. This connection to food can inspire healthier eating habits, especially when they have been involved in planting, caring for, and harvesting crops.

Lastly, gardening encourages physical activity and time spent outdoors. Whether digging, planting, or watering, these activities provide exercise while exposing children to the benefits of spending time in nature. Outdoor gardening activities can improve motor skills, increase vitamin D intake, and boost overall well-being, allowing children to disconnect from screens and enjoy the natural world. Creating a child's garden is an enjoyable project and a multifaceted learning experience that nurtures a range of skills, nurtures emotional growth, and encourages healthy, sustainable habits.

Respect for food is respect for life, for who we are, and what we do.

~Thomas Keller

Body Intelligence

Our gardens provide the nourishment that fuels our bodies. Through gardening and cultivation, we nurture our physical, mental, and spiritual well-being. Conscious eating, a mindful approach to fueling ourselves, improves our mental and physical health. Eating fresh, garden-grown produce and maintaining a balanced diet is as essential as breathing, influencing every aspect of our well-being. Have you ever noticed that processed, heavy foods seem less appealing when feeling unwell? This is your body's way of signaling what it needs. Body intelligence—or somatic awareness—refers to tuning into these signals, helping us understand our body's needs and making informed choices about food and nutrition.

Eating, in essence, is a sacred act that nourishes our entire being. Many people do not eat for nourishment; they eat to avoid feeling hungry. We become what we consume, including media and entertainment. External factors significantly influence our internal health. Eating light, fresh, and seasonal foods helps align the mind and body, while a diet primarily composed of heavy, inert foods can leave us feeling disconnected and sluggish. Our reactions to what we eat are often tied to how it makes us feel, which is where true awareness resides. The same is true about the entertainment we consume. Being mindful of how food and entertainment affect us empowers us to make more intentional choices, developing a sense of balance, clarity, and alignment with our true selves.

We may enjoy certain foods that seem like harmless indulgences, but when we examine the consequences of our choices, we can recognize elements of discomfort or suffering. Our feelings act as an internal guidance system, signaling when something doesn't serve our well-being. Reducing suffering requires conscious effort as we evolve and make more mindful choices. Self-care is closely linked to our overall health and well-being, and eating well is vital to self-care. By aligning our eating habits with our deeper needs, we support our physical health and our emotional and mental balance as well.

When eating, it's more important to be with the food and less with the active mind. Enjoy the bounty by tasting the flavors and textures. Chew each morsel with reverence and respect for all it took and all who assisted in its becoming. This practice can develop your connection with food and improve digestion. Mindful eating means recognizing that the earth nourishes you, along with the labor of others and your own efforts. By consciously expressing grace, gratitude, and appreciation for the food we consume, we cultivate a deeper, more conscious relationship with it.

Distinguishing between true hunger and emotional eating enables us to nourish our body when it truly needs food rather than eating out of boredom or stress. By understanding the emotional relationship with food, better choices can be made, leading to a more balanced, mindful approach to eating. Body intelligence encourages selecting foods that support physical and mental well-being. Over time, we learn which foods energize us and which might leave us feeling sluggish. Since everybody is unique, being aware of and attuned to personal needs helps identify specific dietary requirements based on activity level, metabolism, and health goals.

Incorporating fresh, clean, whole foods into our diet while consciously avoiding processed and fast foods is a practice we can begin immediately. Hydrating and eating foods that minimize mucous production helps stabilize a healthy gut. Foods rich in fiber and iron support digestion, help regulate blood sugar levels, and improve oxygen transport. These nutrients promote heart and colon health, boost cognitive and immune function, and produce energy.

As we develop and practice body intelligence, we understand how food fuels our bodies for physical activity, guiding us in selecting the proper nutrients for optimal performance and recovery. Eating per our body's needs allows us to age with nature organically and naturally, minimizing the need for pharmaceuticals. Nutrient-rich foods strengthen our immune system, helping the body fend off illnesses. Additionally, nutrition significantly influences brain function and mood; healthy eating can improve concentration, reduce anxiety, and support mental clarity. The gut microbiome plays a significant role in mental health, and a nutrient-dense diet supports gut health, improving mood and cognitive function. Being attuned to your body helps us recognize our satisfaction levels, leading to better portion control and less overeating.

It's important to remember that this journey isn't about perfection; it's about living with intention and making healthy choices. By developing body intelligence, we can cultivate a healthier relationship with food, in and out of the garden. This leads to improved health and a more intuitive approach to eating. We can improve our physical health and overall quality of life by prioritizing clean, conscious eating. Body care is an act of love and transformative self-care.

> You are the truth. Observe yourself and understand yourself as you are.
>
> ~Jiddu Krishnamurti

Be Here Now As You Are

A farmer and a gardener know what a seed needs to grow: time, patience, nurturance, and a good foundation. Similarly, the care and attention we invest in nurturing our inner landscape reverberate throughout our external reality. Just as a well-tended garden thrives and blooms, our inner world benefits when we cultivate it with love, mindfulness, and compassion. This internal sanctuary, our true home, accompanies us wherever we go, offering solace, strength, and stability amidst life's changes. By recognizing ourselves as stewards of our inner garden, we reclaim the ability to shape our reality and let the rose of our hearts blossom.

Appreciating our many blessings cultivates creative diversity. When we find peace within ourselves, we are better equipped to serve others. Gardening embodies this appreciation, allowing us to create spaces that nurture and sustain life. We experience this gift firsthand. We hold all the tools and resources to empower ourselves and each other. Gardening allows us to nurture life and encourages creative expression, diversity, and the harmonious growth of all things. It becomes a practice of intentional creation, where every plant and flower contributes to balance and beauty.

Loving the garden within and nurturing our inner landscape is a meaningful act of self-care and empowerment. Just as we tend to a physical garden by enriching the soil and removing weeds to keep it healthy, we must also put effort and intention into nourishing our inner sanctuary. Investing in our emotional, mental, and spiritual well-being is a personal responsibility we all share. Returning to the source of creation and remembering who we are is the highest form of healing. Understanding who you are beyond human confinement is our most extraordinary form of liberation. It is also a privilege—an opportunity to cultivate a life rich with creativity, meaning, connection, and growth. It's not about doing better than others but more about doing better for others.

The Earth is the ultimate garden landscape. Focusing on the microcosm of our garden allows us to let go of aspects or ideas of ourselves that may inhibit our growth while helping us discover and nurture our true nature. In doing so, we cultivate a sense of inner peace and fulfillment and radiate a positive energy that uplifts and inspires those around us. Our garden flourishes and benefits the macrocosm as we learn to develop emotional stability through daily self-awareness practices.

Nature accepts us as we are. As we tend to our inner garden with love and attention, we contribute to life's beauty and richness, both within and around us. The only purpose is to be present in each moment, aware of the seeds of thought being planted. Prioritize what makes us healthy more than what makes money. Nurturing balanced energy will create health and abundance. Invest in dreams and consider what to grow for desirable future harvests. There's no need to worry about the future; if it's meant to be, nature will find a way.

Becoming a Master Gardener of our life's garden is a lifelong journey. The garden already exists within us, waiting to be uncovered. Our responsibility is to clear away what conceals it and enrich it with our unique flair and character. Beneath the surface lies the essence of who we are—ready to shine. Society's projections often act as brambles, obstructing the expression of our truth. By tending to the garden daily and cherishing it as a personal creation, we can delight in its beauty and allow it to expand and bloom.

Embrace the lessons that unfold along the journey, understanding there is no race to win. Clear away the overgrowth of worry and fear, allowing light to penetrate the darkness under the ivy. Treat each step on the earth as a sacred connection to the ground beneath us. Approach life's garden with grace, viewing it through eyes of love and compassion, and dissolve the illusion of powerlessness. Love heals, and within that healing lies humanity's greatest strength.

Master Gardeners Of Life

Congratulations on being part of this journey and showing up with intention. You are continually becoming the master of your destiny. Thank you for embracing the process of living, learning, growing, and becoming your true self. You belong here, and your unique talents and skills hold immense value. In life's garden, everything grows with purpose.

You will face many storms but will emerge stronger because of them. When your purpose feels unclear, remember that your presence alone often carries meaning. The sun will break through the clouds in time and shine upon your soul. Free yourself from entanglements, and boldly explore new ways to connect with your inner light. Resist the urge to dim the light of others, for they, too, are finding their paths to beauty.

You are a Master Gardener of Life. Your passion breathes life into every space you enter, and your loving attention nurtures growth. This is the essence of your inner light. Cultivate a positive mindset and find joy in your thoughts. Interrupt negative patterns as they arise, and create peace within your internal garden—your true home. Treat yourself with kindness and patience, knowing you are a cherished and sovereign flower in life's garden, meant to bloom.

Your purpose lives within you. Nurture its growth and fulfillment, for this is your gift and contribution to life's garden. Embrace your being, transform your desires with love, and celebrate the joy of your own nature. Keep going, keep growing, and embrace your journey of becoming while loving yourself as you are.

Suggested Reading:

Braiding Sweetgrass by Robin Wall Kimmerer

The Old Farmer's Almanac by Carol Connare and Judson D. Hale Sr.

Native American Ethnobotany by Daniel E. Moerman

Restoration Agriculture by Mark Shepard

The Garden Against Time by Olivia Lang

Mastering the Art of Vegetable Gardening by Matt Mattus

The Vegetable Gardener's Bible by Ed Smith

The Complete Gardener by Monty Don

Finding The Mother Tree by Suzanne Simard

Cass Turnbull's Guide To Pruning

The Pruner's Bible: A Step-by-Step Guide to Pruning Every Plant in Your Garden by Steve Bradley

The Preservation Kitchen by Paul Virant and Kate Leahy

The Late Bloomer: Myths and Stories of the Wise Woman Archetype by Clarissa Pinkola Estes, PhD

YouTube and Social Media Recommendations:

Charles Dowding
Epic Gardening
Self Sufficient Me
MIgardener
The Ripe Tomato Farms
GrowVeg
Huw Richards
Gabriel Miller
Roots and Refuge Farm
Daisy Creek Farms with Jag Singh
Grandmother Flordemayo
Sandra Ingerman
Navajo Traditional Teachings
Sadhguru
The Shift Network
Vandana Shiva
Rowen White

Follow on social media platforms: @AYAGardens

ABOUT JAMIE SLOAN

Jamie Sloan is a certified horticulturist and Master Gardener with over 30 years of experience in the field and a degree in horticulture. A dedicated steward of the land, she has spent a lifetime cultivating not only gardens but also a deep understanding of the interconnectedness between humanity and nature. As a world traveler, she has explored diverse cultures, philosophies, and environmental practices, continuously seeking wisdom from ancient traditions and modern science alike.

Beyond horticulture, Jamie Sloan has a rich background in the music industry, holding a degree in communications and audio engineering. As a DJ for 30 years, she has brought people together through sound, recognizing music as another powerful form of connection, movement and storytelling. Additionally, her love for food and community led her to work as a chef in renowned restaurants, further deepening her appreciation for nourishment—both physical and spiritual.

A lifelong student of philosophy and stoicism, Jamie Sloan believes in using this one opportunity of life to be of true benefit to the planet and humanity. Her work reflects a commitment to environmental health, sustainable living, and the preservation of nature's wisdom for the sake of future generations. Through writing, teaching, and hands-on practice, she aims to inspire others to cultivate a more conscious and harmonious relationship with our inner and outer worlds.

www.ingramcontent.com/pod-product-compliance
Lightning Source LLC
Chambersburg PA
CBHW061603110426
42742CB00039B/2709